THE GLOBAL GOVERNED?

When refugees flee war and persecution, protection and assistance are usually provided by United Nations organisations and their NGO implementing partners. In camps and cities, the dominant humanitarian model remains premised upon a provider–beneficiary relationship. In parallel to this model, however, is a largely neglected story: refugees themselves frequently mobilise to create organisations or networks as alternative providers of social protection.

Based on fieldwork in refugee camps and cities in Uganda and Kenya, this book examines how refugee-led organisations emerge, the forms they take, and their interactions with international institutions. Developing an original theoretical framework based on the concept of 'the global governed', the book shows how power and hierarchy mediate the seemingly benign notion of protection. Drawing upon ideas from anthropology and international relations, it offers an alternative vision for more participatory global governance, of relevance to other policy-fields including development, humanitarianism, health, peacekeeping and child protection.

KATE PINCOCK is a research associate at the Refugee Studies Centre, University of Oxford, and a researcher for the Overseas Development Institute. She received her PhD in International Development from the University of Bath, and her research focuses on forced migration and gender in East Africa.

ALEXANDER BETTS is Professor of Forced Migration and International Affairs, and William Golding Senior Fellow in Politics at Brasenose College, University of Oxford. He was previously Director of the Refugee Studies Centre, is a World Economic Forum Young Global Leader and was named by *Foreign Policy* magazine as one of the leading global thinkers of 2016.

EVAN EASTON-CALABRIA is a senior research officer at the Refugee Studies Centre, and Junior Research Fellow at Wadham College, University of Oxford. Her research focuses on refugee self-reliance and the history of forced migration and development.

CAMBRIDGE ASYLUM AND MIGRATION STUDIES

At no time in modern history have so many people been on the move as at present. Migration facilitates critical social, economic, and humanitarian linkages. But it may also challenge prevailing notions of bounded political communities, of security, and of international law.

The political and legal systems that regulate the transborder movement of persons were largely devised in the mid-twentieth century, and are showing their strains. New challenges have arisen for policymakers, advocates, and decision-makers that require the adaptation and evolution of traditional models to meet emerging imperatives.

Edited by a world leader in refugee law, this new series aims to be a forum for innovative writing on all aspects of the transnational movement of people. It publishes single or coauthored works that may be legal, political, or cross-disciplinary in nature, and will be essential reading for anyone looking to understand one of the most important issues of the twenty-first century.

Series Editor

James Hathaway, James E. and Sarah A. Degan Professor of Law, and Director of Michigan Law's Program in Refugee and Asylum Law, University of Michigan, USA

Editorial Advisory Board

Alexander Betts, Professor of Forced Migration and International Affairs, and William Golding Senior Fellow in Politics at Brasenose College, University of Oxford, UK

Vincent Chetail, Professor of Public International Law, and Director of the Global Migration Centre, Graduate Institute of International and Development Studies, Switzerland

Thomas Gammeltoft-Hansen, Professor with Special Responsibilities in Migration and Refugee Law at the University of Copenhagen

Audrey Macklin, Professor and Chair in Human Rights Law, University of Toronto, Canada

Saskia Sassen, Robert S. Lynd Professor of Sociology, and Chair of the Committee on Global Thought, Columbia University, USA

Books in the Series

The Child in International Refugee Law Jason Pobjoy

Refuge Lost: Asylum Law in an Interdependent World Daniel Ghezelbash

Demanding Rights: Europe's Supranational Courts and the Dilemma of Migrant Vulnerability Moritz Baumgärtel

Climate Change, Disasters and the Refugee Convention Matthew Scott

The Global Governed?: Refugees as Providers of Protection and Assistance Kate Pincock/Alexander Betts/Evan Easton-Calabria

THE GLOBAL GOVERNED?

Refugees as Providers of Protection and Assistance

KATE PINCOCK

University of Oxford

ALEXANDER BETTS

University of Oxford

EVAN EASTON-CALABRIA

University of Oxford

CAMBRIDGE
UNIVERSITY PRESS

University Printing House, Cambridge CB2 8BS, United Kingdom

One Liberty Plaza, 20th Floor, New York, NY 10006, USA

477 Williamstown Road, Port Melbourne, VIC 3207, Australia

314–321, 3rd Floor, Plot 3, Splendor Forum, Jasola District Centre, New Delhi – 110025, India

79 Anson Road, #06–04/06, Singapore 079906

Cambridge University Press is part of the University of Cambridge.

It furthers the University's mission by disseminating knowledge in the pursuit of
education, learning, and research at the highest international levels of excellence.

www.cambridge.org
Information on this title: www.cambridge.org/9781108494946
DOI: 10.1017/9781108848831

First published 2020

Printed and bound in Great Britain by Clays Ltd, Elcograf S.p.A.

A catalogue record for this publication is available from the British Library.

Library of Congress Cataloging-in-Publication Data
Names: Pincock, Kate, 1987– author. | Betts, Alexander, 1980– author. | Easton-Calabria, Evan Elise, author.
Title: The global governed? : refugees as providers of protection and assistance / Kate Pincock, Alexander Betts,
Evan Easton-Calabria.
Description: 1. | New York : Cambridge University Press, 2020. | Series: Cambridge asylum and migration studies |
Includes bibliographical references and index.
Identifiers: LCCN 2019038871 (print) | LCCN 2019038872 (ebook) | ISBN 9781108494946 (hardback) |
ISBN 9781108816700 (paperback) | ISBN 9781108848831 (epub)
Subjects: LCSH: Refugees–Legal status, laws, etc. | Emigration and immigration law. | Asylum, Right of. |
Forced migration. | Humanitarian law.
Classification: LCC KZ6530 .P56 2020 (print) | LCC KZ6530 (ebook) | DDC 341.4/86–dc23
LC record available at https://lccn.loc.gov/2019038871
LC ebook record available at https://lccn.loc.gov/2019038872

ISBN 978-1-108-49494-6 Hardback
ISBN 978-1-108-81670-0 Paperback

CONTENTS

FIGURES

TABLES

SERIES EDITOR'S PREFACE

Could we – should we – think differently about the ways in which refugees are assisted and protected? Is it possible to turn traditional thinking on its head by seeing refugees not as the objects of protection and assistance, but instead as the architects and managers of solutions?

In this important book, Alexander Betts, Evan Easton-Calabria and Kate Pincock suggest that the answer to both questions is an emphatic 'yes'. Drawing on their academic backgrounds in political science, history and anthropology, the authors of *The Global Governed? Refugees as Providers of Protection and Assistance* push us to broaden our thinking about how the refugee regime should be understood and operated. Specifically, they draw on a series of original East African case studies to challenge the traditional privileging of states and international organisations as the "providers" of protection and assistance, showing how refugees can and do organise collectively to provide social protection to each other.

Having demonstrated the ability of refugees to provide rather than simply to receive, the authors pointedly challenge the view that 'protection is a form of assistance that is presumed to be inherently benign ... [T]his representation frequently masks that it is malleable, highly contested, and frequently used to legitimate the authority to govern.' Put simply, the way in which protection and assistance are presently structured can amount to an exercise of power over refugees. If this is so, ought we not to adopt a more critical stance about the roles of the official actors and their non-governmental partners who direct the current system of refugee protection and assistance that is – at least in theory – rooted in a commitment to refugee empowerment? And given the demonstrated ability of refugees themselves to author and manage answers to their own predicaments, is the time not right to think hard about a new theory of global governance in the refugee context – one in which refugees are recognised as governors, rather than just governed?

This book beautifully combines rigorous empirical research design with deep theoretical engagement. Its thesis is timely, challenging us all honestly to acknowledge the ways in which refugees have traditionally been denied agency over their own lives, and offering a theory of how that can and should change.

James C. Hathaway
Editor, Cambridge Asylum and Migration Studies

ACKNOWLEDGEMENTS

The dominant public view of refugees is as victims in need of humanitarian assistance. And while many people fleeing conflict and persecution may be vulnerable, we also need to recognise that refugees frequently mobilise to help themselves and their communities. Rather than simply being passive recipients of international aid, refugees are sometimes the *providers* of protection and assistance. Whether through formal organisations or informal networks, they collectively organise to provide support to others in areas as diverse as education, health, livelihoods, finance or housing. And yet their role as providers of social protection is rarely recognised or supported by the international humanitarian system.

Our aim in this book is to highlight and better understand the role of refugee-led protection and assistance. When does it emerge? How does it interact with the humanitarian system? What role should it have in relation to aid delivery? These questions matter for international responses to refugees. Providing answers could identify opportunities for more effective and legitimate forms of refugee assistance. But our answers also matter more broadly for the theory and practice of global governance. By challenging the dominant perception of the provider–beneficiary relationship present in policy fields such as development, humanitarianism, peacekeeping and health governance, we can begin to critically interrogate our assumptions about the presumed passivity and victimhood of the supposedly 'global governed' and reconsider the meaning of participatory global governance.

The Refugee Studies Centre at the University of Oxford has a long history of research relating to the agency of refugees. Ever since Barbara Harrell-Bond published *Imposing Aid*, the centre's work has focused on recognising the capacities of forcibly displaced communities rather than simply focusing on their vulnerabilities. It has covered the economic, political and social lives of refugees and pushed back against the top-down imposition of humanitarian aid. This book very much builds upon that tradition. But it focuses on a hitherto largely unexplored aspect of refugee agency: the ways in which refugees collectively organise to provide the very services – protection and assistance – usually associated with large humanitarian organisations.

The research in the book emerges from a joint Economic and Social Research Council (ESRC) and Arts and Humanities Research Council (AHRC)-funded Global Challenges Research Fund project entitled 'The Global Governed? Refugees as Providers of Protection and Assistance'. The project, which ran from 2016 to 2018, aimed to examine the range of forms of organisational forms through which refugees provide social protection to other refugees. It was conceived as interdisciplinary, encompassing anthropology, political science and history. While all three authors have interdisciplinary backgrounds, Kate was the anthropologist, Alex the political scientist and Evan the historian.

We chose to focus our fieldwork on East Africa, notably on camp and urban contexts in Uganda and Kenya, because this reflects all three authors' regional expertise, and because these contexts offer contrasting policy environments. Between the authors we also had a range of established contacts with refugee-led organisations across our research sites. The basic division of labour for the research ran as follows: Alex was principal investigator and shaped the research design, Kate undertook the bulk of the ethnographic fieldwork, and Evan contributed to both fieldwork and the conceptual development of the project. Writing was a joint effort.

However, the book also relied upon the contributions of many people other than the authors. We are especially grateful to the following refugees for their input and guidance, and for connecting us to their communities: Bahati Ghislain and Jamila Hussein in Nairobi; William Bakunzi and Abdalla Majeed in Nakivale; Ruddy Tutu, Kafi Bashir and Abdikadir Zamzam in Kakuma; and Robert Hakiza and Ter Manang Gatwech in Kampala. Their openness to our research allowed us to gain access to the conversations and insights that have informed this work. We are also grateful to the international organisations and NGOs that have engaged with our work, including UNHCR staff, who not only allowed us access to compound accommodation but also made time to respond to our many questions.

A draft manuscript benefitted immensely from the feedback of participants at several workshops. In November 2018, the Refugee-Led Organisations Network hosted a workshop in Kampala that provided us with input from a number of refugee-led organisations. Also in November 2018, we held a book workshop in Oxford, during which colleagues from a range of disciplinary perspectives generously highlighted ways to improve the manuscript. At the European University Institute in Florence, we presented the research at a symposium on civilian self-protection, from which we received especially helpful suggestions. We are particularly grateful to Matthew Gibney, Betcy Jose, Josiah Kaplan, Tom Scott-Smith, Emily Paddon Rhoads and Cory Rodgers for reading and commenting on draft chapters.

Maurice Herson provided detailed and invaluable suggestions on improvements to the manuscript in terms of both style and substance. The main title for the book originally emerged from a suggestion by Rorden Wilkinson over dinner in November 2015. We are incredibly grateful to our colleagues at the Refugee Studies Centre. Naohiko Omata and Olivier Sterck generously shared ideas and observations based on their parallel work in Kenya and Uganda. Isabelle Aires provided administrative support for the project, including coordinating our fieldwork-related travel and budgeting. At Cambridge University Press, we wish to thank Finola O'Sullivan, Laura Blake and series editor Jim Hathaway for their contributions to the book. Finally, this book would not have been possible without funding from the ESRC and AHRC.

Introduction

When we think of the global refugee system, we tend to envisage international aid organisations delivering large-scale assistance to vulnerable populations, usually in camps. As people flee conflict or persecution and cross borders, the dominant picture is of UN agencies and international non-governmental organisations providing basic needs such as food, clothing and shelter. This is certainly one part of the story, but it risks obscuring the many ways in which refugees collectively organise to help themselves and their communities.

Refugees engage in collective action and self-help across economic, political and social contexts. Economically, refugee entrepreneurship often leads to the creation of businesses, cooperatives or financial instruments. Politically, refugees may mobilise to contest homeland governments, protest inadequate assistance in exile or simply to ensure adequate representation in camps and cities. Socially, faith-based organisations, cultural associations and sports teams often proliferate among refugee communities. That refugees, like all human beings, have the capacity to help themselves and to collectively organise – what social scientists call 'agency' – is now widely recognised.

In spite of this, one area of striking neglect is the role that refugees play as providers of protection and assistance to other refugees. Rather than simply being passive recipients of assistance, they often organise among themselves, whether through formal organisations or informal networks, to support vulnerable members of the community. Formal international assistance is rarely sufficient to allow refugees to meet their basic needs, and so refugees themselves often provide alternative sources of support.

To take an example, the organisation Hope of Children and Women Victims of Violence (HOCW), based in Kampala, Uganda, was created in 2008 by Congolese refugees and a Ugandan pastor, and expanded through the support of international volunteers who raised funds and provided materials. Located on the outskirts of Kampala, the organisation provides various livelihood activities for both refugees and local Ugandans, as well as English lessons and programmes for children. The initiative began after women expressed the need to diversify their skills, as the only work the majority could find in Kampala was washing clothes; it started in 2013 with a tailoring programme, and now runs a range of programmes including arts and crafts, hairdressing, mushroom-growing and business skills training. An estimated 40 per cent of training participants at HOCW are Ugandans, encouraging interaction between refugees and the host community.

Below the radar, there are more than thirty refugee-led community organisations operating in Kampala. Many are formally registered and employ staff; others are informal networks and have relatively few resources. They are mainly based on nationality groups, although some assist across communities. They offer support within and beyond their communities in areas such as vocational training, counselling, youth engagement, access to credit and informal education.

But refugee-led assistance does not just occur in cities. In camps and settlements, formal provision is often inadequate, even though basic needs are in theory provided, and so refugee-led initiatives emerge in these contexts too. In the Nakivale refugee settlement in Uganda, the Wakati Foundation, run by Congolese refugee Alex, employs refugees through small-scale public works projects, building latrines and sports facilities such as basketball courts. The Foundation negotiates contracts with aid organisations and wealthier refugees, enabling it to also undertake voluntary work helping refugees across the settlement to build houses or community structures like churches. Wakati thereby represents a source of employment, vocational training and community development.

These examples are far from isolated. Refugee-led assistance and protection can be found in every contemporary displacement crisis, from Myanmar to Venezuela. They emerge in both emergency and protracted crisis situations. They encompass activities as diverse as education, health, livelihoods, finance and housing. Shanti Mohila ('Peace Women') is a group led by Rohingya women like sixty-year-old activist Khalunisa in the Kutupalong-Balukhali camps of Cox's Bazar in Bangladesh. It provides counselling services to hundreds of victims of sexual and gender-based violence. The Union Venezolana en Peru, created by Venezuelan politician Óscar Pérez, provides integration and legal support to 100,000 Venezuelans. The Project for the Legal Support for Syrian Refugees and Palestinians (PLSSRP), established in Beirut by Syrian lawyer Brahim al Qassem, has offered legal aid to refugees since 2013.

Despite these accomplishments, however, refugee-led organisations (sometimes referred to as refugee community organisations, or RCOs) generally receive little international recognition or support. UN agencies privilege formal 'implementing partners' and 'operational partners', and these are usually international or national NGOs, not refugee-led organisations. Small-scale, refugee-led organisations are often unknown to international policymakers and can rarely meet the accounting, auditing, vetting or compliance requirements to make them eligible for humanitarian funding.

International organisations like UNHCR routinely promote refugee 'self-reliance': encouraging refugees to live autonomously. However, self-reliance is predominantly viewed in relation to economic agency rather than political or social agency. While refugees' entrepreneurship and business leadership are widely encouraged, community and political leadership are greeted with more ambivalence. Political mobilisation is sometimes restricted by host governments unless it takes place within carefully choreographed contexts like refugee camp elections. Community mobilisation, meanwhile, has never been seen as an integral part of self-reliance.

In its 2018 Uganda refugee programme budget, for example, UNHCR allocated just over 1 per cent of its $480 million country budget to 'community mobilisation', its umbrella category for working directly with refugee and host communities. However, even such community mobilisation activities rarely provide refugees with the freedom to address the needs they themselves identify or to pursue their own scope of work; these activities are more likely to focus on trainings to 'sensitise' refugees in matters such as healthcare and hygiene. Therefore, despite explicit funding and programmes to engage with refugees, refugees remain persistently neglected as actors capable of providing protection and assistance. This lack of engagement stems from the top-down structure of humanitarian assistance, which generally privileges large, established international and national organisations over grassroots ones. The enduring perception is that refugees are people in need of help rather than people capable of providing assistance to others. In many field contexts, there remains widespread ignorance among humanitarian professionals about the existence of RCOs.

At the global level, the rhetoric around refugee-led organisations is gradually changing. At international conferences and summits, there is increasing recognition of the need to support refugee-led initiatives. The World Humanitarian Summit in 2016 placed a strong emphasis on 'localisation', recognising crisis-affected people themselves as important first responders in crisis. The leaders of refugee-led organisations were occasionally included in panels during the 2017 consultations for the Global Refugee Compact. In June 2018, the Refugee Council of Australia convened a Global Summit of Refugees in Geneva, alongside UNHCR's Annual NGO Consultations. Its aim was to build a 'new international movement for refugee-led advocacy'.

Meanwhile, a range of other networks and events, including Oxfam's International Refugee Congress held in Istanbul, the Refugee-Led Organisations Network based in Kampala and the Refugee Voices Network in Berlin have emerged to promote a greater voice for refugees within the global refugee system. In December 2019, the Global Refugee-Led Network (GRN) played an active and visible role at UNHCR's inaugural Global Refugee Forum. A smattering of NGOs – from the St. Andrew Refugee Service (StARS) in Cairo to the Finnish Refugee Council (FRC) in Kampala – now provide capacity-building programmes for RCOs. These initiatives share the central message that local people, both refugees and host communities, deserve a voice in debates relating to their own assistance and a seat at the table of global governance. Their varied geographical provenance demonstrates that the agency of refugees is now recognised around the globe.

But to what extent is this changed rhetoric enacted in practice? At an operational level, and in different field locations, how does the reality vary from country to country, from camp to camp or from city to city? When are the national representatives of UN agencies and international NGOs encouraging refugee-led organisation and when are they not? How do refugee-led organisations interact with formal refugee governance? When do refugee-led organisations receive recognition and support? How do refugees strategically navigate institutional barriers to creating organisations? Under what conditions do particular kinds of refugee-led organisations flourish and grow?

In this book, we aim to understand the role of refugee-led organisations within global refugee governance. We do so by taking an in-depth and comparative look at four sites in two countries in East Africa: Kampala and Nakivale (in Uganda) and Nairobi and Kakuma (in Kenya). Rather than assuming refugees to be simply passive 'beneficiaries' of governance, we explore their role as neglected 'providers' of governance. Rather than simply examining how refugees are symbolically included at the Geneva or New York level, we delve into the operational practice across specific field locations in camp and urban contexts, exploring what it tells us about traditional conceptions of the provider–beneficiary relationship within global governance. Ultimately, we seek to interrogate whether, and to what extent, refugees are significant actors within global refugee governance.

We focus particularly on how refugees organise to provide social protection, defined as activities designed to reduce populations' poverty, vulnerability or risk. These are areas that are traditionally state-led, but which, in a refugee context, cannot be provided by the country of origin or of citizenship and so are commonly transferred to an 'international protection' provider. National and international actors usually provide an important part of social protection, through ensuring safety and access to basic services. However, much more neglected is the role that refugees sometimes play as providers of social protection, whether they are formally recognised or not.

This topic matters for the refugee system. It offers an opportunity to render visible a neglected group of providers of protection and assistance. Understanding when and how refugee-led social protection takes place may offer an opportunity to unlock a neglected source of additional assistance. In some cases, allocating resources to refugee-led organisations may even be more efficient than funding international organisations as intermediaries. Generally, RCOs function at far lower cost than international NGOs, and if they had access to just some of the resources available to international actors, it seems plausible that their capacities might expand beyond their current scope. Furthermore, recognising refugee-led social protection could be argued to have inherent value as a means to support the autonomy and dignity of refugees as people capable of self-governance.

However, studying refugee-led social protection also has implications for global governance more broadly. The refugee system represents just one example of a policy field characterised by a provider–beneficiary relationship. Health, development and humanitarian governance are analogous contexts. In each of these areas, recipients of aid are usually cast as objects of governance rather than subjects involved in shaping global governance. Despite this, from global pandemics to hurricanes, we have seen that affected populations often mobilise not just to help themselves but to offer vital assistance to vulnerable members of the community. In this regard, the supposedly 'global governed' cannot be assumed simply to be passive takers of global governance; they may be makers of the very global public goods that a given international regime was created to provide. Rethinking the role and position of the global governed represents an opportunity to challenge presumed hierarchies and consider alternative possibilities for more participatory forms of governance.

Research Questions

We begin with a puzzle. At the global level, there has been growing acknowledgement by international organisations of the role played by refugee-led organisations. Beyond the rhetoric of Geneva and New York, however, practice varies markedly. In some cases, refugee-led organisations proliferate and flourish, albeit usually under the radar, and in others they struggle to become established. In some cases organisation is through RCOs and in others it is simply based on informal networks. Some places are hotbeds of community organisation and other places are not. Across particular urban and camp contexts, RCOs vary in number, institutional form (for example, whether they are organisations or networks) and the degree of funding and recognition that they receive. Based on this starting observation, our central research question is: *what explains variation in the scale and scope of refugee-led social protection?* Put simply, when and where do refugees become significant organisational providers of social protection?

A range of alternative possible explanations exist. Variation could conceivably derive from the different institutional contexts that enable or constrain community mobilisation (structural explanations). Are international organisations or national governments creating a conducive environment for RCOs to formally register, establish partnerships, receive funding or access transnational networks? Variation might also derive from the refugee communities themselves (agency-based explanations). What role does culture and nationality play? Are some communities more positively disposed to particular forms of organisational development? How important are individuals, including through their ideas, networks, capabilities, preferences and personalities?

Our first step is to describe what is happening empirically. Part of our contribution is simply to offer an in-depth look at refugee-led social protection and its interaction with global governance. However, describing is also a precondition for explaining. We therefore build our analysis around three main sub-questions, applied to each of our research sites.

First, *what is the institutional context within which refugee-led organisations operate?* Here, we aim to understand the position of key international organisations, NGOs and national authorities towards refugee-led organisations. What rules exist to allow the delegation of social protection tasks to RCOs? How are organisational statuses such as 'implementing partner' or 'operational partner' conferred? Are any pots of money or other resources made available to RCOs? What attitudes do international and national humanitarian staff have towards RCOs?

Second, *what does the landscape of refugee-led organisations look like?* At the moment, international organisations do not systematically map out refugee-led organisations in camps or cities. How many RCOs or social protection networks exist? What activities do they undertake? How many people do they serve? What are their organisational histories? What areas of specialisation are selected and why? How do activities vary across ethnic and national communities? Which organisations have access to funding and from whom? To what extent are RCOs part of wider RCO networks or umbrella organisations? Which organisations are formally registered or have a partnership status?

Third, *what kinds of interactions take place between formal governance and refugee-led organisations?* Here, we examine the practices of interaction between these 'top-down' and 'bottom-up' levels of governance. How do power and hierarchy shape interaction and mutual recognition? To what extent do UN organisation or international and national NGO staff have knowledge and awareness of RCOs? How are everyday interactions between the leaders and staff of RCOs and international and national organisations structured? To what extent are some RCOs able have greater degrees of access to international actors?

Beyond description, we then aim to offer an explanation for variation in relation to these three main sets of sub-questions. Why are some institutional contexts more open or closed to refugee organisations? Why do refugee organisations, individually and collectively, emerge in the forms that they do? What shapes the quality of the interaction between 'informal' refugee-led initiatives and 'formal' international organisations? The goal of asking these questions is to begin to build a theory of the conditions under which refugee organisations emerge and flourish (or do not).

Refugees, Protection and Governance

Our focus is the role of refugee-led organisations in global governance. There is currently relatively little research that looks at RCOs; even less that looks at them as providers of social protection; and virtually none that situates them within global governance. Nevertheless, three sets of literatures offer starting points for the development of our theoretical, empirical and methodological focus, and we aim to make a contribution to each. The three bodies of existing literature broadly relate to the population (refugee studies), activity (social protection) and organisational context (global governance). Here we identify how each one represents a valuable point of departure but offers an incomplete account of the phenomenon we are interested in.

Refugee Studies

Work on refugees' agency has long been a central theme within Refugee Studies. Barbara Harrell-Bond's (1986) seminal critique of the humanitarian system sought to highlight how, far from being passive humanitarian subjects, refugees have capabilities. The dominant camp-based humanitarian model, she argued, risked creating long-term dependency and exerting unnecessary degrees of control over the lives of displaced populations. Drawing upon ethnographic work with Ugandan refugees in Sudan, she showed the dehumanising effects of top-down aid delivery when it is detached from basic rights and freedoms. She advocated instead for approaches based on self-reliance capable of restoring refugees' autonomy.

Subsequent work on refugees' agency has been diverse, and primarily focused on individual agency in a social context. It has highlighted the ways in which refugees make choices, despite their constraints. And the work covers a variety of domains, from development projects (Chambers 1986) to migration decision-making (Richmond 1994; Van Hear 1998) to decisions to repatriate (Hammond 2004) to retaining homeland connections (Kibreab 1987; Horst 2008) to asserting their claims for rights (Grabska 2006), much of it analysed through ethnographic case studies.

A significant and growing strand of this work focuses on refugees' economic agency, demonstrating refugees' capacity to help themselves economically. Karen Jacobsen's (2005) pioneering work on the economic lives of refugees provided a qualitative account of the many and diverse ways in which refugees work, make a living, and engage in exchange across camps and cities, often despite significant regulatory constraints. This has spawned a growing literature examining the complexity of refugees' economic lives and drawing attention to their capacity to be economic contributors to host societies (Werker 2007; Maystadt & Werwimp 2009; Krause 2013; Ruiz & Vargas-Silva 2015; Betts et al. 2016; Carrier 2016).

Most of the work on refugees' agency has focused on the individual level. However, in some areas, research has also emerged examining the community level; in particular, there is research on refugee-led organisation. On the one hand, there is work looking at refugees' capacity for political self-governance. For example, focusing on Burmese refugees in Thailand, McConnachie (2012) shows how several of the refugee camps along the Thai-Burmese border are part of a model of self-governance, embracing forms of legal pluralism within which rules, norms and their enforcement are shaped and determined by the practices of the community, co-existing with the national legal framework. On the other hand, research has also focused on refugees' transnational political mobilisation (Horst 2008; Van Hear 2016; Mylonas 2017; Jacobsen 2019). In particular, there has been a focus on refugee diasporas' mobilisation relating to conflict (Lischer 2005; Lyons 2007; Salehyan 2009), authoritarian transition (Betts & Jones 2017) and peace-building (Bradley, Milner & Peruniak 2019; Horst 2019; Milner 2019; Purkey 2019), mainly relating to the country of origin.

Within a European and North American context, there has been a growing body of literature on refugee community organisations, including with the aim of providing assistance to other refugees (Gold 1992; Zetter, Sigona & Hauser 2002; Zetter, Griffiths & Segona 2005; Hopkins 2006; Phillimore 2012). Broadening from a more general literature on migrant organisations (e.g. Cordero-Guzman 2007), this work has examined a range of questions and variables, including how community organisations shape integration and social inclusion (Hopkins 2006; Phillimore & Goodson 2008; Phillimore 2012) and how external policy shifts – including by central government or local authorities – affect RCOs (Zetter & Pearl 2000; Griffiths, Sigona & Zetter 2006; Bloch 2008).

Most of the literature relating to RCOs, though, has been undertaken in the Global North, and particularly in the UK. Similar analyses in non-Western contexts have not been undertaken. Indeed, what has been almost entirely missing from the literature is research on how refugee communities engage in organisational mobilisation across the developing world. Refugee-to-refugee community support has been a theme of the emerging literature on 'South-South humanitarianism' (Fiddian-Qasmiyeh 2015). For example, Fiddian-Qasmiyeh (2015) highlights how, in the Baddawi refugee camp in northern Lebanon, long-present Palestinian refugees welcomed and assisted Syrian 'new refugees' in acclimatising to the camp and obtaining basic necessities.

Meanwhile, a related literature has emerged looking at forms of civilian 'self-protection', including by internally displaced populations (Baines & Paddon 2012; Kaplan 2013; Jose & Medie 2015). That literature focuses in particular on how individuals affected by armed conflict engage in strategies to avoid direct threats to their physical integrity. While these works draw attention to the role of displaced populations as actors in the provision of protection, they stop short of theorising the diverse ways that refugees themselves engage in community mobilisation for assistance and protection in the Global South.

Social Protection

'Social protection' commonly refers to programmes and policies aiming to reduce populations' poverty, vulnerability and risk; these were traditionally state-led initiatives. The term has recently become common in international development, as well as among international agencies working to alleviate poverty, whether in collaboration with or in the absence of states. Refugees are an increasing target population for social protection programmes, yet the definition of social protection seems to vary particularly for them as compared to national populations.

Social protection in development practice is often understood as the support provided to enable access to goods such as healthcare and education, with these sectors perceived as beyond the remit of social protection itself. Most development banks work with variations on the following definition from the Asian Development Bank: 'social protection is defined as the set of policies and programs designed to reduce poverty and vulnerability by promoting efficient labour markets, diminishing people's exposure to risks, and enhancing their capacity to protect themselves against hazards and interruption/loss of income' (Asian Development Bank). The World Bank states: 'Social protection systems help the poor and vulnerable cope with crises and shocks, find jobs, invest in the health and education of their children, and protect the aging population' (World Bank). The policy debate has emerged alongside a growing academic literature on social protection within Development Studies (Holzmann & Jorgensen 1999; Devereux 2002; Devereux & Sabates-Wheeler 2004; Barrientos & Hulme 2009; Barrientos 2011).

Devereux and Sabates-Wheeler (2004) have offered a series of critiques of the ways in which social protection has been invoked within development policy and practice, positing what they call a 'transformative' approach to social protection. First, they identify the need to expand the definition, arguing that the definition of risk should be expanded beyond economic shocks to include a full range of social risks, including the structural causes of poverty. Second, they highlight the need to recognise a role for non-state actors: the state is not the only provider of social protection, and informal, collective and community level sources are important. Third, they outline a series of levels of intervention: protective, promotive, preventive and transformative forms of social protection, describing existing mechanisms that fall into these categories as either 'safety nets' or 'springboards'. For our purposes, a key insight of Devereux and Sabates-Wheeler (2004, p. 8) is about the role of informal providers of social protection. They write:

> In poor countries, due to a variety of constraints that restrict the range of social protection services offered by the welfare state, the concept of social protection must be widened to include both private and public mechanisms for social protection provisioning ... An important role exists for non-formal systems of social protection, for instance, those based on kinship and traditional institutions of reciprocity and dependency.

Indeed, other authors within the social protection literature have also highlighted the key role of informal community mobilisation. Davis and Baulch (2009) examine 'everyday forms of collective action' in Bangladesh, showing that the support provided by NGOs is minimal when compared to local community leaders who coordinate a range of responses to social protection gaps. Some of these ideas have subsequently been applied to the context of migration. Sabates-Wheeler and Feldman (2011) explore the challenges that migrants face in accessing social protection, given their distinctive lack of citizenship-based rights. While the book focuses on social protection as the primary responsibility of the state, it recognises the role of social networks as relevant when these formal mechanisms fail.

Du Toit and Neves also look at the role of informal social protection among migrant networks in South Africa. They highlight the role that social capital plays in ensuring access to community-based systems of reciprocal support, suggesting that 'these networks are partly made up of – and provide the underpinnings for – deeply sedimented and culturally specific discourses and practices of reciprocal exchange' (du Toit & Neves 2009, p. 3). Crucially, they avoid romanticising these informal structures, highlighting instead the role that wealth, power and social status play in mediating exchanges and access to support.

So, while this literature draws our attention to the role of informal networks in addressing social protection gaps, including for migrants, it leaves some important questions unresolved. First, there remains limited focus on refugees. The work that does exist on informal refugee networks' role in social protection remains focused predominantly on Europe and the United States (Zetter et al. 2005; Williams 2006; Allen 2010). The major exception to this has been an examination of the role of remittances as a form of informal social insurance within Somali refugee communities (Horst 2006; Lindley 2009; Carrier 2016). Second, the social protection literature as a whole lacks an account of organisational emergence, whether in terms of individual organisations and networks or clusters of organisations and networks. Even Sabates-Wheeler and Feldman's work on migrant-led networks (Sabates-Wheeler & Feldman 2011) tends to assume that the networks are pre-existing rather than examining their emergence. Third, existing work tends not to account for interaction with the wider institutional context. How do 'formal' and 'informal' or 'top-down' and 'bottom-up', interact, for example, and how do these interactions vary contextually?

Global Governance

One of the distinctively original contributions of this book is to situate refugee-led organisations within the theory and practice of global governance. Most of the work on social protection either examines informal social protection in isolation from its wider institutional and political context or is simply concerned with its relationship to the state's provision of social protection.

In contrast, our specific focus on refugee-led social protection in the Global South requires consideration of the relationship to international institutions. This is because while social protection relating to development generally involves exploring interactions between states and citizens, social protection relating to refugees generally involves a three-way interaction – between state, international organisations and refugees. Moreover, in low- and middle-income countries that host the majority of the world's refugees, the relationship between international organisations and refugees may sometimes be even more salient to refugees' social protection than that between the state and refugees. This is because, in the refugee context, their country of citizenship is no longer a viable provider of social protection; and international protection is provided by a combination of host state and international community. In many host countries, governments allocate the bulk of responsibility for social protection to UN agencies and their NGO partners. These features make refugee-led social protection in the Global South analytically distinctive.

The global governance literature offers a useful starting point for considering the interaction between international organisations and refugee-led organisations. This is in part because it includes a focus on the role of non-state actors within forms of global collection action. In contrast to a purely intergovernmental focus, global governance is generally defined as encompassing all processes and activities that lead to collective action in relation to transboundary issues. Moving beyond International Relations' traditional focus on explaining inter-state cooperation, it is an area that now includes a focus on actors as diverse as international and intergovernmental organisations, NGOs, advocacy networks, firms, mayors, municipal authorities, legal associations, faith-based organisations, rebel groups and resistance movements, all of whom are recognised as shaping the rules and organisational responses to complex global issues.

However, within this context, refugees have rarely been recognised as actors within global governance. Work on International Relations and refugees has generally conceived of refugees as the 'problem' to be addressed through intergovernmental action. And yet, we know that refugees do mobilise to influence agenda-setting, negotiation, implementation, monitoring and enforcement of global rules and policies relating to refugees. They are actors in their own right within global governance. While some work has been undertaken examining how refugees mobilise to engage politically with international organisations (Betts & Jones 2017), there has been a lack of research on refugees' role in the direct provision of protection and solutions – the very same global public goods that the refugee regime ostensibly exists to provide.

Two areas of global governance literature are especially relevant. First, work on delegation examines how authority is sometimes devolved from governments, to international organisation, and sometimes downwards to NGOs (Abbott et al. 2015). Using Principal-Agent theory, (Hawkins et al. 2006) examine how international organisations are given a mandate to fulfil specific tasks by governments. However, such organisations sometimes acquire a degree of autonomy in how they implement their mandates because of 'agency slack', or the inability of a Principal to oversee all aspects of the organisation's work. Barnett and Finnemore (2004) use this framework to examine what they call 'organisational pathology' within UNHCR (i.e. why the organisation's preferences and behaviour sometimes do not align with those of its main donor states). While Principal-Agent theory is a parsimonious starting point for looking at relationships of delegation, it is too functional, linear and apolitical to capture the dynamics of delegation across levels of governance.

Tana Johnson's (2014, 2018) work builds upon and addresses some of these limitations. She focuses on the politics that take place at particular stages of delegation. Her early work focuses, for example, on how international organisations insulate themselves from state influence in order to preserve autonomy. Her subsequent work focuses on the next level down – how NGOs position themselves vis-à-vis states and international organisations to have greater influence and authority. Her contribution is important because it shows that delegation of authority, at all levels, is highly political, involving competing interests, power, hierarchy and contestation.

Work on delegation usually stops at the level of international organisations and international NGOs and remains centred on New York- or Geneva-level politics. There is, however, a rich empirical opportunity to go further downstream and consider how power and interests mediate interactions between international organisations, international NGOs, national NGOs and community-level organisations such as RCOs. Within the refugee and humanitarian contexts, for example, the practice of designating 'implementing partners' and 'operational partners' is inherently political and yet unexplored within work on delegation. Indeed, given that in these regimes over 90 per cent of staff numbers and resources are allocated at this level, this is far from a trivial dimension of international organisation.

Second, while global governance research tends to focus empirically on New York, Geneva and the headquarters level of international organisations, this is gradually changing. On a theoretical level, Amitav Acharya (2004)'s work on 'localisation' has had an important impact on the study of international institutions. He highlighted that the way in which particular international institutions operate in practice varies across regions, countries and local contexts, adapting to the particular norms, interests and power structures already present. Furthermore, as Betts and Orchard (2014) show, the implementation of global norms and standards is mediated through national and local politics, meaning that the same global structures can lead to different observed outcomes at an operational level. While these approaches offer a means of examining institutional practice at the local level, they are in some ways linear, top-down reflections, and risk sidelining a local agency, or feedback loops whereby that local agency shapes the behaviour and decision-making of international actors.

On an empirical level, there has been, in Vrasti (2008)'s words, an emerging 'ethnographic turn' within International Relations, with some authors drawing upon concepts and methods within Anthropology to explore local level political practice. In certain policy fields, notably peacekeeping, there has been a move towards using ethnography to examine international institutions' encounters with local actors and processes. Work on peacekeeping in the Democratic Republic of Congo provides a particularly nuanced role for interactions between the staff of international organisations and local actors, including the populations that interventions are intended to serve (Autesserre 2010, 2016; Baines & Paddon 2012; Campbell 2018; Von Billerbeck 2017). Within the refugee context, there has been some work examining how international norms and organisations play out at a local level (Betts 2013; Schmidt 2013; Betts & Orchard 2014; Miller 2016).

Across all of this work, however, the dominant focus is on the international institutions themselves, albeit focusing on their operations at different geographical scales. Local actors mainly matter insofar as they change or shape the activities and impact of international norms and organisations. This is because international institutions are the primary focus, albeit at a national or local level. In contrast, we aim to reverse that assumption. By taking the activities of refugees themselves as the analytical starting point, and then examining how these are shaped by the encounter with international institutions, we flip the lens.

The Global Governed?

We introduce the concept of the 'global governed' as a means to critically interrogate the relationship between the 'governors' and the 'governed'. Our goal is to analytically turn global governance on its head, beginning with a focus on affected populations. While the theory and practice of global governance privileges states, international organisations, and other powerful transnational actors, our aim is to shift the primary analytical lens to the subjects of global governance. The goal is to see them not as passive objects of external governance, but as integral actors in the making of global governance, participating in the making of rules and norms and the creation and provision of global public goods.

We define 'the global governed' not as a population as such but as a mode of thought. It represents an ontological move to start from the bottom-up and to understand global politics from the vantage point of the affected communities, and from there outwards to interpret the experience of interaction with traditionally privileged actors such as states and international organisations. It is an approach familiar to anthropologists, but one that has remained marginal to academic International Relations. Indeed, Weiss and Wilkinson (2018) have argued that International Relations scholarship has generally failed to examine global governance from the 'everyday' perspective of those who are governed, themselves describing such populations as 'the globally governed'. However, they neither theorise nor develop in-depth case studies relating to the concept.

While the kernel of feminist (Tickner 1992; Shepherd 2009; Enloe 2014), Marxist (Gill 1993; Barkawi & Laffey 2002), post-colonial (Rao 2010; Seth 2011), and post-structuralist (Campbell 1998; Der Derian 1989; Edkins 1999) approaches to International Relations has been to reassert the voices of the marginalised and to challenge power, hierarchy and domination, the mainstream study of global governance with its stronger access to public policy makers has seldom incorporated such perspectives. This may be in part because the knowledge structures on which international public policy is based are primarily state-centric, but it may also owe much to the distancing and sometime impenetrable language adopted by post-positivist approaches to International Relations. Our aim is to shift the empirical focus to the lived experiences of affected populations, but to do so within a language and framework that can retain relevance to the mainstream theory and practice of global governance.

The 'global governed' has particular relevance for a subset of areas of governance, notably those with a presumed provider–beneficiary relationship. In areas such as refugee, humanitarian, development, health and peacekeeping governance, for instance, there is a dominant logic that international institutions understand best how to serve the collective interests of their subject communities. Given the presumption of an 'emergency' or 'crisis', the authority to govern is transferred from the community to a group of external actors. Where other community-based actors are engaged as providers, it is usually on the terms of the international institutions. As the purse-holders and partners of the national government, the latter retain the power of delegation and usually exercise significant authority over the populations they serve, including the community-based organisations through which they may choose to deliver services.

Beyond academic International Relations, a body of work has emerged that interrogates the relationship between international institutions and the global governed in some policy fields. In particular, the 'post-development' literature has emerged as a means of critically examining the interaction of international institutions and subject populations in the domain of development governance (Ferguson 1990; Scott 1998; Escobar 2011). Some of these ideas have been exported to other policy fields; for example, there is an embryonic 'post-humanitarian' literature (Chouliaraki 2013; Duffield 2018). The strength of this work is that it critically and ethnographically engages with top-down governance, recognises alternative forms of bottom-up governance, and explores interactions between international institutions and affected populations.

And while the post-development and post-humanitarian literatures mainly adopt a Foucauldian epistemology, we suggest that this is not a necessary or especially helpful aspect of the work; the key move should be seen as ontological rather than epistemological. Power relations within the everyday interaction of international institutions and affected populations can be understood in ways that are not just about discourse. Viewed from this perspective, the prefix of 'post-' should be regarded simply as an interrogation of the presumed benevolence of global governance. It represents a recognition that assistance models, across development, humanitarianism, health and peacekeeping, for example, are imbued with power, and that their complex interactions with subject populations need to be empirically examined from the perspective of the subject populations.

We therefore regard the 'global governed' as an umbrella concept for this research agenda. Applied to the refugee context, we use the concept of 'post-protection' in order to critically interrogate the relationship between global refugee governance and refugees. As with other aspects of the global governed literature, we use it to problematise top-down forms of protection, identify alternative bottom-up conceptions of protection and examine the role of power in mediating interactions between the governors and the governed. As with development and humanitarianism, 'protection' is a form of assistance that is presumed to be inherently benign; this representation, however, frequently masks that it is malleable, highly contested and frequently used to legitimate the authority to govern. Our argument is not that protection is necessarily bad but that an inherent relationship between protection, power and governance exists, and this needs to be better understood.

Methodology

In order to explore our main research questions, we engage in comparative ethnographic analysis across four main research sites in two countries: Kampala and Nakivale in Uganda and Nairobi and Kakuma in Kenya. Our case selection is guided by the aim of exploring both urban and camp contexts, to look at the same national groups across different sites (Somali, South Sudanese and Congolese), and to work across different institutional contexts within the same region. Given that our goal was not positivist theory testing but theory building, we did not start with a fixed idea of the type of variation we would encounter across the four sites in terms of the institutional context, refugees' activities or international organisation/community-based organisation interaction. Nevertheless, knowing that Uganda and Kenya have contrasting regulatory frameworks and assistance models – the former state allowing refugees the right to work and freedom of movement and the latter not – suggested that our inductive ethnographic work might lead to observed variation as the basis for comparison. While we do therefore seek to engage in comparative analysis across the four sites in order to compare and contrast, we do not do so with the aim of building generalisable insights.

Our principal ethnographic methods were semi-structured interviews, focus groups and participant observation. We used 'snowballing' to gain access to RCOs and refugee-led networks, initially through existing contacts in Uganda and Kenya established through other research projects. In our fieldwork, we tried to achieve a number of different tasks: first, to map the landscape of refugee-led initiatives relating to social protection; second, to engage in several in-depth case studies of refugee-led CBOs and refugee-led networks. In addition to our qualitative research, we also conducted a small-scale but representative 'social protection survey' in order to acquire quantitative data relating to refugees' perceived sources of social protection, including the relative importance of international and community-based sources of social protection. This survey involved incorporating a module of 'social protection' questions into a wider (n=8159) survey on the economic lives of refugees and surrounding host communities.

A key challenge of our fieldwork involved building collaborative relationships with our research communities, especially with refugee-led organisations. A small number of key nodal actors served as partners, helping us to navigate the communities and attain introductions. In order to improve trust, we made repeated site visits over the course of a fifteen-month fieldwork period. We also trained and employed refugees from the communities we researched as peer researchers, who provided invaluable insight into our project while better facilitating the trust of our informants. They received training in qualitative methods, including unstructured and semi-structured interviewing and participatory mapping. This enabled them to undertake independent follow-up ethnographic research with participant individuals, organisations and networks over the fieldwork period.

At the end of fieldwork, peer researchers were also involved in shaping our findings by offering feedback and sharing observations. We are committed to sustaining these relationships over time, aware of the challenges relating to the abrupt termination of relationships by researchers departing the field. Following the end of our fieldwork, we set up an email database and sent monthly updates to participants and peer researchers about the progress of the project.

Argument

One of the main contributions of this book is simply empirical: it is to render visible the contributions of refugees to providing social protection. Our case studies show that, despite significant constraints, refugees often engage in a diverse array of social protection activities, including through formally registering community-based organisations. In most cases, though, it is almost impossible for these organisations to be recognised as implementing partners or operational partners in their own right by UNHCR. While UNHCR staff generally encourage refugee-led initiatives, they often struggle to even name most of the refugee-led organisations, and prioritise relationships with established international and national NGO partners.

RCOs face the chicken-and-egg problem of not having the funding or recognition to build capacity but not having the capacity to acquire funding or recognition. Despite this, there are notable outliers that succeed against the odds. Furthermore, the motives and politics surrounding RCOs are complex, sometimes involving individuals with mixed motives that balance altruistic concerns with community status or career advancement.

More specifically, we show that there is variation across our four case studies; in the absence of an overarching global or national policy framework or strategy on RCOs, institutional practice is determined on an *ad hoc* basis. Given that it is a low priority for UNHCR, the practice is usually a reflection of the broader organisational culture of the particular national or sub-national branch of UNHCR. In some cases, it is more open and supportive; in other cases, less so. In turn, the scale and scope of refugee-led social protection is partly an outcome of the institutional context: whether and how refugees can get recognition and support; whether they can work in partnership with UNHCR and international NGOs or whether they are forced to work outside the formal structures of governance.

However, we also argue that these structures are not entirely deterministic; while they influence patterns of RCO formation significantly, there is also an agentic side to the story. A small number of outliers succeed in spite of structural constraints, notably because of their own charismatic leadership, networks and ideas. There is, we show, a common pattern underlying the emergence of these outliers: a story of *inspiration-opportunity-network*. Individual refugee leaders are inspired by an experience, have a chance opportunity to connect to expatriate support, and through this acquire access to a wider transnational networks and funding. Put simply, they succeed in spite of, rather than because of, the formal humanitarian system.

In the next chapter, we outline the theoretical framework on which this book is based, unpacking the concept of 'the global governed', its relationship to post-development, post-humanitarian and post-protection concepts. We then apply these ideas to outline a simple heuristic framework to describe and explain variation in the scope and scale of refugee-led social protection across the four sites.

We then turn to four empirical chapters that introduce refugee-led social protection initiatives. The chapters each follow the same structure: offering an overview of the landscape of refugee-led social protection, outlining the institutional context within which refugee-led social protection takes place, examining in-depth the types of RCOs that exist within the different national communities, and looking at UNHCR-RCO interactions, before seeking to explain our observations. We conclude by highlighting the book's implications for theory and practice.

2

Theoretical Framework

Across the low- and middle-income countries that host 85 per cent of the world's refugees, protection and assistance is provided to refugees by United Nations organisations in collaboration with a network of NGO 'implementing partners'. Whether in camps or urban areas, the dominant humanitarian model is usually premised upon a provider–beneficiary relationship: international organisations are the protectors and refugees are the protected. Food, clothing, and shelter are delivered top-down, and refugees are largely seen as passive recipients of aid. Of course, there is some nuance to this: a variety of consultations and participatory exercises take place, but these are generally chosen by the international actors and used to legitimate external intervention. Protection invariably becomes governance.

In parallel to this model, however, is a largely neglected story: refugees themselves frequently mobilise to create community-based organisations or informal networks as alternative providers of social protection. They mobilise bottom-up to provide sources of assistance to other refugees in areas as diverse as education, health, livelihoods, finance and housing. They usually do so despite a lack of access to external funding sources, recognition or encouragement. Sometimes, these informal sources of social protection may even be regarded by refugee recipients as more important than formal sources of assistance. Indeed, when asked to whom they would turn for social protection in an emergency, nearly 90 per cent of refugees in the city said they would turn to their own communities (see Appendix).

And yet refugee-led organisations (sometimes referred to as refugee community organisations, or RCOs) generally receive little international recognition or support. UN agencies privilege formal 'implementing partners' and 'operational partners'; these are usually international or national NGOs, not refugee-led organisations. Small-scale, refugee-led organisations are often unknown to international policymakers and can rarely meet the accounting, auditing, vetting or compliance requirements to make them eligible for regular humanitarian funding. Consequently, refugee-led initiatives are generally locked out of formal funding mechanisms and access to elite policy networks. The few RCOs that thrive tend to do so in spite of, rather than because of, the way that the formal humanitarian system is constructed.

These observations have practical implications. They highlight a vast, untapped resource of potentially effective and legitimate providers of social protection. They invite reflection on the conditions under which forms of self-protection and self-governance may be complementary to, or perhaps even more appropriate than, external governance. They challenge policymakers and practitioners to consider possibilities for more participatory approaches to global governance, not only for refugees but for affected populations more broadly.

Examining refugee-led organisations, though, also matters for theory. It can teach us a lot about the relationship between protection, power, and governance. On a normative level, what determines the legitimacy to protect and govern following conflict or crisis? On an explanatory level, what explains variation in the scale and scope of self-protection and self-governance activities that emerge among affected populations? In this chapter, we outline a framework for thinking about these questions. We move from the general to the particular: starting with global governance, moving onto refugee protection and then focusing specifically on RCOs in East Africa.

The Global Governed?

Within International Relations, global governance relates to all actions aimed at facilitating collective action, usually in order to address policy challenges with a transboundary dimension (Held 1995). Central to global governance is the recognition that the relevant actors are not just nation-states but also include non-state actors, such as NGOs or businesses, whether involved as participants in rule-making or as regulated by those rules (Hall & Biersteker 2002; Scholte 2002). And, yet, some actors are more analytically equal than others. Across the global governance literature, affected communities – the supposed beneficiaries – have only rarely been considered as important actors within global governance (Weiss and Wilkinson 2018). While victimhood is widely recognised, agency and transformative capacity are usually underplayed.

Our distinctive theoretical contribution is to advance the concept of 'the global governed', which we use critically and interrogatively to reassess the position of the subjects of global governance. We define 'the global governed' not as a population as such, but as a mode of thought: a way of way of analytically re-privileging the subjects of global govern-ance. The move is ontological: shifting the primary analytical focus from the governors to the governed. The aim is to explore the putatively governed as actors in their own right. Rather than being bracketed off as passive takers of rules, norms and aid, our aim is to see them as integral actors in global politics, with their own values, interests and power relations. The goal is not to romanticise; it is to repoliticise.

We suggest that this move has particular relevance within a sub-set of areas of govern-ance, notably those with a presumed provider–beneficiary relationship. In areas such as refugee, humanitarian, development, child protection, health and peacekeeping governance, for instance, there is a dominant logic that international institutions understand best how to serve the collective interests of their subject communities. Their legitimacy emerges from a sense that during a crisis or emergency the subject population's capacity for agency or self-governance is sufficiently diminished as to require external governance. As the money-holders and 'partners' of the national government, they retain the power of delegation and usually exercise significant authority over the populations they serve. They can act as gatekeepers and veto players vis-à-vis initiatives that emerge from within the community. And yet the traditional assumptions about hierarchy may obscure important sources of collective action by the so-called beneficiary population or undermine pathways to more complementary forms of collaboration with international organisations. So how can we advance this ontological shift and what does it imply in terms of a research agenda, whether for the refugee context or more broadly?

We think about social protection as a form of governance. And while liberal thought dominates work on global governance, there are already critical modes of thinking about how power and hierarchy operate within governance, some of which are especially germane to an examination of a subject population's own 'bottom-up' collective action. In particular, the 'post-development' and 'post-humanitarian' literatures offer a starting point for critically examining the interaction of international institutions and subject populations within global governance (Ferguson 1990; Rahnema & Bawtree 1997; Sachs 1997; Scott 1998; Duffield 2001, 2018; Chouliaraki 2006, 2013; Escobar 2011; Duffield 2018). These literatures are a useful starting point because of their focus on power, and because they broadly offer a research agenda that enables, first, exploration of the emergence and consequences of 'top-down' governance'; second, the interaction between governance and subject populations; and, third, the scope for alterative 'bottom-up' approaches to governance.

Arturo Escobar (2011)'s *Encountering Development* represents the seminal text of the post-development literature. It examines development as discourse, focusing on the social construction of the 'Third World', 'the South', and 'less developed' countries. Escobar is interested in how development interventions, which are often unwelcome or even harmful, come to be justified. He provides a historical genealogy of the creation of development and under-development and examines how elite-led global ideas relating to development are privileged over and above local conceptions of development, even when they often fail to meet their own stated objectives. Escobar's aim is to expose the power relations underlying development and render visible marginalised local approaches to development. In his own words, the goal is 'the liberation of the discursive field so that the task of imagining alternatives can be commenced' (Escobar 2011, p. 14). To do this, he draws upon his own ethnographic research with Colombian indigenous communities to demonstrate how local populations sometimes have alternative visions of development.

Relatedly, James Ferguson (1990) undertakes an ethnography of the World Bank's work in Lesotho. He examines the paradox of how, despite repeated failure, 'development' is able to retain its conceptual legitimacy, and repeatedly reinvent itself, whether at a global or national level. He explores a series of World Bank rural development projects in Thaba Tseka in Lesotho. He shows how the Bank, drawing upon generic templates and development 'expertise', tries to find more efficient ways for local pastoral communities to exploit their cattle. The interventions repeatedly fail, and each time the World Bank returns with slightly tweaked project proposals, undeterred by previous failure. Ferguson's ethnographic work reveals the sources of failure: the Bank's inability to understand local-level, context-specific dynamics. First, its state-centric framework cannot see that the Lesotho economy is based upon transnational migrant labour; it is intertwined with the economy of South Africa in ways that are not captured in Bank data. Second, the Bank's generic programme models cannot see that the role of cattle in Thaba-Tseka is not primarily to provide income but is rather a source of savings and status. Third, as a non-political organisation, it cannot recognise and understand how local and national politics alter and fundamentally shape how global templates play out in local contexts.

James Scott (1998)'s *Seeing Like a State*'s examines the emergence of the state. He too implicitly recognises a relationship between governance, protection and control. As states emerge, they seek 'legibility': the ability to render their populations transparent and knowable. Forms of standardisation, from currencies to weights and measures to language to freehold tenure, change forms of social organisation in order to enable effective governance. They are, for Scott, legitimated by a high modernist aesthetic, one that represents social transformation as inextricable from progress and linear improvement. Scott's subsequent work examines the ways in which subject populations sometimes resist incorporation into 'top-down' governance models that purport to be in the collective interest. He examines everyday forms of peasant resistance, and the ways in which, for example, communities in Burma have resisted the expansion of state governance (Scott 1987, 2009).

The post-development literature has application to areas of global governance beyond development. Lilie Chouliaraki (2013), for example, uses the phrase 'post-humanitarian' in the subtitle of her book on humanitarian communication. The work offers a critical analysis of the evolution of visual representations of humanitarian crisis, and the ways in which they are used by the media and humanitarian organisations. She examines representations of human suffering and the ambiguous relationship between solidarity and instrumentalisation. On the one hand, images may create empathy for distant, vulnerable strangers; on the other hand, they also serve to offer personal fulfilment to the viewer as a means to serve a variety of functions, from fundraising to political mobilisation. The work is path-breaking and draws upon broadly post-structuralist theory; however, it leaves significant untapped potential – beyond the realm of communications – for the insights of post-development to be adapted and applied to the humanitarian sphere.

Mark Duffield (2018)'s recent *Post-Humanitarianism* goes furthest to apply the post-development literature to the context of emergency aid. He uses the concept to examine the role that digital technology plays with humanitarian assistance, identifying it as a technique of control that allows transnational threats to the rich world to be contained within poorer societies. In doing so he identifies the role that humanitarianism plays as a tool of governance, in which surveillance and securitisation are further facilitated by the emerging role of innovation, business and technology.

The strength of the post-development approach is that it identifies the connection between assistance and governance, and the role of power therein. Furthermore, it offers a research agenda for understanding the relationship between provider and beneficiary in global governance, encompassing five broad questions. First, *how has governance emerged historically*? The work uses a range of methodologies, including genealogy and archaeology, to reveal the historical and cultural contingency of dominant discourse relating to assistance. How has the discourse evolved over time, and what explains how and why it has taken particular forms or been adopted by powerful actors in the ways it has? Second, *what does governance do*? For example, what practices are legitimated or made possible as a result of the discourse? What are the sources of legitimacy and authority for particular forms of institutional design and behaviour? What outcomes result, including harms and unintended consequences? Third, *what does governance marginalise*? For example, what kinds of norms, practices and behaviours are silenced, obscured or ostracised as a result of the dominant discourse? What tools of exclusion are used to render certain voices, ideas or values illegitimate or irrelevant? Fourth, *what bottom-up alternatives exist*? For example, to what extent are there emancipatory or subaltern voices, behaviours and ideas that exist below the radar? How might participatory or collaborative approaches to protection enable or constrain inclusion of these perspectives? How can emic perspectives be recognised through the use of ethnographic research methods? Fifth, *how can we think critically about these alternatives*? For example, how can we recognise and understand the power dynamics that exist within local communities? To what extent are even local voices subject to co-optation or instrumentalisation by powerful global actors?

These are precisely the empirical questions that are useful for understanding the relationship between protection and governance that we are interested in. And it is the

critical engagement with power at both the 'top-down' and 'bottom-up' levels that empirically distinguishes the post-development and post-humanitarian literatures and makes them
relevant to our interest in the relationship between protection and governance. However,
these literatures generally have a post-structuralist and Foucauldian underpinning, being
concerned with how institutional discourse constitutes the subject position of aid recipients,
reinforcing power asymmetry. Yet, there is nothing axiomatic about this. Indeed, the
different post-development and post-humanitarian authors arguably interpret Foucault in
fundamentally different ways. For example, while early Foucault insists on a purely discursive approach, denying any scope of agency or external critique, mid-career Foucault
identifies a greater role for material interests, choice and strategic resistance. Some authors
such as James Ferguson are implicitly more rooted within an early Foucauldian approach,
as indicated by an almost exclusive analytical focus on discourse, in contrast to Escobar and
Duffield for example, who place greater emphasis on the agency of both the powerful and
the subjugated (Eribon 1991; Macey 1993; Halperin 1995). Escobar and Duffield's more
direct critiques of Northern hegemony also suggest the type of epistemological investi-
gations into a discourse's truth claims that become present only after Foucault's early work
and are more characteristic of *A History of Sexuality* (1976) than *Madness and Civilization*
(1961), for example.

Furthermore, an insistence on a Foucauldian underpinning to post-development may
risk romanticising the local, neglecting material interests, and sidelining agency (Herzfeld
2005; Resch 1992). First, we should avoid romanticising the local. One of the biggest
criticisms of Escobar's work in particular is that is reifies the global/local binary, sometimes
demonising the global and romanticising the local. Although he recognises that many
grassroots, community-based approaches to development are hybrid structures that intern-
alise elements of mainstream development discourse, he frequently argues that local
responses are inherently better than those that emerge from the global level. He writes,
for example (Escobar 2011, p. 223), that 'the task of conceptualizing alternatives must
include a significant contact with those whose "alternatives" research is supposed to
illuminate', focusing on grassroots groups, local knowledge alternatives, and social mobilisation. He accentuated (Escobar 2011, p. 215), 'the defense and promotion of localized,
pluralistic, grassroots movements', critiquing the Colombian National Food and Nutrition
Plan and its relationship with the World Bank during the 1970s.

Rather than assume a normative hierarchy or a clear separation between global and local,
we examine community-based organisations through a critical lens. We recognise the
interdependence between the global and the local. For example, global discourses are
sometimes adopted, internalised and reproduced by local actors. Sometimes, the practices
of even local actors may have harmful intended or unintended consequences for other
members of the community. Consequently, we aim to adapt the post-development
approach by taking seriously the idea that agency and political economy operate 'all the
way down'. In other words, power and interests can and should be recognised and
understood at all levels of analysis, including within community-based organisations. Our
basic analytical tools are no less relevant within and among the local communities.

Second, we need to account for the role of agency. Foucault's account of behaviour is
highly structuralist. In his early work at least, there is no subject position outside of the
discourse; no neutral vantage point from which to understand the overall social structure.
A structuralist denial of individual agency, as is often attributed to a Foucauldian post-
development approach risks marginalising refugees' agency and the scope for progressive

social change. Therefore, we aim to strike a balance between recognising the centrality of power but also leaving open the scope for individuals and communities to recognise and challenge structural constraints.

Third, we must recognise material interests. A Foucauldian approach to post-development also tends to underplay the role of interests. The emphasis on discourse marginalises explanations for behaviour based on gain. In that sense, the post-development approach contrasts with neo-Marxist approaches that tend to balance a focus on discourse with a focus on material interests. A political economy approach is especially important in the context of refugee protection, in which the distribution of scarce resources creates winners and losers. Protection is effectively a value chain that confers money and status on particular individuals and organisations (Morris 2019). To fully understand protection, it is crucial to follow those value chains and ask *cui bono* (who gains)?

Instead, we regard the moniker 'post-' as implying an attempt to go beyond the narrative that governance is inherently good. As an approach, a research agenda that critically examines the interaction of providers and beneficiaries need not necessarily privilege discourse over material concerns. The value of adopting a 'post-'approach, whether to development, humanitarianism or protection comes from critically engaging with the relationship between assistance and governance and rendering visible the role of power therein. It offers a starting point, historically missing from academic International Relations, for examining the interaction between 'top-down' and 'bottom-up' levels, between the 'provider' and the 'beneficiary', while problematising such binaries.

We suggest that the concept of the 'global governed' represents an umbrella concept for these different 'post-' approaches. It can be defined as an ontological focus on the beneficiary or affected populations in global governance. While none of this is new to anthropologists of humanitarianism (Ticktin 2011; Bornstein 2012; Scott-Smith 2016) this alternative gaze is rarely adopted by the global governance literature in international relations, or by international public policy-makers (Autesserre 2010, 2016; Cloward 2014; Paddon Rhoads 2016). To be clear, the move is ontological rather than epistemological. It does not rely upon seeing the world in purely discursive terms; it relies upon critically understanding how global governance works through a dual regard for the ways in which 'top-down' governance constrains and enables subject populations and the potential for alternative, 'bottom-up' forms of collective action.

Post-Protection

Applied to the refugee context, we develop the concept of 'post-protection' in order to critically engage with the relationship between global refugee governance and refugees. A focus on refugees provides three specific and relevant analytical features: first, it involved global, national and local engagement; second, in the absence of the state it inherently involves questions about the authority to govern; third, it has a temporal quality, evolving from an emergency phase to varying degrees of normality. All of these features create a context within which the authority to govern is both contested and contestable.

To protect is to govern. But what determines the legitimacy of that governance? The premise of liberal political thought, from Locke and Hobbes onwards, is that people should be able to rationally consent to be being subjected to coercion and, by extension, governance. What normatively legitimates protection as a form of governance is the idea of an emergency.

Within international law, nation-states are the highest authority. The default is that they have sovereignty over their territory and jurisdiction, and hence the primary duty (and right) to protect is held by the state over its citizens. If the conventional state-citizen relationship breaks down because that state is unwilling or unable to provide protection, then there may be grounds for the authority to protect to transfer temporarily to the wider intergovernmental states system. The task of protection may then be delegated downwards: to a United Nations agency or further downwards to an NGO 'implementing partner'.

The presumption that authority can be transferred and delegated in that way stems from the notion of an emergency. The urgency created by a threat to life, and the presumption that a community cannot self-govern, legitimates the role of an outside 'protector'. For children, people who are not *compos mentis* or people in immediate danger, we accept a transfer of responsibility from the individual to another actor better placed to choose and act on that person's behalf. Such a context may justify 'paternalism' in Michael Barnett's (2011) words. Indeed, within international relations, it is normatively recognised that there may be circumstances under which people can legitimately take control (or 'custodianship') over other people's populations (Wilde 2010).

However, the treatment of a population as subject to an 'emergency' rather than as an ongoing political unit may be more normatively problematic for refugees than in other forms of humanitarian crisis. After the initial crisis and influx, protracted refugee situations are often calm, peaceful and relatively 'normal'. The salient analytical differences compared to surrounding populations is that they are on the territory and under the jurisdiction of another state, and that they are protected from forcible return to danger. But many protracted refugee situations simply would not conform to the normative test of legitimating governance without consent.

This is where 'post-protection' comes in as an analytical lens for critically engaging with the risks of protection as a form of top-down governance, and a means to recognise alternative forms of refugee-led protection. One of the risks of 'protection' is that, like 'development' and 'humanitarianism', it is seen as inherently benign. And yet it is almost infinitely malleable. Protection is what might be described as an 'essentially contested concept' (Gallie 1955). 'Protection' requires a threat, a protected object (a 'beneficiary'), and a protector. The first two elements are the same concepts inherent to security (Booth 1991; Waever et al. 1993; Paris 2001). The conceptual addition, though, is the *protector*, an actor who can legitimately intervene to mitigate the threat to the beneficiary. In comparison to 'security', the conceptual move to 'protection' is, therefore, to posit a relationship between a 'protector' and a 'beneficiary' based on an inherent power asymmetry. The rest of the content, both means and ends, remains undetermined.

The malleability of 'protection' is revealed by its varied uses by different policy actors. As with security, definitions vary on a spectrum between narrow and broad. At the minimalist end of the spectrum, for those engaged in the protection of civilians during armed conflict, protection relates simply to avoiding threats to physical safety. An intermediate perspective, used across the UN humanitarian system, defines protection as 'broadly encompass[ing] activities aimed at obtaining full respect for the rights of all individuals in accordance with international law – international humanitarian, human rights, and refugee law' (IASC 2006). At the maximalist end of the spectrum lies social protection, which includes action to address vulnerability. For example, many development banks work with the following definition: 'social protection is defined as the set of policies and programs designed to reduce poverty and vulnerability by promoting efficient labour markets, diminishing people's exposure to risks, and enhancing their capacity to protect themselves against hazards and interruption/loss of income' (Asian Development Bank 2001, p. 1).

The designation of a particular referent population as in need of protection, and of a third-party actor as a legitimate protector, has consequences. It legitimates a relationship between provider and beneficiary and confers on the latter the power to govern in the interests of the protected population.

The problem comes when the designation of 'protection' confers harm upon the 'beneficiary' population. Barbara Harrell-Bond (1986) has long documented the damaging consequences of 'imposing aid' within refugee camps. Long-term encampment, dependency, opportunities for rent-seeking or corruption, abuse and exploitation, infantilisation and a range of unintended consequences all emerge from her depiction of what takes place in UN-backed camps as the most archetypal example of an international protection space. She depicts the context of refugee camps for Ugandan refugees in Southern Sudan, highlighting the consequences of paternalism, lack of accountability and the ways in which power shapes interactions between international 'helpers' and refugees. Since then, social distance between providers and beneficiaries has arguably become even more disparate as compounds, cars and hotels have increasingly come to characterise the experience of the 'protectors' (Smirl 2015).

But a more straightforward dilemma also comes simply from denying a legitimate right to self-governance. The greatest risk of this top-down protection model is simply that it silences, neglects and excludes alternative visions of protection. It leaves little scope for refugees' own self-protection initiatives, for refugee-led social protection or for refugees' own networks and organisations to play a meaningful role. The terms of protection are pre-determined by external actors and processes, and broader questions like dialogue, participation, welfare and human flourishing are sacrificed at the global altar of protection. If international protection is to enhance welfare and promote human flourishing, then it would surely need to at least consider recognising emic forms of protection and giving voice and recognition to alternative providers of protection, including refugees themselves.

As Rebecca Sutton (2018) highlights, international law – and its instrumental use by particular actors – can play a central role in legitimating some protection actors, to the exclusion of others. Focusing on the role of International Humanitarian Law (IHL), she shows how IHL simply cannot recognise civilian self-protection because it defines the 'civilian' as a negative, in opposition to a 'combatant'; hence the notion of civilian agency is ruled out. For Sutton, international law plays a sociopolitical role in shaping humanitarian practice. Far from being simply doctrinal, it has, first, constitutive properties, creating categories that may reinforce power asymmetries, and second, instrumental properties, enabling actors to use an open-ended interpretation of international law to advance their own interests. Her analysis of IHL might be extended to consider the legitimating role of international refugee law.

In the refugee context, the main source of protection standards is the UNHCR 'Protection Manual', a repository of protection policy and guidelines. It mainly contains legal and policy sources organised thematically, most deriving their authority from intergovernmental consensus or UNHCR's own policy standards. As the guidance to the Manual notes: 'documents from external sources are generally not included'. The range of legitimate sources includes international treaties, UN General Assembly resolutions, UNHCR position papers, summary conclusions from UNHCR-led meetings and expert opinion mainly by

UNHCR legal staff. The Manual is mainly comprised of doctrine and policy rather than specific operational guidance.

UNHCR's own interpretation of the scope of international protection is broad and open-ended. When it is defined, though, it is often with a circularity of definition in relation to the mandate and work of the organisation, so as to effectively describe them as indistinguishable. One UNHCR Protection Note states: 'Given the broad scope of the overall objective of international protection, it is appropriate that the UNHCR Statute describes the protection function of the High Commissioner as encompassing virtually all the activities undertaken by [the] Office on behalf of refugees' (UNGA Note on International Protection 1994; UNHCR Statute Para 8). In other words, protection is what UNHCR does, and what UNHCR does is protection.

While UNHCR recognises the need to delegate protection tasks, these are delegated at the discretion of the organisation and the content of protection is derived from UNHCR's own protection standards: 'international protection involves seeking – in collaboration with Governments as well as non-governmental organisations (NGOs) – to meet the whole range of needs that result from the absence of national protection' (UNHCR 1994). In other words, standards of international protection are set by the UN system and by UNHCR, and either UNHCR implements these standards itself or it determines to whom such standards are delegated – usually to an Implementing Partner managed by national or international staff.

A post-protection approach allows us to critically interrogate the presumed benevolence of top-down approaches to protection and to draw attention to alternative, bottom-up approaches. Within the literature on civilian protection in armed conflict, research has already explored the role of civilian self-protection (CSP) (Baines & Paddon 2012; Kaplan 2013; Jentzsch, Kalyvas & Schubiger 2015; Jose & Medie 2015; Masullo 2017; Suarez 2017; Sutton 2018). It has examined the range of strategies adopted by crisis affected communities when faced with armed conflict or mass atrocities, including through nonengagement (e.g. flight, seeking protection or information sharing); nonviolent engagement (e.g. protest, collaboration or deception), or violent engagement (e.g. self-defense or joining militias or rebel groups) (Jose 2018).

The CSP literature demonstrates that, even during an emergency, there are myriad examples of civilian agency, including those that relate to protection activities. However, the CSP literature tends to define civilian self-protection fairly narrowly as 'actions taken to protect against immediate, direct threats to physical integrity imposed by belligerents or traditional protection actors, primarily selected and employed by civilians, and employed during an armed conflict' (Jose & Medie 2015; Jose 2018).

We suggest that the focus on self-protection can be broadened. Our focus differs from the civilian self-protection literature in four regards. First, we focus on refugees. This shift on focus from emergency to protracted crisis makes a difference in terms of time, which arguably makes the normative case for considering self-protection even stronger. Second, we focus on collective action by refugees to protect others rather than just action by individuals to protect themselves. Third, we focus on social protection rather than simply protection against threats to physical integrity. Fourth, we focus not just on civilians but on the interaction between international actors and affected communities. In that sense, our focus on refugee-led protection complements but broadens the existing CSP literature. A focus on self-protection strategies, whether by civilians in armed conflict or by refugees in a protracted crisis, can be considered contributions to the bottom-up dimension of a post-protection approach.

Refugee-Led Social Protection in East Africa

We apply our concepts of the global governed' and post-protection to examine refugee-led social protection in East Africa. The 'global governed' enables us to ontologically focus on the collective action of refugees themselves, and the ways in which they mobilise to provide social protection. 'Post-protection' offers a heuristic framework through which to critically examine the interaction between top-down international institutions and bottom-up refugee community organisations (RCOs). The main empirical question we are interested in exploring is: what explains variation in the scale and scope of refugee-led social protection?

In that sense, we use the global governed and post-protection frameworks as a means to shift the ontological focus. We use them in order to explain observed variation in practice. In the absence of a clear policy framework at the global level, there is considerable variation in the degree to which refugee-led organisations are supported, encouraged or emerge in different countries and contexts. This reflects the logic that ambiguous global norms lead to variation in national and local level practice (Percy 2007; Betts & Orchard 2014). In order to analytically operationalise our core concepts to explain variation, we draw upon a basic structure-agency framework. For each of our four empirical contexts, we examine the national institutional context as 'structure', and the capacities of refugee leaders to facilitate collective action as 'agency'.

Structure: What Explains Variation in Institutional Context?

Our argument is that UNHCR's receptivity (or otherwise) to RCOs is shaped largely by organisational culture at the national level. Meanwhile, RCO emergence is shaped by a combination of institutional constraints and the agency of individual charismatic leaders within the community working to transcend those barriers. Table 2.1 provides a descriptive overview of the variation seen across our four main research sites, Nairobi, Kakuma, Kampala and Nakivale. Each label is simply a heuristic characterisation of the institutional structures and refugee agency observed in each context: a way of simplifying our overall story.

In *Kampala*, the institutional context can be characterised as a 'monopoly'. InterAid has been the exclusive implementing partner (IP) of UNHCR for over two decades. Despite questions being raised over its performance and relevance, its mandate has rarely been questioned by UNHCR. This monopoly status has been renewed each year in the context of a tripartite agreement between UNHCR, the Government of Uganda and InterAid, with the Government strongly 'encouraging' InterAid's privileged position. Some NGOs, such as the

Table 2.1 Descriptive overview of the variation seen across our four main research sites – Nairobi, Kakuma, Kampala and Nakivale

	Top-down (structure)	Bottom-up (agency)
Nairobi	Contract	Compliance
Kakuma	Market	Struggle
Kampala	Monopoly	Activism
Nakivale	Co-optation	Scepticism

Finnish Refugee Council, Oxfam and HIAS, offer capacity-building for refugee-led organisations (RCOs), but outside of this RCOs receive almost no recognition, resources or collaboration from UNHCR or InterAid.

Two officers working in the protection unit on community-based protection affirmed that UNHCR worked with refugee-led organisations but were only able to provide one concrete example – that of YARID receiving funding from UNHCR's Global Youth Initiative Fund. Although they named two other refugee-led organisations, it was clear that no ongoing work with these organisations occurred. 'Sometimes we support refugee organisations in events,' one officer explained, 'generally this is in-kind, like helping with tents or chairs ... I actually don't know of other refugee CBOs [besides YARID] who received money from UNHCR in the last year.' When we asked whether they could imagine refugee-led organisations working with UNHCR as implementing or operational partners, one officer laughed and the other said 'They are too small and sometimes they disappear; it would be hard for UNHCR.'

The response of refugee leaders is 'activism'. Estimates by refugees themselves on the numbers of formal RCOs in Kampala vary from around twenty-five to over a hundred in 2018, not including unregistered organisations and associations. We also identified at least three – YARID, Bondeko and HOCW – that have raised funding in excess of $100,000 at some stage in their existence. But even their interaction with formal humanitarian governance is limited, and they have instead established parallel coordination structures. In November 2018, The Refugee Led Organisations Network (RELON) launched as a network for Kampala's organisations, with over twenty organisations represented. Neither InterAid nor UNHCR accepted the invitation to participate in the launch. Despite the limited relationship with IOs, RCOs are active across the Congolese, Somali and South Sudanese communities.

In *Nairobi*, the institutional context can be characterised as 'contract'. UNHCR is open to working with refugee-led CBOs, and its IPs do work collaboratively with several. However, the terms of the collaboration are largely defined top-down. Tasks are subcontracted to several CBOs and their staff by IPs. However, there are few opportunities for CBOs to access recognition, collaboration or funding on the basis of their own agenda or based on the priorities of the community. Meanwhile, the refugee response can be characterised as 'compliance'. Most CBOs wish to preserve their relationships with UNHCR and the IPs and so accept collaboration on the terms that are available.

In Nairobi, UNHCR is encouraging of RCO involvement in service delivery. However, it focuses mainly on encouraging its implementing partners to involve RCO-leaders as community workers. These community workers are employed as 'incentive workers' because of their networks and community knowledge. Through fostering relationships with well-known, reputable refugees, NGOs are able to access communities and broaden their reach and impact. But international NGOs often regard the degree of collaboration as limited by RCO capacity. The head of the Danish Refugee Council's community outreach programme explained what this 'building up' takes: 'We help them to organise, write their constitution, get registration ... We see informal groups, and the next step is to formalise because to bid for contracts and funding you must formalise.' However, she explained, 'There are very few groups which have thought through their projects properly, and many are just trying to pay themselves salaries rather than do something properly ... there is such a big gap in service delivery which refugee-led organisations can complement, but the problem is that many are trying to do too much.'

Many RCOs in Nairobi are content to work within this framework. Those that are able to position themselves as community intermediaries can get disproportionate access to international structures, which enables them to pursue their own more independent activities. Congolese organisations like the Union of Banyamasisi Refugees in Kenya and Family of Banyamulenge, for instance, represent the needs of their communities with UNHCR. Special interest groups are also sometimes able to access support and recognition, but this depends on what issues are prioritised and funded at an international level. The LGBTI refugee-led organisation CESSI receives financial assistance from UNHCR through the Danish Refugee Council, for example.

Observing these relationships, many refugee leaders are content simply to retain a positive working relationship even without formal status or recognition. The organisation Kintsugi runs with no institutional funding for operational costs, but their leader Bahati, who has a good working relationship with UNHCR and other agencies, hopes that framing their work as inclusive of LGBTI refugees and people with disabilities will lead to recognition and opportunities. Meanwhile, Christian Musenga, a paralegal trained by national NGO Kituo Cha Sheria, has also recently begun his own CBO, hoping to capitalise on the opportunities that are perceived to come from having a relationship with the big players in refugee protection.

In *Kakuma*, the institutional context can be characterised as a 'market'. UNHCR expects refugee-led CBOs to compete in order to meet a demand for social services. Either they can provide services that the community is willing to pay for, or they can compete to partner with IPs. Although UNHCR encourages refugees to register CBOs and welcomes their participation, it is reluctant to interfere with the market or to arbitrarily support one CBO rather than another. The result is that refugee CBOs face 'struggle', being caught in a chicken-and-egg dilemma: they need resources to develop capacity and competence, but they cannot access those resources without first demonstrating competence.

The market-based logic of Kakuma is endemic. The hashtag #IamKakuma alludes to a series of impressively unique features: the first camp to host a TEDx event, the home of more than half of the Refugee Olympics team, and the venue for a pioneering study that reveals Kakuma to be a $56 million economy ripe for investment (World Bank 2018). Together, UNHCR and the Turkana County Government are trying to reinvent Kakuma, based on a market-based model that can better serve both refugees and the host community, and a newly created market-based settlement called Kalobeyei, which includes 'cash-for-shelter' and an innovative cash-based assistance scheme. And the logic shapes UNHCR's attitude to RCOs. UNHCR's chief of sub-office, Sukru Cansizoglu, explained 'I want UNHCR to do less ... refugees are capable of doing lots of what IPs are currently doing.' What Sukru envisages is a system of social protection in which the market decides who provides what: either RCOs can sell their services directly to the community or they can compete by offering services to international NGOs. This, he suggests, requires 'an entrepreneurial mindset'. He uses the example of Lokado, a host Turkana organisation, to illustrate what is needed: 'Lokado recognised that it had a comparative advantage working with implementing partners including the Danish and Norwegian Refugee Councils and Lutheran World Federation as an intermediary with the communities'.

However, few RCOs can thrive in this marketplace. While around thirty RCOs have registered as CBOs with local government in the regional administrative capital, Lodwar, most struggle for funding or recognition. Only one RCO – SAVIC – has its own building and external funding, and it is an exception. It was founded by two Congolese refugees who spent time as community organisers in Tanzania and then *chose* to come to Kakuma to set up the organisation. SAVIC collaborated with the Xavier Project in order to apply for UNHCR Innovation Funding, enabling it to scale its work on sex and gender-based violence and vocational education and obtain a building. Visibility in turn led to chance meetings with American and Chinese philanthropists, who have since funded a variety of initiatives, including expanding its buildings and purchasing thirty bicycles so its staff are able to move around the camp with more ease.

In *Nakivale*, the institutional context can be characterised as 'co-optation'. Many refugees accuse UNHCR and its IPs of 'stealing' their better ideas. Some IPs have justified independently pursuing ideas generated with refugees on the grounds of the limited capacity or competence of refugee-led CBOs. We found several examples of this type of co-optation. This has created a climate of mistrust. The response of refugees has been 'scepticism': lacking confidence in the formal organisational structures, they often disengage, with many community leaders reluctant to register CBOs or to work collaboratively with UNHCR and its implementing partners.

UNHCR in Nakivale is heavily controlled by the Ugandan Government's Office of the Prime Minister, and its staff are subject to rapid turnover, especially among nationals. This contributes to an environment of pervasive mistrust between refugees and UNHCR. Neither UNHCR nor OPM has much faith in the capacity of RCOs. Henry, a longstanding UNHCR staff member, explained that he is not aware of refugee community initiatives other than those groups that were started by agencies like American Refugee Committee, but tells us that 'one of the big changes I have observed is that refugees now are more educated. There are more political refugees and they understand technology.' But he notes that in terms of refugee-led social protection, 'They are not there yet. Self-reliance is happening at a slow pace. Refugees resist because of the weather and environment in the settlements, which make work hard for them. We build the schools and pay the teachers, but refugees do not want to stand on their own feet and sell chapati to pay the school fees.' But he suggests that if RCOs are going to thrive they must learn to compete: 'UNHCR encourages refugee CBOs to compete in an open market with transparent bidding procedures ... it's not up to us to assist you with further opportunities, you will need to figure out the next step.' Meanwhile, Esau, OPM's deputy camp commander, especially singled out the Congolese; 'they have a poor attitude to work and education. The majority of refugees who bother us about resettlement are Congolese.'

Refugees are in turn deeply suspicious of UNHCR, its motives and its relationship to OPM. Shauri, a Congolese refugee living in Nakivale since 2014, explained that the organisational culture is shaped by the government and UNHCR simply follows what the government wants, saying 'They just move between each other's offices, sharing information. You can't trust any of them. They are all Ugandans, working together.' But refugees also recognise that UNHCR staff want to benefit from the visibility of being outwardly seen to support refugees. Shauri set up League for Peace and Joy of the Young Generation in 2015 to provide professional opportunities to young refugees. However, Shauri was disheartened by the message from UNHCR:

> UNHCR use young people to show that they're doing something by putting on performances and competitions and taking photos for publicity. We only see them on World Refugee Day, International Women's Day and World Youth Day. We are sometimes invited to give ideas to UNHCR directly but maybe 1 per cent get considered ... UNHCR does not see refugees as having knowledge or a vision of their

own. We can do more than just sing and dance and play music. Refugees are losing hope because of the limitations that are placed upon us; we should be free to express ideas and contribute to change in Nakivale. What use is knowing how to dance when we need to get jobs when we go back to Congo?

One RCO leader of the Wakati Foundation, Alex, recounted working with the American Refugee Committee (ARC): 'they wanted to know how they might be able to support Wakati Foundation in our work'. Back in 2015 ARC was in charge of sanitation on behalf of UNHCR, and needed to build some new toilet blocks, so after some discussions, Alex suggested that Wakati Foundation could be subcontracted to do this work. As part of this process ARC asked for them to submit a budget in order to be considered. The budget came in at a third of the cost that ARC had anticipated spending. 'They were so pleased and surprised that we could do this work for them at such a price', Alex recounted, smiling. But when the toilets were built, the organisation would not name Wakati Foundation as the builder. Instead, emblazoned on the sides is the note 'built by ARC with support from UNHCR'. Alex was furious. 'This is so disheartening for the boys who have worked on this, not to have their work recognised.' The dispute over the toilets was eventually resolved, and Wakati Foundation is now named as the builder of the facilities on the blocks. But Alex is wary of working with them again. 'It is better that we stay independent. These organisations, they do not work for refugees. They will exploit us if they have a chance.'

Agency: What Explains Variation in RCO Emergence?

The quantity and quality of refugee-led CBOs is partly a result of these institutional opportunity structures. The presence or absence of recognition, collaboration and funding opportunities serves as a major constraint on the creation and growth of CBOs. However, despite the constraint, there are rare examples of CBOs flourishing, largely due to particular community entrepreneurs, with particular sets of networks, motives and sources of social capital. These 'outliers' – like SAVIC in Kakuma and YARID in Kampala – serve to highlight the agency of refugees. However, they also show how hierarchies and inequalities within the communities based on gender, language and education limit the refugee actors to whom community entrepreneurship is available. Across all the case, these outliers show how CBO creation is generally only available to a small 'elite' group of refugees.

As previously mentioned, RCOs face a chicken-and-egg dilemma. In order to receive recognition and funding, they need to have capacity. But in order to have capacity, they need recognition and funding. As Farhan, founder of a Somali-led RCO in Kenya, explained, 'we want international organisations to engage us directly ... but if you don't have the money, you won't get the money'. The challenge, as he highlighted, is that RCOs are expected to compete immediately. They are expected to either be able to offer services to NGO implementing partners or be able to provide services for a fee to the community. But most need support to develop in order to be competitive within this type of social protection 'marketplace'.

The few RCOs that thrive usually do so by bypassing the formal humanitarian system. The 'outliers' that build significant capacity usually have a strikingly similar background. Usually, the process involves three steps. First, it involves an individual refugee arriving in the host country, experiencing personal challenges, interacting with another NGO, and then deciding to create a CBO. Second, the key event that leads to take-off is often a chance meeting with an actor from outside the community who connects the refugee leader to a wider network. These networks generally include foundations, governments, philanthropists and academics. Third, the breakthrough comes when people or organisations within a transnational network provide funding. This story of *inspiration-opportunity-network* lies behind the narrative of nearly every successful refugee social protection entrepreneur we met in Uganda and Kenya. But within this process, individual leadership matters. From Felicity Susan at URISE to Robert Hakiza at YARID to Charles K. at CESSI to Bahati Ghislain at Kintsugi, charismatic leaders make a difference.

Across our four research contexts alone we mapped out over eighty registered RCOs providing social protection services to tens of thousands of refugees. They vary in scale, scope and specialisation. Most focus on the nationality group of the founders, and some target refugees across communities. They are shaped by gaps in formal service provision, cultural norms and the experiences and aspirations of their leaders. Most are small and struggle to access funding or recognition. Despite this, a few outliers flourish, mainly because of their founders' exceptional leadership and the creation of transnational networks that offer opportunities for funding. Here we outline some examples:

First, *Hope for Children and Women Victims of Violence (HOCW)* is a Kampala-based organisation started in 2008 by Congolese refugee Bolingo Ntahira. Initially an informal community self-help group, it expanded when international volunteers helped connect Bolingo to potential donors. HOCW provides various livelihoods activities for both refugees and local Ugandans, who make up 40 per cent of its beneficiaries. It has a well-regarded English language programme, with refugee teachers representing several different nationalities and teaching classes based on ability and nationality. HOCW is responsive to the needs of the community in Ndejje, where it is based, and started a tailoring programme to help its members, who are primarily poor women, to diversify their skills. Today it runs a range of activities in addition to its central livelihoods and English programmes, including child sponsorship, modern agricultural training and psychosocial counselling. It currently assists over 1,300 refugees and Ugandans. In 2018 HOCW ran all its operations, including activities, overheads and staffing costs, on a budget of $104,000.

Second, *Solidarity and Advocacy with Vulnerable Individuals in Crisis (SAVIC)* is an organization that works with vulnerable young people in Kakuma camp, northern Kenya. SAVIC was registered in Kenya in 2010 by two Congolese refugees named Muzabel Wulongo and Vasco Amisi, who met in Tanzania's Kigoma camp in 1996. They ended up in Kakuma when the Kigoma camp closed, and both recognised the need for a similar kind of sexual and reproductive health training that they had been involved in delivering as youth chairmen back in Tanzania. Although Muzabel was resettled to the United States in 2014, he remains involved in directing and fundraising for SAVIC, successfully securing funding from various American foundations as well as getting contracts to deliver training from Swiss Contacts and the Xavier Project, two of UNHCR's implementing partners in Kakuma. Since 2010 SAVIC has trained 6,000 young people, with 2,000 graduating from SAVIC programmes in English, tailoring, ICT and financial literacy, and 2,500 girls educated on sexual and reproductive health. In 2018 SAVIC held assets worth $165,000 and has an operating budget of $200,000 a year.

Third, *Kobciye*, meaning 'empowerment' in Somali, is a community organisation in Nairobi that was started in 2009 by the father of the current director, Afrah Abdullahih. Afrah's family had been resettled in Ottawa, Canada, in the early 1990s from Somalia. In 2001, Afrah's father returned to Somalia and Kenya to work as a Child Protection Officer for UNICEF, but he felt he could make a bigger impact through his own organisation, focusing on youth empowerment. Kobciye's community centre in Eastleigh opened in 2010; it offers training in leadership, conflict resolution and life skills to residents of Eastleigh, whether refugees or Kenyans. Members can also study accounting and computer literacy. Kobciye holds various community events, including an annual sports tournament known as the Unity Cup, a youth conference on countering violent extremism and has also hosted a technology and entrepreneurship summit. Kobciye trains over 450 students a year, and also has wider impact through its conferences and outreach activities. In 2018 it ran all these programmes and activities on a budget of $125,000.

Fourth, the *Wakati Foundation* – meaning 'the passing of time' in Swahili – was created in 2013 by Alex Mango, a Congolese refugee who lives in the Nakivale settlement. The organisation employs refugees to undertake small-scale public works projects such as building latrines and sports facilities, and it builds houses and community structures for vulnerable people who are struggling to set up secure homes on their allocated land. The idea for the Wakati Foundation came to Alex when he saw the impact of displacement on the mental health of refugees, which was driving young men to drink and use drugs. Many of them had skills that they were unable to use and felt hopeless and frustrated by the passivity expected of them in the settlement. Alex has used his own education in community development and business acumen to negotiate and subcontract building work from implementing partner organisations including the ARC (now known as 'Alight'). The Wakati Foundation also has connections to the Congolese diaspora, which supports its activities through remittances. In 2018, the Wakati Foundation operated on a budget of $75,000, supporting at least 250 families.

Fifth, the *Community Empowerment and Self-Support Initiative (CESSI)* was started by Ugandan refugee Charles K. in 2015, shortly after he came to Kenya. Charles had been in the middle of a Masters degree in Community Development when he was forced to flee the country during a spate of homophobic violence. Soon after arriving in Nairobi, Charles came up with the idea for a community organisation that would assist LGBTI refugees, who were particularly vulnerable due to being excluded from many of the informal community-based sources of social protection available to other refugees. CESSI delivers livelihoods training to LGBTI refugees so that they can set up their own small businesses, including hair salons and restaurants. Charles' connections and advocacy for LGBTI refugees means that CESSI benefits from local partnerships with organisations, including UNHCR and the Danish Refugee Council, that are trying to work with LGBTI refugees and help them to run their programmes. CESSI's affiliation with a local Kenyan LGBTI organisation called Health Options for Young Men enables them to legally receive funds from outside Kenya. CESSI currently has 156 members from Uganda, Ethiopia, Rwanda, Burundi, Somalia, Congo and even Yemen, and its 2018 budget was $45,000. Overall, then, the picture that emerges is that refugees are important and neglected providers of protection and assistance.

Despite abstract commitments to work with refugee at the global level, there is significant variation in how international organisations actually work with refugee-led organisations at the national level. RCOs generally struggle to access funding and recognition. However, despite facing structural constraints, a small number of 'outlier' organisations manage to thrive and provide social protection within their communities. Usually there is a common pattern behind these unlikely success stories: an individual inspired to work on behalf of the community has a chance opportunity, which allows access to a transnational network of support, thereby enabling her or him to bypass the formal humanitarian system.

3

Kampala

In April 2017, an article in the *Guardian* newspaper asked: 'Is Uganda the world's best place for refugees?'[1] It described the welcoming nature of Uganda's refugee policies, which offer refugees the right to work and freedom of movement. Under the government's Self-Reliance Strategy, refugees in Uganda's settlements are provided land to farm and basic material assistance. Yet 100,000 refugees have chosen to forfeit access to formal assistance and instead live in the capital city of Kampala. Just south of the central bus station, the slums of Kisenyi have become a hub for Somali businesses selling everything from electronics to hijabi fashions, imported from all over East Africa. In Nsambya, a surburb to the south-east of the city, majority Congolese refugee neighbourhoods have sprung up. And near Makerere University in the northern quarter, thousands of South Sudanese refugees live, study and work.

In Kampala, direct assistance to refugees is virtually non-existent. Instead, the explicit focus of UNHCR and the Government of Uganda services to refugees is 'protection': a category encompassing status determination, processing, documentation, and counselling. A host of international and national non-governmental organisations work as operational partners for UNHCR, with the shared objective of integrating refugees into Uganda's healthcare and education systems. Yet the only Implementing Partner of UNHCR in Kampala is InterAid, a Ugandan NGO which since 1995 has delivered the Urban Refugee Programme under a tripartite agreement with UNHCR and the Office of the Prime Minister, which is responsible for refugee management on behalf of the government of Uganda. As well as integration of refugees into existing services, InterAid provides psychosocial counselling to refugees traumatised by conflict.

Yet beyond these formal institutions, a diverse landscape of refugee community-based organisations (RCOs) has flourished in Kampala. These initiatives support refugees, and often Ugandans too, to build lives in the city in spite of the lack of support and assistance available to them. Filling the gap in services available from the Urban Refugee Programme and the limited alternative assistance offered by formal institutions in the city, refugees have set up numerous initiatives. These include language classes and financial literacy classes to promote integration with the host community; peace promotion projects to bring together young people from different ethnicities; and business training in areas such as hairdressing, tailoring and agriculture to help them thrive in Kampala.

---

[1] Bhekisisa, M. D. R., 2017. *Is Uganda the world's best place for refugees?*, Guardian Africa Network: The Guardian.

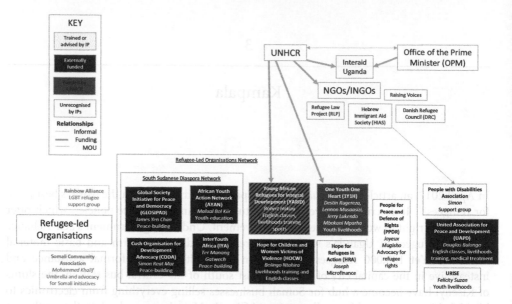

Figure 3.1 Refugee-led, national and international organisations in Kampala

Figure 3.1 maps the main international, national and refugee-led organisations we encountered during our research in Kampala. The figure is not intended to be comprehensive but serves to illustrate the types of connections and partnerships that exist between formal international and national organisations and those led by refugees, and those that exist between the refugee-led groups. In particular, it shows the limited extent of engagement between formal institutions and RCOs in their various forms. Most refugee-led organisations were not receiving assistance from UNHCR's implementing partners in Kampala; and a significant number had managed to find alternative streams of funding instead.

The figure offers an overview of the variety of organisational forms that refugee-led protection and assistance take across the main nationality groups in Kakuma. For example, there are relatively few formally registered Somali RCOs. Several of our Somali informants were sceptical about the ability of either international NGOs or UNHCR to provide assistance to urban Somali refugees. Some Somalis feel this way based on direct comparisons of what the international community provides with what they think Somalis need and what they are able to offer each other; a common saying is that 'Somalis will always help each other out', and so many believe that the most important source of support for newly arrived refugees is from within the community, rather than from external sources.

For Somalis, the formal provision of social protection is not a priority; it is coordinated along hierarchical lines through a community umbrella organisation, the Somali Community Association (SCA). The SCA exists to ensure that those in need are assisted within the community, and regularly advocates to the Office of the Prime Minister (OPM) for the continued security of the Somali community as a whole. Its form is thus shaped through both Somali cultural norms around authority and leadership, and by the institutional structures it sees as most relevant; OPM does not expect to work through an RCO, and Somalis do not expect assistance from those who might be.

In contrast, formal organisations proliferate among the Congolese community. The Refugee Led Organisations Network (RELON), a Kampala-based network of RCOs recently created by Congolese refugees, is illustrated in Figure 3.1 by a line around its nine member organisations. Congolese refugees are the most numerous nationality group in Kampala. Partly reflecting this, Congolese-led RCOs have proliferated, engaging in activities as diverse as providing business training, teaching English, and exerting political pressure on the formal refugee system in Kampala. The formal registration of groups of refugees as community-based organisations rather than just 'self-help groups' is very common among the Congolese community. Legitimacy and authority are key issues here; certain Congolese organisations are able to generate support both within their communities and from international donors, whilst others feel marginalised.

The most established Congolese RCOs, like Hope for Children and Women (HOCW) and Young African Refugees for Integral Development (YARID), have followed the rules laid out by the international refugee regime in terms of replicating what they believe a credible community operation looks like in order to gain recognition and support. Yet they have also been able to draw on social solidarity amongst the Congolese to create this network; whilst institutional recognition matters for funding, connections at a grass-roots level still matter, particularly for RCOs that lack the capacity to engage with international institutions and donors. This challenge helps to explain the emergence of RELON, which we discuss in this chapter.

The experiences of South Sudanese in Kampala highlight another important strand of the story of social protection in the city: its political economy. South Sudanese refugee leaders – generally the heads of pre-existing organisations in South Sudan – sometimes explained that they chose to settle in Uganda due to its straightforward laws on grassroots organisations and relatively benign stance on refugees. Kampala is therefore something of a utilitarian destination for South Sudanese human rights defenders like Inter-Youth Africa, the Global Society Initiative for Peace and Democracy and Africa Youth Action Network, which have fostered international contacts interested in supporting the South Sudan peace process. However, South Sudanese refugees do not look to the government of Uganda for anything more than this; their sources of support remain transnational, namely international organisations invested in South Sudan's future. Markedly better connected to formal international actors than other nationalities, South Sudanese social protection initiatives in Kampala present an interesting case for thinking about where money to facilitate refugee activities comes from, to whom, and for what reasons.

Institutions

As is clear from Figure 3.1, funding for RCOs rarely comes from UNHCR or its operational and implementing partners. Only two RCOs in Kampala – YARID and One Youth One Heart (1Y1H) – appear to have been funded by UNHCR. In both cases, that funding has come a specific youth innovation funds (the Youth Initiative Fund) coordinated as a one-off competition by UNHCR Headquarters in Geneva. Such opportunities are very much the exception. However, even when this funding has been awarded, the money has not always been forthcoming. For example, YARID's award was for a 'Soccer for Peace' programme in 2016. The funding that YARID won through the UNHCR Youth Initiative Fund competition was contested by UNHCR Uganda, who pointed out, following UNHCR Headquarters' decision to award, that YARID was not an implementing partner of UNHCR and therefore should not be permitted to receive the agreed funding. YARID's Director explained:

> It was impossible to get the money. We spent six months arguing how the money would be spent. Eventually we got it in November, and they told us we had to spend it by December! Geneva controlled the money and was saying to UNHCR in Kampala 'we don't care if you give them the money'. I even told the Senior Programme Officer I was no longer interested, and she said they would send it to Interaid. Eventually, it was channelled through Windle Trust International. They wanted to charge administration costs but UNHCR stopped them. We had to do the project in just six weeks. The next year they said they would do the same funding. But UNHCR requested lots of documents. First, we signed a tripartite agreement. And then they said it was not valid. Then we signed a new agreement. Then they said it would not work because we needed to be a UNHCR Implementing Partner. But we are not able to become an IP.

Indeed, within Kampala, the general view of UNHCR staff is that to receive UNHCR funding requires the status of 'implementing partner' (IPs) but that RCOs are unlikely to meet the requirements to become an IP. One UNHCR staff member, working in the protection unit in community-based protection explained, 'Sometimes we support refugee organisations in events,' one of them explained, 'generally this is in-kind, like helping with tents or chairs ... I actually don't know of other refugee CBOs [besides YARID] who received money from UNHCR in the last year.' But another colleague from the same unit did not think it realistic for refugee-led organisations to become UNHCR implementing or operational partners: 'They are too small and sometimes they disappear ... It would be hard for UNHCR.'

The InterAid Monopoly

In 2015 UNHCR Uganda published a call for expressions of interest for partnership with organisations to collaborate in the implementation of UNHCR assistance projects across Uganda, including in Kampala.[2] This call was welcomed by many refugees as a chance to dismantle the supremacy of InterAid, UNHCR's sole Implementing Partner (IP) in Kampala. InterAid is a Ugandan organisation which has implemented Kampala's Urban Refugee Programme since 1995 and is meant to support all nationalities of refugees residing anywhere in the city. One refugee leader in Kampala wrote to UNHCR about this directly, stating: 'It is encouraging that UNHCR is making a public call for partnership after working with only one partner in Kampala for over a decade. I believe it's going to play a big role in improving the services delivered to refugees in Uganda.' The letter went on to highlight UNHCR's exclusion of refugee-led organisations:

> ... Under the current guidelines, refugee-run organisations do not have the possibility to become implementing partners of UNHCR. I believe this needs to change, as refugees are in a unique position to support each other – if resources are available. The Uganda Refugee Policy gives refugees the right to work, freedom of movement and the right to organize themselves in associations or organisations but it seems that they are not enjoying fully that opportunity because of lack of support and resources from big Organizations include [sic] UNHCR. Today the bottom up approach is recommended

---

[2] http://web.monitor.co.ug/Tenders/2015/06/16/unhcr-partners23062015.pdf

to make sure affected communities are involved in all stages of the assistance and integration process to make sure they become responsible of their own destiny. This includes collaborating and partnering with refugee-run organisations. I would like here to inform you that refugee-run organisations exist in Kampala and I believe they have the potential to be implementing partners of UNHCR in different areas ... Therefore, I request for refugee-run organisations to also be considered in this call of partnership and suggest a meeting with leaders of refugee-run organisations to discuss this possibility further.

This letter to UNHCR went unanswered, and later in the year InterAid was announced as the continuing – and sole – UNHCR implementing partner in Kampala. Our own requests for meetings with UNHCR Uganda or InterAid with refugee-led organisations during our research were met with either silence or disinterest. At the launch of RELON in November 2018, only the Office of the Prime Minister sent a representative, despite invitations having been sent to numerous community support workers at both UNHCR and InterAid. One refugee offered a perspective on InterAid:

> What InterAid does is fight refugee-led organisations because they see us as competition. UNHCR is working with four local organisations and they are all national organisations. In Kampala it is just InterAid, and they have been the only urban IP for twenty-five years. The UN audit on the corruption scandal said one of the organisations was involved in corruption. It wasn't named but all the refugees know who it was.

It is unsurprising that RCOs expressed reluctance towards 'partnering' with InterAid. Many refugees we spoke with expressed a feeling that effective, active RCOs were overlooked for funding when there were opportunities for partnership in project implementation to which funding was attached. This was primarily attributed to InterAid's fear of competition. InterAid was perceived to prefer to partner with organisations which they could direct and control. One CBO in Kampala that InterAid partnered with and appeared to provide for financially was Refugee Now, which described itself as a platform for urban refugees to improve their lives. However, other refugees alleged that it was run by InterAid staff, with refugees included only as tokenistic evidence of InterAid's 'community' basis. Overall, refugees did not speak highly of the existing opportunities they saw for engaging with refugee-serving institutions in Kampala.

The experiences of the RCO URISE illustrate the frustrations refugees feel towards the opportunities for engagement that InterAid presents. A youth group led by a charismatic young Congolese refugee called Felicity, URISE had formed in 2017 when its members met through participating in music, dance and drama (MDD) groups put together by InterAid. Their objective was to foster the talents and ambitions of young people and expand opportunities for them. InterAid had groups that did MDD, but URISE wanted to move beyond that to train other young people in the community in these areas, which included creative pursuits like music, art and design, but also computer programming and business. In turn, they envisioned that young people would be able to make money through the skills they developed.

URISE members were involved in other activities to make money to support their 'showcasing' activities. Many of them had received skills training from international non-governmental organisations (INGOs) in Kampala, including Kampabits and the Butterfly Foundation, which did not specifically target refugees, offering assistance to disadvantaged young people in general. These skills in art, graphic design and computer programming were what they hoped to be able to teach to other young people. After painting the murals of the Antonio Guterres Urban Refugee Centre at Kabusu, which URISE had hoped would show InterAid what they were capable of, Felicity had heard that InterAid was looking for someone to manufacture paraphernalia for their Youth Solidarity Summit. URISE bought a printing press and used it to make sample t-shirts, mugs and badges. They took them to InterAid – but InterAid, she said, chose a Ugandan youth group to design and produce the shirts for the summit. 'They were three days late delivering the items – they nearly missed the event,' Felicity said resignedly. 'The lack of opportunities for refugees is a big challenge, especially for young people. But who should you go to when the person to whom you are reporting your challenges is the same person stopping you?'

UNHCR Uganda's approach to refugee-led organisations can be understood as a continuation of its ongoing 'provider/beneficiary' model, with RCOs falling under the mandate outlined in the 'community-based protection approach' it claims to take (UNHCR 2013: 6). Refugees' participation under this approach positions them ultimately as beneficiaries, rather than engaged through meaningful delegation of responsibilities or supported to orchestrate their own ideas. The refugees we spoke with were keenly aware of this dynamic, sharing experiences of countless 'sensitisation trainings' in areas such as health and gender-based violence to which community leaders tend to be invited. Yet these trainings were not followed up with the provision of material or equipment to act upon their presumed 'newly acquired' knowledge. Any funding allocated on paper for such activities, according to refugees, was rarely actually received.

An institutional culture in which there is no institutional support for activities, let alone capacity building, forces RCOs to remain small. To refugees, this is not accidental, but seen as a deliberate strategy for retaining the status quo in Kampala. And to the leaders of RCOs, UNHCR appears remote. One explained, 'Of course, I understand the challenges they have with the government. The government is on top. UNHCR cannot work at all without the government . . . I have tried to get a meeting with the UNHCR Representative since he came here. I have written at least three times but never had a response . . . We never see anyone on the ground except for the community services people, and they are basically the same as InterAid'.

Working within the System

These institutional barriers to participation within the formal humanitarian system have been unable to deter refugees from setting up their own civil society organisations. Uganda's legal environment is key to understanding why RCOs have been able to proliferate despite the challenges they face. Since the late 1980s and 1990s, community-based organisations, associations and networks have been an important part of good governance programming in Uganda, with international donors seeking to engineer the development of civil society through which to implement poverty alleviation programming (Dicklitch 2001). In 1986 there were fewer than 200 NGOs registered with the government; by the end of 2013 there were over 12,500.[3]

---

[3] Uganda National NGO Forum (2015) *A position paper and clause by clause analysis of the NGO Bill 2015.* Available at: http://chapterfouruganda.com/resources/reports-analysis/cso-position-paper-ngo-bill-2015.

This legal environment has led to the emergence of a multitude of community-based organisations, including those created and run by refugees. Yet, although the process of registering a CBO is straightforward and relatively inexpensive thanks to the 1989 NGO Act and subsequent amendments, it is also a legal requirement for all NGOs operating in Uganda to register with the NGO Registration Board of the Ministry of Internal Affairs. The legislation added in 2006 and 2016 builds on this requirement and seeks to control CBOs and discourage involvement in overtly political activities.

This has implications for refugee-led organisations seeking to grow and mobilise refugee communities towards common goals. At the launch of RELON, refugee representatives were sternly reminded by the OPM representative in attendance that their role was to 'stick to non-political activities, conform, and do genuine work to promote peaceful coexistence'. 'We face a lot of bureaucracy and censorship here' explained Augustin of Youth Action Empowerment Initiative, a South Sudanese organisation which he registered in 2015. 'Our services are reduced to advocacy and we cannot do anything transformative. We are limited by this system.'

In Kampala, there are refugee assistance organisations that fall outside the tripartite agreement between the government, UNHCR and InterAid. The Finnish Refugee Council (FRC), International Rescue Committee and Jesuit Refugee Service are operational partners (OPs) of UNHCR, running a variety of programmes for refugees in Kampala. Other INGOs that refugees mentioned were the Windle Trust Uganda (WTU), which gives a few scholarship opportunities each year to refugees from the settlements to attend urban universities. The Lutheran World Federation does some advocacy work; like WTU, it is funded by UNHCR, but neither LWF nor WTU are considered implementing partners. FRC has been working in settlements and camps since 2004, but it only opened an office in Kampala in 2009, offering training in English and Business. In 2018 it coordinated and implemented projects across Kampala under the areas of Youth, Business (Livelihoods), Literacy, Capacity Building for Refugee-led Organisations and Psychosocial Care. Other international NGOs like Oxfam have been working actively to promote a greater voice for RCOs within Kampala but without the resources to offer direct funding.

It is in part through the recognition of the necessity for informal support networks that the capacity-building programme began. FRC's project officers in Kampala recognised the struggle of refugees in the city to make a living without extra support for shelter and food, and this was significant in the direction of its programming. But it was FRC's unique capacity-building programme which several refugee leaders reported to us as being instrumental in their ability to formalize and grow. Through this programme, FRC sought to directly support and build up refugee-led CBOs – indeed, it was the only NGO or INGO we identified that was working directly with refugee-led organisations in Kampala rather than seeing refugees solely as beneficiaries of programming.[4]

Each year ten to twelve organisations are selected to take part in a two-year training programme, which includes courses on organisational management and leadership, finances and developing mission statements and business plans. At the end of the programme it offers refugee-led organisations 5 million Ugandan shillings (approximately US $1,500) to start or expand activities that contribute to their organisation's sustainability.

---

[4] In 2018 Oxfam Uganda began working with RCOs in Uganda's northern settlements and hopes to continue this work, but does not currently work with urban refugee-led organisations.

An example was the creation of a baking oven given to the Bondeko Refugee Livelihoods Centre to train refugees in baking and selling bread to cover organisational overheads. Refugees involved in FRC's programme found this financing useful but moreover felt that their own work and skills in creating organisations was called upon and acknowledged through this support.

Refugee Agency

How have refugees responded to and interacted with these structures, given the dynamics of power that exist between refugees and the Ugandan host community? Refugee-led organisations that emerge to fill gaps in services find themselves in a delicate situation; able on the one hand to legally register and operate, but on the other having to do so in ways that did not disturb the existing official or organisational balance of power. Whilst capacity building training from FRC is only available to limited numbers of refugees at a time, it offers an important insight into the ways that organisations working with refugees have been able to assist them in navigating this landscape. To some extent, keeping InterAid, OPM and UNHCR on board matters; especially for those who do not have access to international contacts, InterAid and UNHCR can appear to be the only means of solidifying community-based activities into something sustainable due to their monopoly over official refugee provision in the city. But RCOs in Kampala that have been able to thrive have done so by learning how to bypass formal systems of financing entirely.

In brief, Somalis do this through tribal and clan systems of reciprocity and accountability; South Sudanese, via connections to and through peacebuilding activities in Juba. We will return to the specifics of the organisations that form as a result of the cultural, economic and political experiences of these nationality groups later in this chapter. What is significant here is that Congolese refugees, who lack access to such immediate, transnational networks, are the most likely to register new RCOs. Congolese RCOs that are able to succeed do so through what we described in the theory chapter as an 'inspiration/opportunity/network' cycle, in which individual leaders make a significant difference to the trajectory of the initiatives that they embark upon.

Of course, there are many refugees of all nationalities who are unable to access opportunities to bypass the formal humanitarian system in order to grow. But Congolese refugees rely on the 'inspiration-opportunity-network' model more, because the systems of reciprocity and the transnational interest in addressing conflict, on which Somali and South Sudanese refugees can capitalise respectively, tend to be less available. But there are limited funding opportunities from donors willing to support refugees, given the risks that they are perceived to present, and not all RCOs can become stable organisations like YARID, 1Y1H and HOCW.

For some refugees, contending with the frustrating monopolisation of refugee assistance by InterAid has led to antagonism and activism. Refugee dissent has gathered pace in recent years despite the pressures refugees face to remain apolitical. In 2018, a corruption scandal indicted staff at the Office of the Prime Minister, with allegations made by refugees about, amongst other issues, mismanagement of government resources.[5] A recent online message

---

[5] Refugee Scandal: OPM suspends 4 officials. February 6, 2018. www.monitor.co.ug/News/National/Refugee-scandal–OPM-suspends-4-officials/688334-4293038-mtpxyx/index.html

sent by one refugee activist to a refugee network in Kampala detailed a survey he had undertaken on issues refugees want raised and the names of specific officers who refugees would like dismissed for corruption – at InterAid, UNHCR and the Office of the Prime Minister – on the basis that:

> As the investigations into refugee scandals [over inflated numbers] continue, if you move around and ask questions to refugees privately they will tell you what they know and who abused them ... they will also tell you to speak quietly because the names are for big people ... in most cases some [refugees] will tell that is a sign of disrespect to mention the names of a big person or authority ... [but] this is an opportunity for you to contribute for the better future of refugees here in Uganda. On what do you think investigations should focus and which officers do you think have abused refugees and you would like him or her out?[6]

The Congolese activist leading this assertive call to action, Pecos, was the founder of a CBO in Kampala (called PDDR), which he has since left to start another organisation (called Foundation PPDHR). Having left the Democratic Republic of Congo as a political refugee, he has since committed to human rights activism in Uganda. 'Kampala is a hub for recruitment by armed groups in DRC. I wanted to make an organisation which would intervene in this problem, but it was too political and my fellow refugees objected. UNHCR told me that I only had two options if I wanted to stay here in Kampala – be a human rights defender or keep quiet and wait for resettlement. I chose to defend human rights, but whenever I speak up, I risk being arrested' Pecos explained.

Yet Pecos is viewed with ambivalence by the leaders of other refugee-led organisations. He is seen by many as a much-needed whistle-blower, but his unpredictability and his sometimes hostile comments, for example about LGBTI issues, means he is equally perceived as a potentially destructive force for advocacy work that organisations are doing to promote their inclusion in more formal assistance efforts. In 2017, he was ousted by the other staff of his original organisation. This example illustrates that many RCO leaders are aware of the need to self-regulate the behaviour of other RCOs in order to safeguard their collective reputation. They are especially are concerned that, in critiquing InterAid and UNHCR, they are not perceived as a liability by the international community and can still access alternative funding opportunities.

The Refugee-Led Organisation Network

In 2016, four Congolese refugees who were running their own registered CBOs came together to discuss how they might bring refugee-led organisations in Kampala together to combat the institutional dominance of InterAid. Together they formed the Refugee-Led Organisation Network (RELON). One of these founding members was Robert, who runs YARID. Whilst we sat in his office before the meeting, Robert described the objectives of RELON. The first was practical; by coordinating the activities of refugee-led CBOs, there were opportunities for mutual learning and improved access to funding opportunities could be achieved. The second motivation was legitimacy and the possibility for influential advocacy that a show of unity might generate. RELON provided a means for refugees in Kampala to 'speak with one voice', in Robert's words, on the issues affecting them. This

---

[6] Refugee activist, WhatsApp message to refugee-led network, May 8, 2018.

choice of language was in itself significant; it implied that someone is there to listen. The coordination and capacity-building of the network and the show of unity it could enable were integral to the third objective: for refugee initiatives to have the choice not to partner with NGOs, and thereby 'avoid corruption at certain organisations'.

Congolese refugees have been in Kampala and working on behalf of their communities since they began to arrive *en masse* in the early years of the conflict in the Democratic Republic of Congo (DRC) in the 1990s. In 2008, community elections were organised by UNHCR across the different refugee nationality groups. Out of these elections established the Congolese Refugee Community of Uganda, and its official leaders worked as intermediaries between refugees and the structures meant to assist them. But since then, several community leaders had created their own CBOs. These CBOs have often worked together, although not in a structured way.

Through his professional and personal connections, Robert began reaching out to leaders of other refugee nationality communities with the aim of making the network more representative and inclusive. At an initial meeting of RELON, ultimately eleven representatives arrived – four Congolese, two Eritreans, four South Sudanese and one Rwandan – all of whom had formed or were in the process of forming community organisations to assist some of the 100,000 refugees in the city. At its most recent count in January 2019 more than twenty-five organisations had joined. The interest taken in the network by refugees from a range of nationalities and backgrounds indicates its value to those working with and for their communities.

The emergence of RELON in Kampala – and the objectives that drove its expansion – spoke to the changing environment for civil society and the growing formalisation of refugee-led social protection in the city. However, RELON faced a number of challenges in its objectives to become the effective, unified actor in Kampala it sought to be. Inequalities in the size and impact of the various member organisations was perceived as a basis for competition rather than an opportunity for strengthening communities. CBO leaders often told us ex post that they felt reluctant to bring ideas and opportunities to the table as they worried that these would be taken up particularly by larger and more connected and well-established CBOs with greater capacity to leverage funding. The variety of backgrounds is also perceived as a challenge for promoting trust. One Eritrean member commented that, far from creating an equal playing field, 'diversity makes for distrust'.

However, one of the problems identified in Kampala was an increasing replication of services by Congolese-led organisations. As Bolingo, head of an organisation called Hope for Children and Women Victims of Violence (HOCW), told us, 'They see the success of CBOs like HOCW and believe copying their work will generate the same results. They just want to create jobs – but that will never lead to success.' These concerns about imitation often led to allegations that people were setting up social protection initiatives as a means to make money rather than make a difference. Accusations of being a 'briefcase' organisation were common amongst Congolese refugees who ran their own organisations. Bolingo, Robert and others observed with regret that when an organisation successfully set itself up and was able to obtain financial support, a slew of other CBOs also suddenly emerged to compete for resources, seeing charitable works as a way to earn money rather than to serve the community. 'Congolese see a good thing and they copy it', remarked Joyeux of the organisation One Youth One Heart. 1Y1H's offices are close to YARID's in Nsambya, a district in central Kampala where many Congolese reside. Joyeux explained that YARID's success in securing funding after starting English classes and soccer teams for young people had led other Congolese groups to pop up, offering the same thing, often even in the same neighbourhood. This replication of services was pointless, he suggested, because funders wanted to see something new and innovative.

Previous research with Congolese refugees in Kampala found that Congolese do not generally form a nationality-based 'community' or settle geographically close to each other in the city due to their relationships to the conflict that drove them away – and the difficulty of knowing who can be trusted (Boer 2015, p. 495). Despite the majority of Congolese refugees in Uganda coming from the Kivus and having a shared cultural and linguistic heritage, it is important not to downplay the political differences that remain within displaced communities. Conflicts are not simply happening 'back home'; Kampala was described to us by one refugee as a 'hub of recruitment for fighting back in DRC' by both government and rebel militias. Particularly since 2000, Congolese arriving in Kampala report that they do not initiate contact with other Congolese refugees due to fears about security. Indeed the main way in which Kampala has been felt to offer safety is through offering many places for Congolese refugees to hide (Russell 2011, p. 296). This deters the solidarity that RELON seeks to foster. It also creates a dilemma for RCO leaders like Bolingo of HOCW, who feel that solidarity is vital for sustainability and progress.

Simultaneously however, Congolese refugees described themselves as hospitable and generous in ways that they felt Ugandans and other nationalities were not – as one refugee we spoke with stated: 'You could lend a Congolese person money and he will never harass you to repay him, but a Ugandan will be angry at you until you return it.' Congolese CBOs were the only groups that had beneficiaries from a variety of different countries, and took pride in offering assistance not only to Congolese but to anyone who came to them in need. After a large number of Sudanese refugees began attending HOCW, the organisation employed English teachers who spoke Arabic to meet their needs. This openness was attributed to being from a country comprising over 400 tribes. 'Congolese have a bigger idea of community compared to Somalis,' as Bolingo explained it. In this way, Congolese CBOs are able to easily reflect the generally non-discriminatory and inclusive ideals of INGOs. The coexistence of tensions within the Congolese community and the openness with which they approach social protection initiatives are not positions which are necessarily mutually exclusive. For Congolese refugees, trust appears to exist more along the lines of personal connections than pre-existing ties such as nationality (Russell 2011).

The development of RELON by Congolese refugee leaders, including Bolingo, demonstrates this interest in the creation of cross-community allegiances in ways which other nationality groups have not been seen to initiate. This may in part be because they constitute the largest refugee population in Kampala – but it also reflects Boer (2015)'s findings that Congolese refugees turn to religious institutions for creating social capital and new support networks rather than automatically turning to those with whom they share a nationality. Distrust between different groups among the Congolese means that establishing formal groups may be understood as a way to introduce mechanisms for accountability and avoid allegations of unfairness. However, this does mean that Congolese refugees may have fewer 'automatic' social resources to draw upon in comparison to other communities. Rather, these resources must be actively built and fostered. The Congolese also must work within an environment where funding is scarce and opportunities for institutional engagement are limited, with InterAid retaining control over which organisations become 'visible' to UNHCR. Such a context makes initiatives like RELON even more important for the opportunity they present to enable RCOs to reach beyond Uganda to international donors – but at the same time it makes them more difficult to consolidate.

Insurance Is the Tribe

The Somali Community Association (SCA) in Kampala was established in 1987, the same year that Ugandan President Museveni took power. Indeed, Museveni was seen by Khalif, director of the Somali Community Association, as a positive force for the protection of Somalis in Uganda. 'Museveni used Somali tracks during the war; we have a good relationship with this government and we work together . . . people here don't like the Somalis, but the government do,' Khalif explained when we first met. For Khalif, Museveni meant security and stability; without Museveni, the peaceful coexistence of Somalis and Ugandans was at risk.

Although Somalis are the second-largest refugee population in Kampala, there were no Somalis at the first RELON meeting we attended. Robert said he sought out Somali leaders to participate, but when we asked Khalif whether he was aware of the initiative, it was clear that any efforts had not been seen as genuine. 'There was a football tournament at YARID,' he told us 'and our Somali teams participated in that'. We explained that this was a different initiative, for refugee leaders rather than children, but Khalif was insistent that he only knew about the youth sport projects. Yet the requirement of RELON that, to be recognised as legitimate, member organisations must be registered as CBOs and have various staff positions filled, would itself make it difficult for the SCA to join. The structures that Somalis have in place for resolving issues within the community follow a very different model to that seen in Nsambya and Ndejje.

The Somali Community Association was an umbrella organisation that encompassed youth and women's special interest groups. These sub-groups held meetings on issues specifically affecting them. However, they did not operate outside the SCA. Its member groups could bring concerns to the chairs of the SCA, of which Khalif was the current head, who constitute the formal leadership. They themselves seek advice and counsel from a group of elders representing the different Somali tribes. This leadership acts as representative and intermediary with the Ugandan government, the police and border control, embassies and NGOs.

Emerging from this intermediary role was one of the SCA's unofficial functions: assistance with border control. If someone is attempting to cross illegally into Uganda, the Ugandan police could call the SCA, who would find their family in Kampala and either verify their identity or organise money for them to be returned to Somalia. As such, their relationship with the Office of the Prime Minister was a strategic but mutually beneficial one. This intermediary role was also what is distinctive about the Somali community's approach to social protection. The SCA relied on coherence and solidarity, rather than seeking to generate it through strategic partnerships like those being orchestrated through RELON. 'Other refugees are jealous of the organised state of the Somalis,' Khalif laughed when asked about comments we had heard from Congolese about the special treatment that Somalis got from the government.

Somali engagement with humanitarian institutions is different from that of Congolese refugees in large part because of the distinct form that social protection takes within the Somali community in Kampala. The Somali Community Association plays an important role as a formalised representative for the purposes of advocacy and intermediation, and in ensuring that traditional loci of justice are incorporated into this model. But many of the activities that would be classed as 'social protection' in the Somali community are simultaneously informal and obligatory. Sub-clan and clan leaders are responsible for ensuring social justice and peace, and they participate in regular meetings to ensure that the community is able to get along. When someone is sick, elders from their tribe will arrange for someone to pay their hospital fees. Assistance within the community is delivered on the basis of necessity and survival. As Khalif put it succinctly: 'for Somalis, insurance is the tribe'.

Obligations to help are built on trust and the idea of the 'tribe' as insurance, but this is not about altruism *per se*, as inherent in the very term insurance is a sense of future returns. Community-based social protection by Somalis in Kampala remains firmly grounded in traditional forms of assistance and support that bolster the independence of the Somali community through drawing on Somali cultural norms. Social protection in Kampala serves to reinforce and solidify a sense of Somali identity and community that transcends tribalism and divisions. However, herein lies another 'chicken and egg' dilemma. UNHCR and other institutional actors perceive that Somalis look out for each other, and hence are less in need of social assistance from external sources; but a lack of external assistance which meets the needs of the Somali community necessitates internal organization.

Security-related issues such as counterterrorism represent the main priority for international funders focusing on the Somali community. Indeed, a focus on preventing young people from crossing the desert to participate in conflict in the Middle East, or joining Al-Shabaab more locally, is the way that appeals for assistance to embassies in Uganda were framed by the SCA. Counterterrorism activities in Kampala have been driven by official consultation and cooperation with actors like the SCA; this is in contrast to the reaction of the government in Kenya, where aggressive, punitive crackdowns on the whole Somali community in Eastleigh in response to terrorist attacks have exacerbated mutual suspicion and resentment. But whilst the Ugandan government's approach has helped to root out extremism, without further opportunities in Kampala young people may be driven to put themselves at risk in other ways. Khalif contrasted the solidarity of Somalis in Kisenyi positively with the experiences of Somalis in Eastleigh in Nairobi, who, he said, were caught up in tribal politics, undermining the solidarity of Somalis.

Indeed, young people are a source of great concern to the elders of the SCA. They are perceived as at risk of losing hope and attempting to leave Kampala for the violence of Mogadishu, the perilous crossing of the Mediterranean, or even to participate in conflicts in the Middle East. Yet making a life for oneself in Uganda through finding work in Kampala or starting a business with a customer base beyond Somalis in the district of Kisenyi in central Kampala requires adaptations which potentially challenge cultural continuity. Strengthening the Somali community is therefore also a way of balancing these pressures by creating opportunities for young people to work and build a future in Kisenyi that reproduces existing models of Somali interconnection rather than breaking (with) them.

The preservation of Somali modes of assistance and survival is also seen as a source of tension among Somalis over the degree to which their community should pursue integration in Uganda. Khalif questioned, for example, whether too much integration was making young, upcoming Somali leaders unwilling to serve their community to the degree expected by older generations. As Khalif opined, 'We don't want our children to become like Ugandans. We are concerned that they do not have the ties to Somalia.' One way that the SCA is attempting to reconcile intergenerational disagreements over integration is through advocating that Somalis be recognised as a tribe of Uganda. This would allow them to retain a distinct identity whilst also accessing the advantages of citizenship.

Indeed, the advocacy being practiced by the SCA was specifically about Somali survival rather than broader refugee issues that might intersect with other communities. The activities of the SCA notably did not extend beyond the Somali population; it was difficult in 2017 to identify social protection activities that existed beyond the umbrella of the Somali Community Association. However, concerns about negative consequences of social change for Somali identity also appeared to be at play. This was particularly evident in conversations with and about the role of Somali women, which reflected a lack of acceptance of the changing roles of women as a result of becoming refugees. Women often associate in informal groups to enhance their collective agency (Ritchie 2017, p. 555) but by formalising activities, women's groups risk being seen as encroaching on masculine spaces.

Directing the focus of activities 'inwards' and strengthening the internal solidarity of the Somali community in Kampala also means that the Somali Community Association lacks 'legibility' by the international community as an actor, in contrast to Congolese organisations following a typical CBO model. In late 2017 a community livelihoods centre, funded in part by the American Embassy, was opened in Kisenyi at a well-attended community event, offering a purportedly rare public acknowledgement of the SCA by international actors. In general, however, Khalif felt that activism and advocacy by the SCA for help from UNHCR fell on deaf ears. Positioning themselves as an organisation for representation and intermediation did, however, create space to engage instead with the Ugandan government, which the Somalis saw as a more significant actor in terms of their social protection within Kampala.[7]

The approach of the Somali community in Kampala towards self-governance must also be understood within the context of conflict in Somalia, where mutual help along tribal lines is the only functional and reliable source of protection. The apparent difference for Somalis in exile is the emphasis on collective solidarity through a shared Somali identity, which offers a means of mutual protection within the perceived hostile environment of Uganda. 'InterAid and the police are corrupt,' explained Khalif, 'we don't look to them for justice'. He also said that InterAid made it difficult for Somalis to get help from other places. 'When we try to access UNHCR support, the Ugandans at InterAid block us from doing so. These other Africans are racist against Somalis.'

UNHCR's approaches to social protection were also, however, felt to be incompatible with existing hierarchies of authority within the Somali community. As one refugee shared, 'NGOs bypass community leaders, but these are the people who keep our community together.' Their approach to engagement mainly consisted of inviting community leaders to their offices for 'training' or participation in consultations. However, sending them back to their communities empty-handed was felt to have sown tension and distrust in Kisenyi. Khalif and the elders who formed the committee of the SCA contrasted this approach with the Office of the Prime Minister, which was seen to work through Somali hierarchies in a more respectful way. The importance of hierarchies may explain the ways that the SCA

---

[7] Later fieldwork in Nairobi also highlighted stratification between more formal providers of refugee-led social protection and informal community-based 'helpers' who do not seek to make themselves visible to institutions. It may have been that similar things were happening in Kampala, but the dominance of the Somali Community Association obscured this.

interacted with other actors in Kampala, such as the suspicion of Khalif towards initiatives like RELON, which followed a distinctly different model. Despite Robert's aims to involve Somalis and transcend differences and unite refugees as one community, when Khalif was asked about membership, he expressed reluctance to be invited into what he perceived as a structure created by Congolese, based on interests and concerns which differ from Somali priorities.

The South Sudanese Diaspora Network

One group of refugees that did not seem deterred from participating in RELON by its Congolese origins and leadership were the South Sudanese living in Kampala, despite having their own established network of organisations which actually predates RELON. The network was created in 2013 when significant international resources shifted towards building civil society in Juba, the South Sudanese capital, after the country gained independence. This facilitated the emergence of a number of community development organisations, many of whose leaders were forced to flee after the outbreak of civil conflict from 2016 onwards. Now called the South Sudanese Diaspora Network to reflect the fact that these organisations were no longer based in South Sudan, it is through this network that South Sudanese refugees shared opportunities and ideas, rather than through RELON – though they had come to the meeting to see whether it would be advantageous to collaborate.

James, the head of the Global Society Initiative for Peace and Democracy (GLOSIPAD), later told us he did not believe in the idea that refugees could work together across communities, describing South Sudanese participation in RELON as being 'for access to further contacts and coordinating with partners and donors' rather than true collaboration. GLOSIPAD's primary focus was peace and reconciliation, an obvious difference from the activities of Congolese and Somali refugee organisations. One Congolese refugee wryly commented that this was because the South Sudanese were still hopeful; their country was still so new, but in Congo and Somalia, people had given up on peace and reconciliation long ago. GLOSIPAD's key activities were described by James as work on gender-based violence, women's rights, documentation, psychosocial support and capacity building. This was broadly reflective of the work of other South Sudanese organisations based within Kampala. It also reflects the extent to which global development discourse has permeated South Sudanese CBOs, whose leaders spoke fluently on peacebuilding in particular. GLOSIPAD was one of several South Sudanese organisations which had joined RELON which were also members of the South Sudanese Diaspora Network (SSDN).

Unlike RELON, SSDN was openly cooperative, with members sharing opportunities that arose from international donors and even taking it in turn to be put forward for opportunities where limited openings were available, such as trips to Kigali and South Africa for training by donors. A thriving WhatsApp group offered ongoing debates and commentary on current events as well as potential avenues for funding. The opportunities were often directly related to the activities of SSDN members, demonstrating a compelling intersection between the declared needs of the South Sudanese, according to the organisational leaders, and the availability of outside support. There was funding for oral histories and victim accounts from Sites of Conscience, the Public International Law Policy Group helped with the creation of a database to record these violations and the Rift Valley Institute paid for training on customary law in peacebuilding. The Konrad Adenauer Stiftung think-tank was funding and organising public dialogue debates on peace in South Sudan at Makerere University in Kampala.

James had started his own CBO back in South Sudan in 2008 to engage young people who, like himself, had grown up in the midst of conflict in the country and to promote peace and reconciliation as an alternative to fighting. This, he explained, was important due to young people being particularly vulnerable to recruitment and mobilisation by both government and rebel forces. James had been made a refugee twice; born into the war between the Sudanese government and the Anyanya rebels in the south in 1978, he had first left South Sudan in 2014 after a wave of violence that specifically targeted his home province. James travelled to one of the refugee camps in northern Uganda and stayed there until May 2016, at which point peace was officially declared and he returned to Juba. However, he was forced to flee to DRC a couple of months later due to insecurity in the city. James made his way to Uganda soon after and settled in Kampala in 2017. He had been encouraged by the Ugandan government to register his NGO under a new name within Uganda in order to engage in peace-promoting activities with refugees who had fled to the country. He described the Ugandan government as 'morally supportive' of the South Sudanese diaspora. This attitude was shared by others in the SSDN who were aware of the role of the Ugandan government in promoting peace in South Sudan, and of its history of hosting South Sudanese refugees.

Educated, male and predominantly Nuer, South Sudanese RCO leaders who participated in RELON and SSDN already had status in their communities and many had experience working with international organisations. They saw themselves as the future leaders of the country. As Simon, head of the South Sudanese Cush Organisation for Development and Advocacy, explained, '85 per cent of our community is illiterate – we are the intellectuals who can go back [to South Sudan] and transform the culture of violence'. Indeed, rejecting their designation as 'refugees', Simon and others claimed the term 'exiled human rights defenders' instead and were involved in politics as well as peacebuilding. Unlike Congolese and Somali refugees in Kampala, South Sudanese refugees like James had little interest in resettlement to a third country, or integration in Uganda. James saw himself returning to South Sudan once there was peace and in particular wanted to continue working with the South Sudanese refugee community and assisting people in peaceful repatriation.

South Sudanese organisations had demonstrated success in securing international support for the particular activities they undertook, evidenced by the international trips for training in peacebuilding and leadership that were being funded by a variety of INGOs; members of the SSDN were consistently busy and moved around a lot. They were also strategic in their use of funds; for example, one organisation's director had managed to get funding to attend a conference in Nairobi through his registered CBO in Juba, but used a proportion of the money to finance the registration of the same CBO in Kampala to create a safer base for their activities. Thanks to this prolific NGO funding, they undertook frequent international travel, including visits to camps and settlements for human rights documentation and training for these activities in Rwanda, Tanzania, South Africa and even India.

An obvious factor driving the successful expansion of South Sudanese organisations in and beyond Kampala is the investment of the international community in securing peace in South Sudan. It is unlikely to be coincidental that South Sudanese CBO operations explicitly reflected and reiterated INGO discourse on conflict resolution in their home country. Their choice of base in Kampala rested on the ease of CBO registration there and the proximity to South Sudan; their engagement with the Office of the Prime Minister, UNHCR and

InterAid was minimal, given the lack of dependence on these providers for activities. Because of this, their interactions were also able to be tactical and opportunistic, with South Sudanese organisations working with partners when opportunities arose, such as distribution of donated items in the camps from other organisations, including InterAid.

Living in Kampala offered South Sudanese refugees a hub for contacts with international civil society. The leaders of organisations like GLOSIPAD and CODA, with their fluent English and business cards, were recognisably elites and not the '85 per cent illiterate' that Simon described living in the camps. They needed to be in Kampala to liaise with donors and capitalise on potential opportunities. Ethnicity, which is broadly seen by the international community as a significant vector of insecurity in South Sudan, was played down by leaders of CBOs in Kampala, who described ongoing conflicts as 'political rather than tribal'. This emphatic public neutrality, despite the population in Kampala being almost entirely Nuer, speaks to the commitment of South Sudanese exiles to ensuring the maintenance of support from the international community. A wealth of experience in working with international partners made South Sudanese RELON members confident and assertive about their activities and how to frame them through the discourse of development. Their experience showed in their capacity to speak the language of development and humanitarianism and anticipate what international visitors want to hear. 'Accountability', 'human rights', 'documentation', and 'good governance' were frequently referenced by South Sudanese refugees describing their organisations.

Yet given the inherently political nature of conflict resolution work, the South Sudanese refugee-led organisations face a challenge in undertaking the very work that the international community is interested in promoting and funding. In the refugee settlements near to the South Sudanese border, organisations work alongside international humanitarian actors like Oxfam to deliver assistance and promote peacebuilding. Yet these activities put them at odds with the anti-political rhetoric of the government of Uganda with regard to refugees. 'Your children are being educated in Uganda,' refugees at the launch of RELON in November 2018 were told by a government representative 'and with this knowledge they can go back home and change their countries of origin'. Yet he was clear that this change was expected to happen only once they had left; 'here in Uganda we cannot stop people talking about their countries of origin, but action is a problem'. As some South Sudanese refugee-led organisations scale up their activities in the north of Uganda in response to the crisis there, they risk being seen as a threat to the hegemony of Ugandan NGOs in the same way that InterAid and UNHCR Uganda appear to perceive organisations like YARID.

Given the efficacy of SSDN, understanding why the South Sudanese were interested in being present at RELON meetings shows how institutional factors shape activities at the community level. Membership by organisations in SSDN and RELON was seen to generate institutional legitimacy and opportunities because donors were perceived to be more willing to link up with a network of multiple stakeholders. This was a key objective of RELON, but it was complicated by inequalities in the size of member CBOs, especially Congolese groups, many of which previously had not worked together and established positive relationships. Of those that had a history of working together, there were personal histories that either created a sense of 'blocs' or produced antagonism, depending on how positive the experience had been. In contrast, for SSDN these relationships were positively seen as opportunities to work together. 'If [donors] want work on documentation and agriculture and you do documentation but do not do agriculture, but know another whose organisation does, you can work together to provide your services to the donor,' explained James.

The members of SSDN were interested in the opportunities that RELON created, but not necessarily in the collaborative element it was seeking to build. Belonging to RELON was seen very functionally as a way to access the contacts of other organisations who had a more established presence in Uganda to find support and resources for work rather than to collaborate with them on projects. Signing up to membership of RELON also could help with visibility: 'It is helpful to be known by the international community, there is funding attached,' explained Simon of CODA. As discussed earlier, James of GLOSIPAD felt that belonging to these networks created opportunities because often donors would link up with networks rather than individual organisations. This strategic approach makes sense given that SSDN already provided its member CBOs with the opportunities for mutual benefit; yet the lack of personal investment by leaders in the success of RELON meant that South Sudanese attendance at meetings was patchy.

South Sudanese RCOs were pragmatic about taking advantage of the benefits of having a presence in Uganda – for example, the ease with which one can set up an organisation and receive international funding – whilst avoiding the difficulties that longer-term displaced populations must contend with. There has been immense financial and strategic investment by the international community in securing peace in South Sudan, and by the political and economic interests of neighbouring countries like Uganda in ending the conflict. Together, these factors create funding opportunities for those working on peace and reconciliation and an environment in Kampala to do so. But South Sudanese organisations are well placed to capitalise on these opportunities because of their history of working cooperatively in Juba during a period when civil society expanded. This has given South Sudanese elites an understanding of the norms and expectations of international organisations which enables them to position themselves and their work through language that reflects the discourse of potential donors.

Outliers

Despite the constraints we have detailed here, some organisations managed to succeed and grow; exploring how this happens serves to emphasise the perversities of the current system for RCOs, and the importance of particular qualities for understanding how these can be navigated by some refugee leaders. We describe this as the 'inspiration/opportunity/ network' cycle and suggest that this is a particularly significant means of bypassing formal institutions in Kampala for Congolese refugee-led organisations. These RCOs lack the international interest and strategic investment of South Sudanese CBOs described previously; yet also do not have culturally derived modes of 'insurance' that the Somali community in Kampala described.

Inspiration

Hope for Children and Women Victims of Violence (HOCW) was started in 2008 by Bolingo, a Congolese refugee who had fled DRC in 2000 after the death of his father. A farmer by trade, Bolingo arrived at the Ugandan border with no money or possessions. A chance encounter there with a local Baptist pastor helped him achieve his goal of reaching Kampala. As an urban refugee, Bolingo was legally required to register with the police station, but no one knew where to direct him other than to UNHCR. At their offices he was not given assistance; instead, he was sent to a bus parked 100 metres from the Old Kampala Police Station, where more than 60 refugees were already living. The bus was overcrowded, and people were struggling to find enough to eat.

But Bolingo, relieved at last to be out of danger, began to see opportunities to build a new life. 'I spent my free time moving around and talking to people, and got to know the community well', he said. One day, a priest named Father Antony Musaala came to visit the site after Bolingo met him in the street and told him about the way that people were living. The priest was shocked at the desperate situation, particularly the lack of shelter. He began to advocate and try to fundraise to help the community, and he managed to secure a building where the refugees were able to sleep. 'Life started there' Bolingo said with a smile. The priest started a charity named Agape Pendo Lamugu (Agape, for short) to help refugees during the six months that they expected to wait for their refugee status to be granted by the government. During this waiting period, refugees were unable to work legally and support themselves, despite a lack of official and other assistance. Bolingo worked closely with the priest; his relationships with people in the community meant he understood what they needed and how best to help. He was given responsibility by the priest to ensure people helped each other and that their needs were met.

In 2003, the charity was able to buy its own land in Ndejje, some twenty-five miles outside Kampala, and received funding and client referrals – essentially vulnerable refugees in need of assistance, for whom there was no emergency aid available in Kampala – from Jesuit Refugee Service (JRS). However, by 2005 JRS itself was struggling to support the number of refugees living in the area. Over the months they funded fewer people, and for less time. The money dwindled and then ran out, but Bolingo remained working for Agape, saying he was inspired by his own experiences to continue to work with refugees. Then in 2008 he took the plunge and started his own initiative. 'When women were asking for help, they were vulnerable. They were raped. This is why we decided to focus on women' Bolingo explained.

Opportunity

Bolingo's experience working with Agape in the early 2000s was a significant part of HOCW's trajectory. In 2007, Bolingo married Emily, another refugee from DRC. A mother of eight, including five adoptees, Emily said with a smile that HOCW had been her idea. She had always dreamed of having an organisation to look after people who had been abandoned and had nowhere else to turn. Back in Goma in Eastern DRC, Emily had been a nurse, but she had also worked for some time as a counsellor for an NGO called Équipe d' Education et d'Encadrement des Traumatisés de Nyiragongo (ETN), which provided training and education to victims of violence. ETN was not a small organisation. It had successfully formed partnerships with the World Food Programme, UNDP and CARE International.

HOCW started with one teacher, fifteen students and one classroom; by 2018 they had twenty teachers, seven hundred students and seven classrooms. The organisation specialised in skills training and language classes, but also ran several savings groups and had a partnership with a medical school in the United States that brought volunteer medical students to the organisation each year. In 2015 HOCW had to expand beyond the buildings that had initially been secured by the priest, and the Slovenian Foreign Ministry bought it the land needed to accommodate the expansion. In 2018 HOCW was one of the largest refugee-led CBOs in Kampala. Buildings had sprung up across its compound in Ndejje, and more building work was being planned to accommodate new classrooms.

Networks

Together, Bolingo and Emily had first-hand experience of the norms of international institutions, such as the need for business plans, clear project proposals and transparent financial systems. They also understood that although visiting volunteers wanted an 'authentic experience', they also wanted some creature comforts such as hot water and good Wi-Fi. This knowledge had helped them to cater the image, and indeed the activities, of HOCW to an audience who could help them to do the work they see as desperately needed by urban refugees. Bolingo smiled wryly when asked about his Slovenian volunteers: 'If you want people to eat with you, you have to make sure they enjoy the meal.'

In addition to running HOCW, Bolingo was one of the founders of RELON. In our conversations about its potential, he emphasised the need to show strength and solidarity in order to encourage international donors to have faith in the capacity of refugee-led organisations to deliver. Indeed, all of the registered Congolese CBOs in Kampala had an online presence through their own websites and made prolific use of social media such as Facebook and WhatsApp groups to promote their work internationally. They also had an international profile, complete with a glossy website and a volunteer programme. They had a positive reputation with INGOs in Kampala like the Finnish Refugee Council, which had trained Bolingo in capacity-building some years before. HOCW had thereby carefully created an excellent reputation – not only with local Ugandans and refugees, but also with the international community.

However, rather than relying on InterAid or UNHCR, Bolingo was clear that the successes of HOCW were related to the international links he has been able to cultivate through chance encounters and opportunities. The priest he met on the border was born in the United Kingdom and had his own connections; the support from the Slovenian Foreign Ministry began after two Slovenian volunteers spent time at HOCW. An American colleague based in California handled the website and the majority of fundraising efforts. Through these connections, others have emerged such as All The Sky Foundation, a Canadian organisation that came and built a library on the site in 2017. Refugees at HOCW are keen to learn skills that don't require additional materials. 'Hairdressing is popular with refugees' Bolingo remarked; 'the skills stay in your hands, so you don't have to meet additional expenses to make money from it.' In the future, Bolingo would like to expand and establish a vocational training centre for both urban and settlement-based refugees in Uganda.

Qualified 'Success'

Whilst the most established CBOs, such as HOCW and YARID, are often perceived by other organisations to have been successful because of funding from UNHCR, our research indicates that this is not really the case. It is reaching beyond the borders of Uganda that enables the greatest growth for refugee-led organisations. Robert's recounting of successfully bidding for funding from UNHCR's Global Youth Initiative Fund provides more background to the story given us by the UNHCR officers we spoke with, who provided this as an example of the agency's successful work with refugee-led organisations. According to Robert, although YARID was told they would receive the funding, the money was initially not being released by UNHCR Uganda because YARID was not a UNHCR implementing partner. It was only through his contacts at UNHCR Geneva that Robert was able to bypass UNHCR Uganda to access the money. As a result of these delays, the success of the project was compromised, as was faith in UNHCR's legitimacy at the national level.

For organisations like YARID and HOCW, flying below the radar is the best bet – and this requires finding other means of generating income. 'If you wait for just ten thousand dollars funding, you'll be waiting forever, and spend that money in a year going to the office and doing what they ask, but it'll never come back to you,' Robert stated. For both YARID and HOCW, international connections had been vital for enabling this strategy. For organisations that cannot directly reach the international community for support, membership in RELON is only one option. Some organisations now aim to develop themselves as social enterprises rather than rely on partnerships at all. This was a perspective repeated by Joseph, the vice-chair of RELON and the organisation Hope for Refugees in Action, which focuses on microfinance and credit for refugees to start businesses. 'Depending on donor money is unsustainable for refugee-led organisations', he explained. 'There is sometimes money for capacity building, but that is all.'

The key to understanding who can take advantage of this process lies in the qualities of leadership that certain refugees possess. Bolingo feels that the organisations he has worked with are drawn to the authenticity of his vision and work. 'I wouldn't be here if I had bad motives. You need heart to do this work. I have made sacrifices.' Regardless of the level of formalisation, strong leadership was characteristic across Congolese organisations, with most activities being centred around whoever had initiated the group and registered it as a CBO. It was through such leaders that relationships with external donors were successfully developed. In the case of HOCW, a volunteer exchange led to a relationship with the Slovenian Foreign Ministry; for YARID, Robert's relationship with someone at Xavier Trust enabled him to obtain funding for an early literacy project; at 1Y1H, Destin's friendship with a UNHCR staff member who believed in a technology solution they were proposing led to two years of funding and their capacity to formalise and establish themselves in Nsambya. In many cases, a personable leader was pivotal in the 'success stories' of Congolese RCOs. Despite its obvious implications for sustainability, when there are no clear routes for engagement and partnership, personal relationships matter even more.

Conclusion

At InterAid and UNHCR Uganda, there was a broadly held perception of refugees as demanding troublemakers who were insufficiently grateful for the generosity that they have been granted by the Government of Uganda. On the other side, refugees saw InterAid, UNHCR and OPM, which have a tripartite agreement on refugee management, as not only in cahoots against refugees, but actively corrupt and untrustworthy. RELON and its members had to tread a fine line with InterAid, UNHCR and OPM: while striving for recognition as important actors, they could also not appear too political and thereby threatening of other formal organisations' work, lest they be challenged or shut down. This made for a delicate balancing act; in Robert's words, 'officially we [YARID] have no issue with UNHCR and InterAid – we simply do not work with them'.

With limited alternative sources of support available to individual organisations from other international organisations in Uganda, the Refugee-Led Organisations Network had taken its own measures to support the impact and expansion of refugee-led organisations. Opportunities such as funding and introductions garnered by its more influential members were brought into RELON. Those who failed to attend meetings – and therefore did not participate in bolstering the image of RELON as an intercommunity force – were also excluded from these opportunities. The power of RELON therefore lay in the continued involvement of bigger refugee-led CBOs and their continued goodwill in promoting and involving others. However, this was not done through pure altruism; the larger Congolese organisations at the centre of RELON perceived solidarity as advantageous for both the funding priorities of international donors and strength in numbers against InterAid and OPM's alleged corruption.

The new opportunities that HOCW had generated had led to new investments. Yet opportunities often do not come without compromise. As mentioned, in 2017 a Canadian organisation called All The Sky Foundation paid for a shipment of books donated by Americans, building materials donated by American businesses and a team of builders to be flown over to HOCW at great expense rather than use local materials or employ local staff. The only books seen being read at HOCW's grand library were the few children's books included, which seemed to be at a more suitable reading level for the HOCW children and youth. This library, therefore, appeared to be more an example of Westerners striving to 'do good' than one of true engagement and collaboration with a refugee-led organisation. The power dynamics at the heart of such partnerships leave refugee-led organisations unable to negotiate terms and challenge problematic activities – just as in their interactions with InterAid.

On top of these challenges was a less tangible barrier to meaningful engagement, but one which would appear much more difficult to overcome: UNHCR and its partners simply did not see refugees as meaningful providers of protection and assistance. This is exacerbated not only by the monopoly of InterAid, but by the government's limitations on refugees' 'political' activities. This idea itself remains ill-defined and vague, and appeared to be used primarily as a threat by OPM to prevent refugees from outright resistance to the status quo. While impressive in their aspiration and the steps taken towards sustainability, refugee-led organisations' long-term success in Kampala relies just as much on the shifting of the institutional power balance as on the actions of RCOs themselves.

4

Nakivale

Nakivale is the oldest refugee settlement in Africa. Established in 1958, it initially provided refuge to Rwandan Tutsi who had fled ethnic violence in their home country. It has been widely recognised as a leading example of the success of Uganda's self-reliance model (Betts et al. 2016). It is divided into three zones: Rubondo, Juru and Base Camp. The hub of the settlement is Base Camp, where UNHCR, OPM (Office of the Prime Minister) and the various implementing partner offices are located. Many shops in Base Camp's main street are run by local Ugandans who are happy to take refugee money for goods and services like hairdressing and electronic charging stations. In contrast to Kampala, according to 2014 census figures, by far the largest group in Nakivale, at around 45 per cent of the population, is Congolese; this is followed by Somalis, who make up 17 per cent. South Sudanese refugees fleeing that country's ongoing civil conflict have generally headed to the settlements in the north; Nakivale, located near Uganda's southern border, is far too remote for them to reach.

In Nakivale, UNHCR Uganda and the local government in Isingiro work together to provide basic social services to refugees. There is a health clinic through which refugees can access free basic medical treatment, a number of primary schools, and a secondary school in Isingiro, a short distance from the settlement, which provides education for children of both the refugee and host communities. There are also a variety of social projects run by agencies to sensitise refugees on gender equality and child protection, with activities undertaken through a network of refugee community workers who are hired and paid on an *ad hoc* basis. These agencies act as 'implementing partners' for UNHCR and the Government of Uganda. In 2017 these included international organisations such as the American Refugee Committee, as well as 'local' Ugandan-registered organisations like Nsamizi Training Institute of Social Development (NSAMIZI) and Tutapona.

But UNHCR-led services are not the only initiatives available to help refugees navigate life in Nakivale – and official forms of assistance were not automatically seen as the most useful or accessible. Over the course of the research, we met over thirty refugees who had their own social protection or assistance activities. These ranged in scope from established RCOs that had secured contracts for work from UNHCR's implementing partners to provide services in the settlement, to groups that had started as livelihoods groups and self-help groups and, seeking to expand their activities and their support base, had since registered as community-based organisations under Ugandan law. Informal protection and assistance extended by refugees to one another also proliferated in Nakivale, despite the range of agencies ostensibly supporting refugees in the settlement. Below the radar, and invisible to UNHCR and its partners, informal networks and individual 'helpers' within communities were the first point of call for many refugees in need.

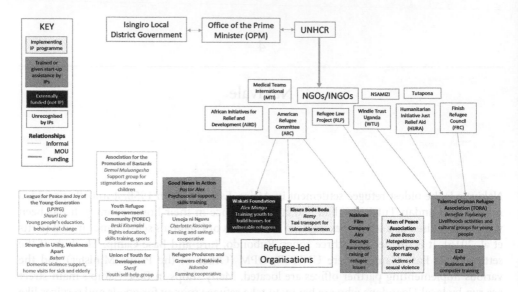

Figure 4.1 Refugee-led, national and international organisations in Nakivale

Figure 4.1 shows the range and scope of the activities of some of the organisations and groups that we spent time with in Nakivale. Whilst not a complete map of social protection and assistance, the figure shows us that connections do exist between UNHCR's implementing partner organisations in the settlement, and RCOs. Yet these links are exclusively based on 'memoranda of understanding'; informal relationships between RCOs and IPs, rather than flows of funding or any privileged status. Indeed, most RCOs were either invisible to IPs altogether, or not regarded as legitimate initiatives.

Figure 4.1 shows the range and scope of the activities of the organisations and groups that we spent time with in Nakivale. One of these, known as the League for Peace and Joy of Young Generation, was started by a group of young professionals who set up classes to teach the subjects of the degrees they had to abandon when they fled their homes; one of their members was a doctor who went out in the night to treat HIV-positive patients, who were stigmatised at the official hospital. A large number of groups, like the Refugee Producers and Growers of Nakivale, Umoja ni Nguvu and Good News in Action, had started as livelihoods groups and self-help groups, and either planned to formalise by registering as CBOs or had already done so.

Yet many of these groups were not recognised by implementing agencies as being significant actors in social protection in the settlement; the existence of some of them was not even known to UNHCR and its implementing partners. Refugees who were working to help their communities did sometimes put themselves forward when these implementing agencies solicited refugee participation, and these were the organisations which UNHCR and its partners were most likely to have heard of. But echoing the experiences of refugee CBOs in Kampala, many of the formal organisations that we met, like Wakati Foundation and Nakivale Movie Company, had been disappointed by past experiences of getting involved with agencies. A common refrain from these RCOs was that their ideas had been 'stolen' by implementing partners.

In Nakivale there were some RCOs that had been able to build constructive relationships with implementing agencies – the most notable being Talented Orphan Refugee Association (TORA) in New Buja, which, as can be seen from Figure 4.1, had MOUs with several formal agencies. Yet, although their leader Benefice had worked hard to create relationships with implementing partners, and these were viewed positively by both parties, the main source of financial support for TORA came from other international networks. As we will explain, the success of TORA was mainly due to Benefice's experience of working with international non-profit organisations in Burundi, his home country, which enabled him to build a wider network than that available to most refugees in Nakivale.

Within the Somali areas of Nakivale, as in Kampala, formalisation of groups was rarer, which is why there are few Somali organisations depicted in Figure 4.1. Rather than register formal non-profit organisations, Somalis engaged in advocacy on behalf their communities through Refugee Welfare Committees and relied heavily on elders to maintain justice and oversee the redistribution of resources to vulnerable members of the community. We met a number of women who mentored and even housed new arrivals, helping them to start businesses selling second-hand clothes or food items imported from the city. But the informality and gendered nature of this kind of assistance rendered it practically invisible to UN agencies and their IPs, whose Ugandan staff often viewed Somali activities as culturally parochial.

Institutions

The Office of the Prime Minister (OPM)

The biannual Refugee Welfare Committee (RWC) elections are a significant annual event in Nakivale and, by coincidence, in 2017 they fell during our fieldwork in the settlement. The elections were organised by OPM, whose commandants would work with the elected representatives to manage affairs in the camp. William, one of these representatives, had been the primary representative for Rubondo for several years. However, recently he had experienced a number of difficulties in negotiating the demands of the Rubondo villagers with the expectations of OPM. 'It is not an easy job' he sighed. 'You have to keep everyone happy.' William recounted a situation he dealt with in which a large storm destroyed the roofs of many houses in Rubondo. Those affected expected that they would be given plastic sheeting to replace the destroyed roofs, but when William went to make this request, he was turned away. 'They said that according to their policy a refugee is given plastic sheeting just once, so there is no sheeting for replacement.' William felt trapped. 'The community say "you are not advocating enough for us"' said William. 'And the implementing partners say "you are raising the community against us!".'

The RWCs were established to formalise representation of, and intermediation between, refugees in different zones of the settlement, and the camp commandant, and were the most visible form of refugee participation in the politics of Nakivale. Yet research by the European Institute for Democracy and Electoral Assistance in 2018 described refugees' experience of representing their communities through the Committees as 'restrictive', with representatives unable to make decisions which OPM did not want (Bekai et al. 2018, p. 51).

The image of OPM in Nakivale has not been helped by a number of ongoing corruption scandals. In 2017 and 2018, a number of government officials lost their jobs after being accused of making refugees pay for services that should be free, inflating numbers of refugees so they could pocket money from international donors and exercising nepotistic hiring practices for contractors in the settlements. Yet, while OPM worked closely with RWC leaders, expecting refugees to hold them to account through the RWCs is unrealistic given the power asymmetries within the camp. William told us 'There was a Burundian guy I heard of who complained to UNHCR Geneva about OPM and they investigated, but he had to leave the camp afterwards because he knew they would make his life impossible.' Stories of retribution like this were commonplace, and regardless of their accuracy, they contributed to refugees' fear of getting on the wrong side of UNHCR when it came to advocating for themselves.

Although OPM commandants went out into the villages every week to meet with community members at public meetings, distrust of Ugandan government staff was expressed by many refugees in Nakivale. One Congolese elder recounted a time that OPM called some Rwandan and Burundian asylum seekers to collect their papers, but then called the police to have them deported. 'Now when people are mobilised for a meeting, they are scared to come in case they are being tricked by OPM', William explained. Implementing partners were tarred with the same brush because the staff are mainly Ugandans. In the courtyard where the organisations' offices and OPM were based, our research assistant Abdallah gestured to their proximity. 'They just move between each other's offices, sharing information. You can't trust any of them. They are all Ugandans, working together.' Alex, from Wakati Foundation, told us that implementing partners wouldn't work with refugee organisations 'because they want to show they are above us, because they are Ugandans and we are refugees in their country'.

One OPM camp commandant, Esau, specifically singled out Congolese refugees as having 'a poor attitude to work and education. The majority of refugees who bother us about resettlement are Congolese.' Esau felt that coming to Uganda and experiencing its education system and its 'rigorous' laws could have a positive influence on the attitudes of refugees. 'The Sudanese who came to us in the 1990s changed their attitudes towards education and became law-abiding – they went back in a much better situation, more enlightened, and better behaved than when they came.' Despite acknowledging the challenges of Nakivale's environment, Henry, a long-time employee of UNHCR, also attributed what he saw as a slow pace of change to 'dependency syndrome within communities'.

This perception of refugees as privileged beneficiaries of Uganda's self-reliance policy places many at risk of being seen as not needing formal assistance. The narrative that they are autonomous, entrepreneurial and self-sufficient is frequently interpreted as a reason to limit formal assistance. By constructing a narrative of refugees as productive subjects, 'the conditions of life and lack of rights that refugees endure' are sometimes obscured (Ilcan, Oliver & Connoy 2015, p. 4), and basic services such as food assistance of frequently been cut (Dryden-Peterson & Hovil 2004). And yet, precisely because significant vulnerabilities remain (Betts et al. 2019), refugee-led social protection is especially important for those living in Uganda settlements like Nakivale.

Many long-term settlement residents remarked that during their time in Nakivale, there has been both an increase in the number and diversity of INGOs working in the camp and a drop in the quality of services. 'Staff are working shorter hours now. They leave early on Friday and then on Monday are in meetings all day, so they only have a few days to meet refugees' we were told by Sam, a refugee who had been in Nakivale for nearly thirty years. It is not really surprising that relations between the refugees living in Nakivale and the Ugandan staff of agencies and OPM are characterised by scepticism and mistrust.

UNHCR in Nakivale

In contrast to the hubbub surrounding the OPM and NGO offices, which were built close together in a single courtyard on the main road of Base Camp, the UNHCR compound is housed in a separate courtyard just down the road, enclosed by a three-metre-high wall. A small office to the right of the main gate houses several security guards, who sign visitors in and out if they can prove they have appointments with the staff inside. The staff themselves emerge only in four-wheel-drive vehicles with the UNHCR logo emblazoned on the side. There are always projects to check in on, meetings to hold and training to be delivered.

It was here that we met with Henry, who before joining UNHCR had worked for InterAid in Kampala for seventeen years. He had been with UNHCR for twenty-eight years, but in Nakivale for only the previous four. Having worked with refugees over a period of time during which the focus had shifted towards a settlement model in Uganda, he had also observed a gradual change in refugee attitudes, but felt that there had been resistance to the drive for self-reliance. 'They are not there yet. Self-reliance is happening at a slow pace.' Henry explained. 'Refugees resist because of the weather and environment in the settlements which make work hard for them. We build the schools and pay the teachers, but refugees do not want to stand on their own feet and sell chapati[1] to pay the school fees.'

Henry was not aware of refugee community initiatives other than those groups that were started by agencies like American Refugee Committee, but told us that 'one of the big changes I have observed is that refugees now are more educated. There are more political refugees and they understand technology.' When we asked about how UNHCR interacted with refugee CBOs, Henry explained that refugee-led organisations were welcome to compete as contractors to supply services for UNHCR, but first must go through certain processes. 'They first develop a constitution, register with the district commercial officer, are given certificates that are presented to URA (the Uganda Revenue Authority) for a tax identification that is required for payment of the services rendered. Based on this documentation the CBO can apply to provide services under the procurement procedures of Uganda.'

The groups Henry described were those that were supported by implementing partner organisations to undertake particular projects, rather than independent refugee initiatives. Activities by refugee CBOs that he could describe RCOs undertaking, such as the distribution of poles to new arrivals, had been on behalf of implementing partners. Henry added that 'UNHCR encourages refugee CBOs to compete in an open market with transparent bidding procedures.' He told us that UNHCR also provided training to refugees in various areas, including leadership and group formation, which enabled them to create CBOs, and that they could also give groups stationery, safety equipment and other start-up items. Alpha, who runs a CBO called E20, had received such training from UNHCR. He was then told that 'it's not up to us to assist you with further opportunities; you will need to figure out the next step'.

Implementing Partners

UNHCR's approach to refugee assistance and protection is based on delegation to its Implementing Partners (IPs). In 2017, these included the American Relief Committee,

---

[1] An example of the kinds of work that refugees could undertake in the informal economy of Isingiro.

Samaritan's Purse, Windle Trust, and NSAMIZI. Livelihoods programming, including vocational training in areas such as livestock management and fishing, had received increased funding in recent years, reflecting UNHCR's commitment to support refugee self-reliance (UNHCR 2014, p. 14). In Nakivale, there was even a technology centre where refugees could pay to learn IT skills and access the Internet. With access to credit being another barrier to refugee entrepreneurship, there was a large savings and loan cooperative called Moban, which was actually started by refugees in 2008 and registered in 2013 with the Ministry of Trade and Commerce with assistance from UNHCR. Moban at that time had over 1,500 members, around a third of whom were Ugandans, and was an important means of financial access in the isolated district of Isingiro where Nakivale was located. But the refugee who started it had been resettled some time before, and its operations were now managed by Ugandan staff.

UNHCR's Global Livelihoods Strategy for 2014–2018 states that empowering communities is a vital part of self-reliance; 'interventions should build upon the knowledge, skills and resources present, and aim to enhance them further while strengthening community leadership and integration' (UNHCR 2014). And indeed, we met staff working for implementing agencies in Nakivale on refugee education, water sanitation and hygiene (WASH), community services, SGBV and food distribution, and most told us eagerly about the importance of working with the community. But in the words of Henry at UNHCR, 'UNHCR's work and policies change almost annually'. He explained that, as long as changes are made from Geneva, implementing partners must stay on their toes to keep up with UNHCR standards. Failure to do so runs the risk of cancellation of privileged IP contracts.

During our time in Nakivale, we met with staff working for Windle Trust Uganda, HIJRA, Samaritan's Purse, American Refugee Committee (ARC) and the Finnish Refugee Council; we visited various training centres and Refugee Welfare Council offices; and we spent time at the Medical Teams International hospital. Richard, an employee of ARC, explained that previously they had had responsibility for health and livelihoods, but they had lost these contracts in the previous funding cycle to NSAMIZI and the Finnish Refugee Council. That January they had switched from youth and community work to WASH and SGBV. This competitive working environment inevitably has implications for the ways in which implementing agencies could engage with and support community-based initiatives.

Refugee Agency

In 2014, a young Congolese refugee called Alex had an idea: he wanted to hold a marathon in Nakivale for World Refugee Day. The "marathon" (in reality a 10K race) would promote peaceful coexistence in Uganda: 'There is a lack of communication between host and refugee communities, they feel we have come to take their land – so the marathon would mix us and bring us together as one.' Alex went to ARC with his idea. They loved the concept and began to make arrangements for the race. Alex had his own social business, called Nakivale Movies Ltd., whose activities included training young people in film-making. Nakivale Movies had been written about widely, including in an article in VICE magazine, and he was proud of his achievements.

At the time, ARC was running a programme called Changemakers 365. Under the terms of Changemakers 365, US$500 was paid out from ARC's funders for each idea brought forward to improve the lives of refugees – a substantial sum in Uganda. The money was meant to be specifically allocated to fund the activities of the refugee-led group who had brought forward the concept. Alex went to ARC to present the idea, and ARC were delighted to support it. Whilst the race had been organised before he had joined ARC, Richard was proud of the two thousand participants it had drawn. The ARC website mentions the run as one of their big achievements of the year.

Yet Alex told us that Nakivale Movies Ltd. did not see a shilling of this money. 'I went to them to complain and they called me a liar. They said that I would have to admit it was not my idea after all, or leave Nakivale', Alex said angrily. 'They also denied me a certificate for Nakivale Movies' he added, making it more difficult for his organisation to formally register as a CBO. ARC then chose to use another group of videographers to document the marathon instead of Nakivale Movies. '(ARC) got the money from UNHCR for this activity, and then they ate it' Alex said. Richard was sad about the outcome, which had led to a breakdown in the relationship between ARC and Nakivale Movies. 'We wanted to use Alex to document the race, but it was a big job, too big for him – in the end we had to use a team from the United States. They filmed the marathon using a drone.'

The Political Economy of Ideas

When asked what refugee-led organisations he was aware of and who ARC worked with, Richard quickly named Wakati Foundation, describing ARC as their 'customers'. 'Wakati Foundation have really benefited from us.' In 2013 Alex Mango had started Wakati Foundation after becoming particularly concerned about the life prospects of youth in the camp. 'They were abusing drugs, wasting their lives lying around. Our people see so many cases of suicide, torture, HIV, unwanted pregnancies from rape,' he told us from the office at the back of his house in Base Camp. Alex decided to draw on his experience in construction to create opportunities for them to do something productive with their time that would also help others, and at the same time help them to improve their coping skills through a programme of psychosocial support.

Wakati Foundation had several projects, including what Alex described as 'emergency education training' for improving resilience, HIV prevention and a sports team. But the largest is Alex's building programme. Alex trained young men in basic building techniques like brickwork, plastering and even electricity. 'We have skills, we can use them to create hope for people.' Alex and his team of trained young men built brick structures and focussed in particular on creating liveable homes for those designated as EVIs (extremely vulnerable individuals) by UNHCR. 'We can move quickly – UNHCR will take a long time to even give you a plastic sheet. UNHCR have their criteria, but my only criteria is "are you in my community and do you have a need?" Then I can help.'

In 2015 Alex Mango was approached by ARC. 'They wanted to know how they might be able to support Wakati Foundation in our work' he told us. At that time ARC was in charge of WASH on behalf of UNHCR and needed to build some new toilet blocks. After some discussion, Alex suggested that Wakati Foundation could be subcontracted to do this work. As part of this process, ARC asked them to submit a budget in order to be considered. The budget came in at a third of the cost that ARC had anticipated spending. 'They were so pleased and surprised that we could do this work for them at such a price,' Alex smiled. But once the toilets had been built, the organisation would not name Wakati Foundation as the builder. Instead, emblazoned on the sides was the sign 'Built by ARC with support from UNHCR'. Alex was furious. 'This is so disheartening for the boys who have worked on this, not to have their work recognised.' The dispute over the toilets was eventually resolved, and Wakati Foundation was later named as the builder of the facilities.

But Alex was wary of working with them again. 'It is better that we stay independent. These organisations, they do not work for refugees. They will exploit us if they have a chance.' He also accused them of mismanaging the financing of the project. 'Their original budget was so inflated. They were just looking to take advantage of *mzungu* [foreigner] money.' With community services being one of the areas for which ARC had been delegated responsibility by UNHCR, working with community groups was seen as a key part of their activities. But Alex suspected that ARC presented the same budget to their funders even when they partnered with Wakati Foundation and made savings. When we asked what he thought would have happened to the rest of the money, Alex shrugged and narrowed his eyes. The difference was 43 million Ugandan shillings. Whilst Wakati Foundation has since sought out other partners, much of the US$75,000 support for Wakati's programming in 2017 came from Alex's own connections – both resettled refugees in Europe and North America and relatives and friends back in DRC.

Perceptions of UNHCR

If refugees were sceptical about engaging with implementing partners like ARC, their perception of UNHCR in Nakivale was no more conducive to building relationships. Refugees largely saw UNHCR as relatively trustworthy but inaccessible. Some also perceived their staff as having less power than OPM, making them less significant in the settlement. Abdulfardah, a Somali elder, told us that 'power here in Nakivale is with OPM, we never see UNHCR'. The perceived distance of UNHCR from refugees was compounded by the 'information black hole' that UNHCR leaves and which is then filled by rumours and distortions, creating further problems for UNHCR when they do try to engage with refugees (Jones 2013).

The detachment of UNHCR was perhaps what led refugees to seek to work with them directly, with some refugees noting that their international staff might be more neutral and sympathetic. However, this lack of understanding meant that they were unable to provide effective assistance since, as Alex of Wakati Foundation said, 'they only know ten per cent of what happens; they don't know what's really going on'. Our own conversations with UNHCR staff suggested that refugee-led initiatives were largely invisible to them, and if they were recognised they were framed as extensions of the activities of implementing agencies rather than expressions of social protection by and for refugees themselves. If this continues to be the dominant understanding of how and from whom humanitarian assistance flow in Nakivale, partnership between UNHCR and refugee-led organisations seems an unlikely prospect.

The only funding opportunity with UNHCR appeared to be an annual talent competition for young people. This took place in celebration of World Refugee Day; the winners received 10,000 Ugandan shillings in prize money, which they could use towards their activities. 'Last year a group called Nyota won. UNHCR told us all that we were all good and should organise ourselves more if we want future opportunities,' explained Shauri, the Congolese leader of an RCO based in New Sudan. In 2015, frustrated at the lack of professional opportunities available in Uganda to young refugees because of discrimination and language barriers, Shauri set up League for Peace and Joy of Young Generation.

The lack of opportunity to be actively involved in shaping the world around them was a source of frustration for the members of League for Peace and Joy. Shauri was not heartened by the message from UNHCR, and, similarly to Alex, felt that refugees were treated dismissively.

> UNHCR does not see refugees as having knowledge or a vision of their own. We can do more than just sing and dance and play music. Refugees are losing hope because of the limitations that are placed upon us; we should be free to express ideas and contribute to change in Nakivale. What use is knowing how to dance when we need to get jobs when we go back to Congo?

Shauri also accused UNHCR of saying one thing and doing another when it came to their support for refugees. 'UNHCR use young people to show that they're doing something by putting on performances and competitions and taking photos for publicity. We only see them on World Refugee Day, International Women's Day and World Youth Day. We are sometimes invited to give ideas to UNHCR directly but maybe one per cent get considered.' Shauri and his group had attempted to meet with UNHCR on several occasions to discuss problems that they were trying to ameliorate in their area of the settlement. They were able to arrange a meeting on the issue of LGBTI discrimination in medical services – one of their group members was a qualified doctor who could not work in Uganda because he could not speak English and left his credentials behind when he fled Congo – but they saw little happening as a result of their discussions.

Looking beyond the settlements for support is therefore a necessity for RCOs doing certain types of work. Jean Bosco is an older Rwandan man who runs the Men of Peace Association, a support group for male surviviors of sexual violence. Their main work was in activism, fighting the 'culture of silence around male sexual violence'. Jean Bosco explained that in 2013 there was a research project conducted in Nakivale by the Refugee Law Project, an organisation working in Kampala with a group called the Men of Hope Association on the experiences of survivors of male sexual violence. Four of the participants, including Jean Bosco, started Men of Peace and began to work with the Refugee Law Project, receiving training in how to identify and support fellow survivors.

But as membership of the support group grew, Men of Peace encountered challenges. 'There was confusion from many about the difference between us and homosexuals. Many implementing partners in Nakivale think that working with us means working with gays, they are not aware of the difference and are scared to work with us.' The Men of Peace Association therefore relied on support from beyond Nakivale to expand their work. Like the Men of Peace Association, the League for Peace and Joy of Young Generation also spoke of LGBTI as a special interest group. Shauri feels that this is why their meeting with UNHCR about the issue of violence against LGBTI refugees had been unproductive. 'The government is more powerful than UNHCR, so it is easy for them to come and stop any activities.'[2]

Self-Reliance in Practice? Congolese Education

Nakivale was also home to a number of refugee-led initiatives that did not seek external support through formalisation. Rubondo, the village to the far side of Base Camp where

---

[2] Men of Peace Association has since changed its name to HOFEMA: Hope for Female and Male Survivors of Sexual Violence, which Jean-Bosco says will handle problems experienced by survivors of both sexes.

William lived, was an area primarily inhabited by Congolese; William explained that this was because it was remote, and the only thing one could do there is grow crops and raise livestock. 'They brought some Somalis here once, and they all left immediately to go to Base Camp.' William said as we walked together, looking at the neat layout of detached housing structures which all backed on to vegetable gardens. 'You can't even get phone signal here, and Somalis need to be connected so that they can do business. They couldn't make a life here.'

In Rubondo, Juru and the other villages which were some distance away from Base Camp and where primarily Congolese farming families were living, a number of small privately-run schools had sprung up that were run by refugees. One of these was Canaan Baptist School in Rubondo, which was opened in 2011 and taught children all the way up to Primary Seven. The headmaster, Ildephonse, had been working there since 2014, after the evangelist bishop who started it had been resettled. 'The performance of students is good here in comparison to Rubondo Primary School (the government-run alternative). There is less congestion, smaller class sizes, and better outcomes for students. Parents are happy to pay for that.'

However, these schools were a source of tension between refugees and Windle Trust Uganda (WTU), the implementing partner of UNHCR for education in the settlement. According to Sharifa, one of their programme officers, WTU worked with the Office of the Prime Minister 'to promote quality education' for refugees. 'Refugees are not allowed to have their own education projects. They can have early childhood centres, but primary schools are not allowed. All schools must go through Windle Trust. We have standards.' She added that WTU actually encouraged early childhood centres to be set up by communities, 'but Windle Trust may come in once they are more established to make sure that they are doing things properly'.

'Windle Trust gave us some support last year in the form of scholastic materials, and they gave our teachers some training, but they didn't provide transport, so it was difficult for us to actually attend it', Ildephone told us when we asked about their involvement with Canaan Baptist School. 'This year, however, there is nothing. They just want a weekly report from us.' When it came to the school itself, the community took the initiative. 'The Church donated the land and church members made the bricks for us to build the classrooms.'

There were a number of reasons for the emergence of alternative schools like Canaan Baptist. Dignité International School in New Congo village delivered teaching in French as well as English and teaching depended on the expertise and background of the teachers, rather than following set curricula. The headmaster was another Congolese pastor. He told us that the school emerged from the frustrations of Congolese who either wanted to learn, or wanted to share their education. It was staffed by young professionals who had not been able to work in the settlement and spent their days giving classes for free, trying to keep up morale and encourage their compatriots not to lose hope and ambition. 'Many of us dream of being able to return home and so we need to know the French education system that operates in Congo; the Ugandan system is not useful for us,' the pastor told us.

It was impossible for every student in the settlement to attend Nakivale Secondary School; for a start, it cost forty dollars per term, a huge outlay, on top of travel expenses. Windle Trust was trying to promote self-reliance by encouraging students to start their own economic activities to pay these costs, but dropout rates were high and only 20 per cent of refugees who started secondary school would finish it (Windle Trust Uganda 2013). The effect of this was also felt at primary level, where students perceived continuing with education to be impossible, so retention rates decreased over the years here too, with few refugees staying to take their primary leaving certificates. The great irony of this was that the lack of educational opportunities due to underfunding of services undermined the possibility for refugees becoming self-sufficient (Ilcan et al. 2015, p. 5).

The impossibility of attaining 'success' through the Ugandan system drove refugees to create their own alternatives, which were both materially more accessible and aligned with an envisaged future that would put them beyond this frustrating paradox. Yet these alternatives devised by communities were being clamped down upon rather than encouraged as innovation because of their 'illegality'. In Sharifa's words, 'we have noticed the number of illegal schools growing and we have a new strategy to get these schools out'.

Somali Alternatives

Officially called Base Camp Three, Little Somalia was home not just to Somalis, but also to Ethiopians and Eritreans. The Somalis in Nakivale had their own Refugee Welfare Committee system, run in a way that accommodated traditional Somali forms of authority, such as elders, who advise the main Somali representative. Somali social protection in Nakivale, as in Kampala, remained contained within the Somali community. 'Trust is a major issue for us', Suleiman, the elected RWC leader for the Somali community, told us 'and we secure it through accountability. Somalis can always find each other, wherever we go. We don't live with other communities here. When OPM gives us land to construct in other places, we do not use it. We live with other Somalis.'

A major part of the role of Somali RWC leaders was to be able to effectively mediate across cultures in order to secure protection and promotion of their communities. One such important privilege that Somalis were keen to protect was the right to nominate representatives to collect their food rations. This, Suleiman explained, enables Somalis to spend significant periods of time outside the settlements working in Kampala without needing to return on a regular basis to queue like other refugees. It also made it possible for Somalis to reduce their dependence on engagement with UNHCR and its partnering agencies. 'Somalis are business people, but Nakivale has limited opportunities for Somali entrepreneurs. How can UNHCR empower thousands of Somalis here in Nakivale to do business?' Suleiman explained.

Elders were often the ones to mobilise assistance through the Somali diaspora, both in Uganda and beyond, when crises occurred. 'In other countries, Somali refugees are the same as here – they take their culture with them' said Abdulfarah, an elder who was part of the advisory council in Little Somalia. 'Somalis abroad give to those in Africa. There was a bombing in Mogadishu, people sent money to help – the money goes to the families first, but is there to help everyone.' Money is usually sent to someone trusted in the community, who distributes it to those they hear are in need. 'Somalis are not good at politics, but we are good at helping each other' Abdulfardah joked.

In 2017, the Refugee Welfare Committee elections sparked discontent amongst the Somali community when Suleiman's re-election was overruled by OPM as 'too close to call'. Rumours flew between Somalis across Nakivale and Kampala. Suleiman's opposition was a young man called Hasan, who was rumoured to be the candidate favoured by OPM because he was educated in Kampala and spoke the local language, Luganda. For OPM, the primary objective was to have a leader of the Somali community that they could work with easily. However, many Somalis felt similarly. Some refugees commented that Suleiman's insistence on standing firm on certain issues was actually causing problems, and that maybe a new person who had a better relationship with the commandant would bring benefits for Somalis in Nakivale. Whilst Suleiman was held in high esteem by the Somalis we met, there were worries that he did not have enough influence with OPM.

A major part of the role of all RWC chairs was to be able to effectively mediate with OPM in order to secure protection and promotion of their communities, which extended beyond the boundaries of Nakivale. The movement of Somalis between Kampala and Nakivale for business was vital to the Somali community in Nakivale. 'Until it is possible to empower Somalis in business here in Nakivale, it will be necessary for Somalis to get certain favours – and to do this we must sit with OPM and implementing partner organisations to advocate for ourselves' Suleiman explained. The dispute over Suleiman's election had created divisions among Somalis in Kampala too; at the Somali Community Association offices in Kisenyi, Khalif told us that hundreds of Somalis who had registered in Nakivale but lived and worked in Kampala had been brought in by bus to cast their vote for Hasan. Khalif was vehemently opposed to Hasan, describing him as a puppet whom OPM wanted to manipulate to keep the Somali community down.

Though Somali representation clearly mattered, social protection and assistance did not just happen at the level of the elder councils and RWCs. With the lack of opportunities in Nakivale, Somalis who lived in the settlement full-time tended to be those who relied the most on the services that implementing partners could provide, and that were unavailable to refugees in cities like Kampala under the Urban Refugee Programme. This meant that Somalis living in Nakivale tended to be the very old and the chronically ill, or single mothers with small children. Older women in particular made up a large proportion of the Somali community in Nakivale.

One such woman was Mama Gello, a widow in her seventies, who invited us to her smallholding and introduced us to some of the other women she knew. When Somali women arrived in the camp with nothing, they were often directed to Mama Gello by tribal elders and community leaders, who were the first point of call for new arrivals. 'Here in Nakivale, we are mostly women and children. I help by giving women materials to sell and they get to keep the money. It's not what I would call a big help – just favours,' Mama Gello told us. 'I am a human and have feelings; I cannot watch someone pass by with their problems. If I can help, I want to; I have the means to do so.' Asked what she would describe as 'big help', she clarified this as acts that required the work of implementing partners, like medical care or making changes to ration cards to secure longer-term food aid; 'but as women, we can do small things, even though it is hard to help here as there is not a lot to share'.

Despite the demeaning way she described her work, the importance of women like Mama Gello was evident. During our repeated visits to her home, there were always various women and children present, who joined us and expressed agreement with her comments. 'When Somali refugees arrive in Nakivale, the offices are often all closed. They need a place to stay the night; we cannot let our people sleep on the streets. The next morning, they go again to find that no one is willing to help straight away. Registering takes time, and in the meantime, what are people meant to do?' It was this gap that Mama Gello filled.

Mama Gello was fiercely critical of the camp authorities for their abdication of their duty to support them because of their presumption that Somalis will help each other. 'They know we will cook for and feed each other, offer shelter; they don't know the specifics.' This echoed Khalif's criticisms at the Somali Community Association in Kampala; those whose mandate was to assist refugees did not know the specifics of Somali community-based assistance, but because it relieved them of a duty of care, they did not make the effort to find out.

Norms like the reciprocity and charity that exist in the Somali community, especially amongst women, can assist in spurring new economic and social life after a conflict (Lyon & Porter 2009). Indeed, this was what Mama Gello's clothes-selling kickstarters for new arrivals propagated. Yet Mama Gello was cautious when comparing what she did to the broader protective role of men in the community. She equated masculinity with being a provider, and said that although some men came to her they were not 'full men'.

Yet whilst opportunities existed for women both to engage in providing social protection directly and to improve their status in the settlements in a way that seemed less available to Somali women in Kampala, this did not automatically translate into improved quality of life for either women or men in the Nakivale Somali community. Other research has documented the changes in gender relations and challenges to male authority, which are common in migrant communities as gender roles shift and women assume new responsibilities and opportunities in displacement (Ritchie 2017). Women also may receive targeted assistance from agencies working with refugees (Hilhorst 2016), which places women in the role of being the primary generator of income and disrupts local processes of integration and development, in which men are usually at the forefront.

These dynamics may be experienced negatively by men, who are more likely to be subject to discrimination by authorities when they attempt to find the kind of work that is traditionally done by men (Ritchie 2017). 'Many refugees leave Nakivale looking for work but then realise that they are unlikely to be chosen above a Ugandan, and so they have no choice but to return to the camp', Suleiman explained. Their other option was to participate in the marginal Somali economies of Kampala and other cities, something many chose to do – treating Nakivale as a form of social insurance. Suleiman was also concerned that the prospect of resettlement generated a level of complacency and passivity amongst some Somalis, who 'think they can just wait for resettlement in the camps. Some of them got to OPM and request to be resettled immediately. They do not know the system'. He described how, when people heard about resettlement opportunities, they 'come back and wait in Nakivale'.

Outliers

Across communities, the accounts that refugees provided served to illustrate a broadly held distrust of implementing partner organisations that purported to work with refugee communities. Even when refugees attempted to formalise their organisations and appeal to the agencies' stated objectives of community empowerment and self-reliance, they found agencies unsupportive and disengaged from the interests of the very refugees they were there to assist. 'They do not want us to develop' said Alex from Wakati Foundation. Yet in Nakivale there were a small number of groups that managed to grow despite the lack of funding for activities from implementing partners. One of these was Wakati Foundation; the other was a CBO called TORA. The 'inspiration/opportunity/network' process we described in earlier chapters provides a framework for understanding the experiences of TORA.

Inspiration

At TORA's office in New Buja, Benefice, a young Burundian man with an infectious smile, invited us in with open arms and shooed away the crowd of small children who had gathered outside the window to listen in on our meeting. Benefice's parents died in 1997, and he was adopted by his grandmother and uncle. In Burundi he had been sponsored by an NGO called Restoration of Hope. 'They told me that I should always try and see a way to help others. It had a big effect on me' he said. After graduating from school, Benefice started a cooperative called Association for Brave People in Development. Its members were other orphans like himself. They did laundry, washed cars and grew crops as a collective strategy to avoid poverty.

In 2015, Benefice's grandmother and uncle both died unexpectedly. During that year, violent political protests had also begun to break out in Bujumbura, and Benefice decided to join tens of thousands of other Burundians and fled to Uganda with his uncle's six children, plus another child that the family had been fostering. At first Benefice had not been sure how he would survive. 'I asked the local community leader if there were other orphans here. He showed me where they were staying and there were so many, and I realised that we could support each other. I convinced some of them to form this association with me. We agreed to contribute a small amount of money (500 Ugandan Shillings) each month, and with that we could buy tools and seeds to grow vegetables, sell them and generate some more income.' The plan worked and the number of orphans who joined his association grew.

But that was not the end of Benefice's plans. As well as protecting orphans and helping them to build a future, he decided to run a cultural programme. 'We have three groups – drama, Burundian dance, and a new programme for a hip-hop dance team.' The terms he used were straight out of a programming manual: 'Our cultural programme helps to promote self-awareness, confidence, emotional coping, personal values, and raises hope amongst our members that they can be more than just orphans' he explained.

Opportunity

At Windle Trust Uganda, Sharifa shared a list of the groups her team had 'supported'. One of them was TORA. 'They were a music dance and drama group which we supported, but now they are trying to be independent. They want to stand alone, but we continue to fund them.' Sharifa said. But according to Benefice, Windle Trust visited TORA in 2015 after they had already started, hearing about them through other refugees. 'They gave us technical support and advice – but no funding' said Benefice. He said the same thing about the NSAMIZI Training Institute for Social Development, which aimed to support refugee self-reliance through skills development programming and whose staff had visited TORA some weeks later. 'They helped us to register as a CBO once we were ready.'

The only material assistance that Benefice had received had been ten ducks from the Finnish Refugee Council's livelihoods programme. They had multiplied under Benefice's watchful eye, numbering thirty on this first visit and thirty-seven when we said goodbye a few months later. In contrast to Sharifa's narrative of their role in TORA's incipience, Benefice was keen to point out that TORA began without outside help and did not depend on it to keep going. 'We did not start TORA to be supported, unlike other groups, who collapse when initial support runs out. We do need help, but [even] without it we move ahead.'

The livelihood security and protection elements of TORA were evidently the most important to Benefice – with TORA's mission statement being 'to ensure access to health, education and security for orphans' and much of their advocacy online centring around feeding the orphans in their care. Yet the cultural element had been what enabled TORA's connections to Windle Trust, NSAMIZI and FRC. 'Windle Trust ran a dance competition in 2016 which we won, and it was a free exhibition for TORA.'

Networks

Leadership is inherently about social capital. Benefice of TORA was young, male, educated, well-connected and had clear legitimacy within New Buja. The deputy Chairman of TORA was one of the RWC leaders for the Burundian community, who was present at all our meetings and voiced his pride at the organisation's success. Yet Benefice was also willing to buy into and fulfil the objectives of implementing partners in order to build relationships with them that could lead to more than donations of ducks.

Indeed, part of the success of TORA has been its ability to frame its activities in a way that speaks to the priorities and interests of implementing agencies. Indeed, Benefice saw the benefit in the technical support and advice that implementing agencies can offer. 'These are useful to us because (the agencies) share information with us. I have learned how to write proposals and make a budget and work plans. I've applied for funding from Cambridge, UNHCR, Restoration of Hope, the Forever Living Project, SwiftCert ... Our dream is that one day TORA will be a big NGO, helping many vulnerable orphans.'

For now, TORA continues to expand its 'friendships' through a steady stream of international visitors – many of whom are brought to TORA by implementing agencies that can claim a hand in its success. 'The only time we see UNHCR is when they come to the field with their visitors, give out t-shirts, and say "smile, smile!"' Alex of Wakati Foundation said, miming a camera being held up. 'And then they leave, and that's it. There is no more contact.' But for TORA, relationships can be continued through their Facebook page, where these photos are reported and shared, bolstering TORA's image as an organisation with many friends. The page is also used to share videos of the orphaned children who are members of TORA and news about events within the Burundian community; it is cautiously apolitical, even when reporting the deaths of refugees in Nakivale.

Analysing 'Success'

Part of the explanation for the emergence of RCOs in the form seen in Nakivale is structural. 'Everyone knows that there is a policy by UNHCR of supporting groups and not individuals' William told us, 'and this is why there have been so many groups coming up in recent years'. The majority of the groups we met had started after 2013. Groups with an income-generating angle were able to get support from implementing partners by emphasising the self-reliance and empowerment that their activities promote. This support was usually via capacity building, training or – sometimes – initial start-up capital.

The compromises that TORA have been willing to make are not for everyone. Alex of Wakati Foundation, for example, was unwilling to compromise on the activities of his organisation, preferring to seek support instead from other places. One such place is the Congolese diaspora. 'Since Congolese started getting resettled, life has really got better for refugees here in Nakivale,' William told us. 'They send money, remittances, also information. As people leave, the level of development of our communities here gets higher.' This reflects the trends of engagement with formal institutions seen in the Somali community of Nakivale too; the imperative for many of those in leadership positions was to retain 'Somali' values and solidarity as far as possible as a point of pride.

However, many refugees lack the ability to access international donors whatsoever. Internet and electricity are expensive commodities. Creating a website requires skills that are difficult and expensive to learn in Nakivale. With the Community Technology Access centre charging for internet use by the hour, it is difficult for refugee-led organisations to have an online presence that can compete with the likes of international agencies. But being able to effectively advocate for support and endorsement by the international community is seen as key, given the limited options for RCOs within Nakivale itself.

Interestingly, this has led to a market in Nakivale in opportunities to interact with outsiders. We were told that a community leader in New Congo called Pierette, whose number we were given by another refugee in Kampala, could help us to access refugee groups. When we called her, a man called Demoul took over the call and made the arrangements. We met with ten refugee groups in the space of a few hours, all of them asking for financial assistance from outside Nakivale to bolster their activities, declaring it impossible to get any support from implementing partner organisations for anything from training to resources. Demoul described himself to us as the groups' 'manager'; when there were visitors to New Congo, he set up the meetings and made sure that people got opportunities to talk to someone who might be able to help them.

Conclusion

Refugee assistance was the bread and butter of UNHCR's implementing partners in Nakivale. Yet paradoxically, the movement towards a 'humanitarian marketplace' (Crisp 2009) appeared to be generating a culture of reluctance within UNHCR's implementing partners to engage with RCOs. The limited scope of 'partnerships' was related in part to IPs' desire to protect limited formal resources, given the pressure they were under to deliver programming on increasingly tight budgets. The high turnover of contracts with UNHCR meant that agencies had to constantly redefine their work and show their value in new and innovative ways. The staff working for these agencies had little time to explore and build relationships with refugee groups that might not contribute to these financially tight and time-sensitive agendas. Since the signing of the New York Declaration on Refugees and Migrants in September 2016, implementing partners for UNHCR have also had to introduce a budget provision for 30 per cent of resources to benefit the host community. At the time of this research, this was only a recent change, and it remains to be seen how refugees will perceive its impact on services.

Whilst some forms of 'self-reliance' in the form of community-led initiatives were being encouraged, as in the case of TORA, this only happened when the activities of RCOs did not undermine the importance and relevance of implementing partner organisations. RCOs' significance was repeatedly downplayed; where it infringed upon the territory that had been competitively carved out by agencies for themselves, as in the case of alternative schooling systems, it was treated as competition rather than a force for good. Genuinely refugee-led social protection and assistance was not being integrated into the broader formal infrastructure through partnership and cooperation; instead, implementing agencies support community groups that they have selected and instructed, and these are invited to participate in 'community services' in instrumental rather than transformative ways (White 1996).

The close relationship between implementing agencies and OPM, and the disconnect that was perceived to exist between UNHCR and refugee-led activities in the settlement, meant that many refugees felt distrustful about such 'partnership opportunities'. Allegations of widespread corruption and credit-seeking against staff in agencies, OPM and UNHCR added to a generalised picture of distrust between refugees and institutions. This environment of distrust fed into interactions between refugee CBOs and UNHCR implementing partner agencies. Refugees who had experience of working with agencies like ARC and Windle Trust framed their interactions with them in terms of co-optation and exploitation. The Refugee Welfare Committees (RWCs) were the only way in which the government of Uganda formally engaged with refugees as agents within the settlement rather than as passive service users. Yet the RWCs too have been largely instrumental, with refugees perceiving their role as intermediaries between the demands of refugees and the ultimate authority of OPM, whose staff have tended to value different 'refugee leadership' qualities than those emphasised by communities themselves.

As a result, some RCOs have deliberately distanced themselves from the formal infrastructure of OPM, UNHCR and international NGOs. Groups like Wakati Foundation have relied on connections with individuals back in Congo and resettled refugees in the West for support. Others have seized the opportunity presented by visitors to the camp to build networks that may lead to funding opportunities. The RCOs most likely to thrive in the settlement have been those with leaders who are willing and able to diplomatically mediate between OPM, UNHCR and the IPs on the one hand, and the refugee community on the other. This usually requires certain traits, such as a willingness to serve as RWC leaders and to avoid overtly challenging or confrontational language in relations with 'top-down' actors. This requirement for obedience and acquiescence is significantly different to the situation in Kampala, where RCOs rely less on support from such structures, and so those who are unwilling or unable to mimic the perceived institutional requirements of a 'good refugee leader' are able to achieve success regardless. The contrast underscores the importance of Nakivale's distinctive institutional and geographical context in constraining and enabling particular forms of refugee-led social protection.

5

Nairobi

Since the 1990s, the Kenyan government has operated a strict system of refugee encampment, with assistance for camp residents provided by UNHCR. A law was introduced in 2014 to formalise the expectation that refugees should live in camps, making residing outside of camps without government permission a criminal offence. Yet despite this, 75,000 refugees reside in Nairobi, the capital of Kenya.[1] The majority of these are Somali or Congolese. The former are drawn to Nairobi because of its large Somali neighbourhood of Eastleigh, described as a 'global hub' for the Somali diaspora. Others choose to seek refuge in Nairobi because of security concerns in the camp; in particular, ethnic groups such as Oromo Ethiopians and Tutsi Congolese, who prefer to live amongst other communities in the city for fear of being targets for political and reprisal violence.

This growing urban population – making up 16 per cent of Kenya's overall refugee numbers – has done little to make Nairobi a more welcoming place for refugees at an institutional level. Indeed, since its creation in 2017, the Refugee Affairs Secretariat (RAS), the government body given responsibility for refugee management, has frequently suspended registration of new arrivals to Nairobi as it copes with a backlog of cases from its previous incarnation as the Department of Refugee Affairs (DRA). It is impossible to understate the impact that this insecurity has had on refugees, for whom documents that confirm their status are essential to their stability and survival. Without them, it is impossible to secure formal employment or medical insurance, or access services like banking. It also exacerbates the harassment that refugees face from the police.

Whilst the passage of the Refugee Act in 2006 had given a mandate to implementing partners to deliver some services in Nairobi of behalf of UNHCR for refugees who asserted that they needed to be in the city and not in a camp for security or educational reasons, 'official' social protection remained strictly limited. Refugees in the city were not officially permitted to work; therefore, most depended on the informal economy – and their own social networks – to survive. Around twenty-five RCOs had managed to establish social protection and assistance programming, including psychosocial support, legal advice and counterterrorism activism.

Figure 5.1 shows the main international, national and refugee-led organisations we encountered in Nairobi. What is immediately notable here, particularly when contrasted with the mapping of RCOs in Uganda, is the extent of the links between the mapped-out organisations. A significant number of organisations were previously funded or were receiving funding at the time of this research, and many other had other relationships with

---

[1] See: www.unhcr.org/ke/wp-content/uploads/sites/2/2018/12/Kenya-Infographics_November-2018.pdf

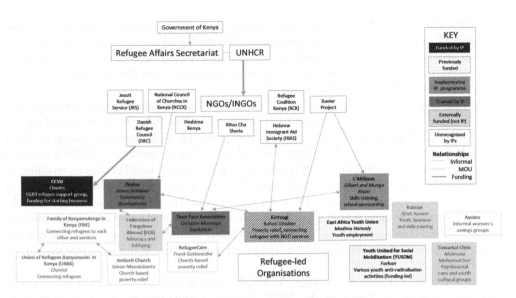

Figure 5.1 Refugee-led, national and international organisations in Nairobi

implementing partners of UNHCR. Additionally, whilst the relationships between RCOs are not formalised in the same way seen in Kampala through the Refugee-Led Organisations and South Sudanese Diaspora Networks, they were still present, illustrating the importance of social networks and solidarity within an unwelcoming political environment.

Being able to mediate between the international community and refugees was an important characteristic for Congolese refugee leaders. At the front line of Congolese social assistance in Nairobi was a network of elected leaders, community representatives, unions and churches; but individual community workers for implementing partner organisations like HIAS and Danish Refugee Council were particularly important actors. Community workers were able to draw on the relationships they built with IPs to get support for their own social protection and assistance operations because they themselves were indispensable to their capacity to deliver formal assistance. Through the connections and knowledge of community workers, organisations were able to access marginalised communities and broaden their reach and impact.

The challenge for RCOs started by community workers was that because their relationships with IPs were instrumental, they were often unable to break out of the 'provider/beneficiary' model discussed earlier, in which implementing agencies are seemingly unable to see refugees as legitimate and significant providers of protection and assistance. The organisation Kintsugi ran with no institutional funding for operational costs, but their leader, Bahati, who had good working relationships with UNHCR and other agencies, hoped that Kintsugi would lead to recognition and opportunities. Christian, a paralegal trained by Kituo Cha Sheria, had also recently begun his own CBO, hoping to be able to capitalise on the opportunities that he perceived to come from having a relationship with the big players in refugee protection.

Congolese associations like the Union of Banyamasisi Refugees in Kenya (UBRK) and Family of Banyamulenge in Kenya (FBK) also worked with UNHCR, its IPs and refugee-led initiatives to refer refugees to services and organise support for refugees whilst they waited for formal assistance. Many of these services were provided by churches, some of whom had registered as community-based organisations. The managing director of one such church-based initiative, RefugeeCare, hoped this formalisation would put them in a better position to access support from funders that was more consistent than the donations it already received from within the local community.

Being able to strategically position one's work shaped the trajectories of some organisations. Being a 'special interest' group had been an important factor in the success of CESSI, an LGBTI refugee support and self-help group set up with financial assistance from UNHCR through the Danish Refugee Council and other organisations. CESSI's business ventures received funding and training set aside specifically for LGBTI refugees, enabling its Ugandan leader Charles to successfully apply for further international funding. A period of USAID-led investment in Eastleigh under the Kenyan Transition Initiatives (KTI) kick-started various Somali community initiatives, including Youth United for Social Mobilisation (YUSOM) and East Africa Youth Union. Rather than disappear once that money ran out, successful RCOs in Eastleigh broadened their support base in the same way that CESSI had done.

In the Somali suburb of Eastleigh, Tawakal Clinic, started by two Somali doctors who became refugees in Kenya in the 1990s, had been providing psychosocial support to refugees since 2006 with help from Kenyan organisations. Kobciye, a Somali-run organisation with links to the diaspora and families in Canada, operated a community centre offered a series of different trainings: members began with basic computer literacy and could then graduate into an alumni programme that offered trainings in leadership, conflict resolution, and life skills. Trusting relationships, made possible by personal connections, were an important feature in the success of both these organisations – whose sustainability was also not contingent on IP support.

Institutions

The Kenyan Government and UNHCR

In recent years, the Kenyan government has become increasingly involved in the monitoring and regulation of refugee movement and work. Ostensibly, this is due to concerns about its own national security. The Westgate Mall attack by Al-Shabaab in 2013 led to a rhetoric of hostility about refugees in Kenya, in particular towards Somalis. The years 2014 – 2016 saw few refugees actually completing status determination through the government's Department of Refugee Affairs. In 2017 the Department of Refugee Affairs was disbanded – an act that was subject to legal challenges from Kenya's High Court (NRC/IHRC 2017) – and the government established the Refugee Affairs Secretariat in its place. But refugees have reported that it is now slower and more difficult than ever to acquire documentation. New arrivals in the city are often sent to camps to register instead. Refugees who have previously registered in Nairobi with UNHCR are now issued 'waiting cards' by the government instead of receiving renewal of their documents, which require updating every two years.

Since 2011, the Kenyan government has required refugees to register their presence with the government before being able to start the process of status determination with UNHCR. During this same time, responsibility for refugee status determination has begun slowly transferring from UNHCR, which previously had sole responsibility for this process, to the

Kenyan government. Whilst UNHCR has continued to be present when community meetings are called, the Refugee Affairs Secretariat has increasingly run the show. At a February 2018 meeting organised to debate how elections for community leaders in Eastleigh should be run, a government representative opened the floor by declaring that refugees were welcome in Kenya but needed to be more grateful. He accused Eastleigh of harbouring terrorists and illegal migrants and asked why there were so many unregistered refugees in Eastleigh. There were a lot of security concerns that the police wished to address before letting the elections go ahead. Al-Shabaab was mentioned; the police wanted to make sure that the elections would not be targeted by those who would take advantage of the crowds to strike against the city as they have before. 'Eastleigh', a police chief inspector for the area told the assembled crowd darkly, 'is the head of the snake'.

To be a refugee in Nairobi was to live in precarity. Refugees reported that they were constantly harassed by the police and exploited by landlords and employers. But the lack of clarity over who was responsible for processing and renewing documentation since the establishment of RAS, and the interminable delays that refugees we met were experiencing as they waited, meant that suspicion towards the authorities abounded. Many Somali refugees felt that the delays were a deliberate effort by the government to deter them from seeking asylum in Kenya altogether. 'They speak of us as guests but treat us like terrorists' declared one refugee. In contrast, UNHCR was perceived as increasingly inaccessible. Formal meetings with the community, such as the one described previously, were led by the government – an intimidating presence – so refugees could not use these fora to speak out about their concerns.

The shifting global policy discourse on refugees has more recently played an important role in reshaping institutional engagement with refugees. In 2016, the Comprehensive Refugee Response Framework (CRRF) was adopted as a formal strategy for the integration of refugees into Kenya. The CRRF demands integration of services for refugees and the host population in signatory countries, whilst also reducing funding for activities that are not sufficiently oriented towards promoting 'self-reliance' for communities. This has seen non-governmental organisations working with refugees in Nairobi begin seeking ways to engage with community-based, bottom-up systems of social protection.

In part this is about saving money; yet staff working for implementing partners of UNHCR also personally recognised the effectiveness of community-based refugee initiatives in reaching those who are most vulnerable. Winnie was the psychosocial programmes manager for HIAS, an organisation that had been implementing psychosocial, legal and livelihoods services in Kenya since 2002. 'It is impossible for us to do everything. We can support one hundred refugees with a livelihoods project; but what is that compared to a thousand refugees entering the city every month? We need refugee-led organisations' she told us. Since September 2017, HIAS had been working to identify refugee-led associations, groups and organisations. Winnie's department at HIAS had applied for funding for a project to first map out the landscape of community-based social protection and then find ways of working together with these initiatives to improve counselling and support for refugees. They were only given half the money they asked for, so only had a year to find out all that they could.

Yet this initiative still centred the work of HIAS in delivering social protection and assistance. 'We are finding organisations, seeing what they are doing, showing them what we are doing ... we want to make sure refugees can access our services' Winnie explained. 'For example, we can educate the groups on mental health issues like depression and they

can then refer their beneficiaries to us, where we have trained staff who can help them.'
Refugee-led CBOs may help significant numbers of people, but Winnie told us that 'direct
assistance is the easy part'. Whilst refugee-led initiatives were able to respond immediately
and effectively to new arrivals and help them find a place to sleep and food to eat, longer-
term planning was difficult for small organisations and informal groups. Refugee-led CBOs
lacked the capacity to deliver the CRRF priority of long-term refugee self-reliance and
sustainable development for the Kenyan host community, especially on a large scale,
without funding and support from UNHCR; their strength was their proximity to their
own communities, rather than knowledge of the challenges facing local Kenyans.

As Winnie indicated, material support for RCOs and their initiatives was sorely lacking
in Nairobi. 'The first thing they expect from us is money, but we ourselves have limited
resources. We can offer them training on how to work on the issues facing their communities, but many don't see the value in it' Winnie explained. HIAS's own training programme sought to expand RCO capacity to deliver transformative and empowering support
to other refugees, in line with the CRRF, yet it was accompanied by none of the resources
that would stabilise their organisations and secure their longevity or allow them to move
beyond their current marginal position. Training, by itself, was insufficient to overcome the
structural barriers that remained for refugees seeking to move from incentive work on
behalf of agencies towards building proper partnerships – partnerships in which refugees
had a meaningful role in determining what social protection and assistance activities had
the greatest impact in their communities.

This lack of funding occurred largely because the programming that organisations like
HIAS had been given responsibility for by UNHCR had to take priority; budgets for this
programming usually did not contain allocations for funding independent refugee activities
that did not specifically align with these priorities. Eliza at Danish Refugee Council, another
UNHCR implementing partner in Nairobi, confirmed the challenges presented by having to
plan in accordance with what funding they themselves were successful in securing. 'We
used to give savings and loan groups seed capital, but when our funding from UNHCR
decreased our role changed to just encouraging and supporting groups in the communities,
mainly to start businesses or expand their existing money-making activities.'

Choosing Partners

The RCOs that were able to succeed in accessing funding were usually those with some
form of connection to implementing partners. This often resulted in them undertaking
activities that were informed by the implementing partners they worked with. We met with
two members of staff at the Danish Refugee Council (DRC) who knew of a number of
Nairobi-based, refugee-led social protection and assistance initiatives that had actually
started as savings and loans groups with the Danish Refugee Council. Indeed, when
UNHCR funding through DRC's Community Savings and Loan Association programme
ran out and they struggled to raise money by themselves, instead of getting mentoring on
business support and expansion under the existing DRC programming, some groups
wanted capacity-building training so they could mobilise as not-for-profit community-
based organisations that could seek funding elsewhere.

These groups included CESSI, an RCO run by a gay Ugandan refugee called Charles who
had left his country after experiencing homophobic attacks. 'CESSI were founded as a
business but weren't making any money' Eliza explained. 'They were doing hairdressing but

wouldn't charge people consistently. We told them that to become self-sustaining they could charge customers and use the money to pay for group members' salaries, further training – but they didn't want to. And actually, they didn't need to, because as a result of being built up by UNHCR money, they were able to get private funders.' Faith, who headed DRC's community outreach programme, explained what form this 'building up' took. 'We help them to organise, write their constitution, get registration. We see informal groups, and the next step is to formalise because to bid for contracts and funding you must formalise.'

However, Faith was critical and suspicious of some of the initiatives that DRC had seen. 'There are very few groups which have thought through their projects properly, and many are just trying to pay themselves salaries rather than do something properly.' Faith wanted to see groups identify a niche for themselves and focus on doing small things effectively. 'There is such a big gap in service delivery which refugee-led organisations can complement, but the problem is that many are trying to do too much.' But DRC currently had no criteria for working with RCOs, instead giving support on an ad hoc basis. This lack of criteria meant that decisions about who to support and why were made on the basis of personal judgement and experience.

As discussed, the main way that implementing partners like DRC and HIAS found they could work with refugee CBOs was through training. Yet the extent and usefulness of such training varied greatly. Refugees saw the value in some of these programmes; for example, a Kenyan organisation called Kituo cha Sheria had been delivering paralegal training to refugees. With the frequent harassment refugees faced from the police, their training programme sought to help refugees understand and defend their rights – and educate others – about how to react in such situations. One Congolese paralegal, Christian, had taught other refugees to start filming on their phones when a police officer approached, and to ask which law they were following when they requested bribes. He wanted to see all big organisations and executive powers upholding the 1951 Refugee Convention and the 2006 Refugee Act. 'I am advocating for the local integration of refugees through focusing on their rights' he stated.

Another organisation, RefugePoint, worked directly with a team of refugee 'community navigators' to identify and meet the needs of refugees across Nairobi. It had been Refuge-Point that had issued new guidelines in January 2018 for what incentive workers like Bahati should be paid for their work, putting pressure on other organisations to raise the incentive pay rates they were offering refugees. 'Before January 2018, the pay from most organisations was bad and you had to be on call twenty-four hours a day' two refugee incentive workers for RefugePoint told us.

> When refugee incentive workers for the Refugee Affairs Secretariat tried to protest against being paid just ten dollars a month for translating, they fired everyone and then recruited again at twelve dollars a month. UNHCR was the best, they would pay US$400 per month and transportation costs, but they needed very few people. HIAS, DRC and National Coalition of Churches in Kenya paid US$200 per month. Refugee Coalition of Kenya paid only US$77 per month.

But refugees felt they had no choice but to accept the wages they were offered; it has taken RefugePoint stepping in to alter conditions, and refugees are slowly seeing rates increase.

'Community is the most powerful tool we have', Martin, RefugePoint's outreach officer, told us. 'We want to see community groups grow, to reach out to them and support them.

Community-based solutions, where refugees are going out and doing things by themselves, are better and more affordable.' RefugePoint relied primarily on private funders for the 'social entrepreneurship' model it described itself taking, rather than bidding for contracts from UNHCR. Indeed, Martin was critical of existing approaches by agencies that work with UNHCR when it came to finding ways to promote community solutions. 'Danish Refugee Council and others are only interested in doing the same things they have always done. There is not enough willingness to take risks.' He added that donors were part of the problem; 'their expectations are about aid and the numbers of people who can be given something, rather than development'.

Refugee Agency

Many of the 'narratives' through which institutions framed their engagement with refugees espoused the importance of community-driven approaches. Yet as seen here, the majority continued to implement programming in fundamentally top-down ways. Successful community-based initiatives by refugees in Nairobi were those that had been able to capitalise on opportunities offered by institutions without challenging these dynamics. The context of the Kenyan legal and political environment makes it difficult for refugees in Nairobi to speak out full stop – let alone push back against marginalisation within social protection programming. Implementing partner organisations like HIAS and the like were seen as the only organisations who had some clout in advocating for refugees with the Government of Kenya.

How have refugees in Nairobi responded to these structural constraints? They have done so largely through compliance within their relationships with implementing partners. In the Somali hub of Eastleigh, much social protection and assistance was based upon Somali solidarity and cultural norms of reciprocity and charity, and it looked very similar to that which informed mutual assistance amongst refugees in Kampala and Nakivale. Yet there was a notable difference. Whilst in Kampala, Somalis largely did not bother attempting to engage with UNHCR and InterAid, in Eastleigh community leaders had fostered strong ties to UNHCR and its implementing partners. They often occupied multiple roles as elected representatives, incentive workers and informal advisors. Although some community leaders created organisations based on the encouragement of implementing partners like HIAS, their personal connections and individual reputations were generally more important in mobilising financial support.

Amongst Congolese refugees, this pattern was clearly evident. Networks were integral to being able to both access and provide protection and assistance. Congolese refugees who were influential within their communities, and were thereby able to mobilise people and resources, were often those occupying roles such as community leaders, incentive workers, businessmen and RCO directors. Their ability to 'shapeshift' relied upon reconciling the conflicting expectations of different stakeholders. Whilst many Congolese refugees would see the leaders of traditional community structures like the so-called Family of Banyamulenge as the first port of call for assistance, these 'traditional' modes of organisations lacked the perceived legitimacy to engage directly with implementing partners. As one such refugee leader, James, put it, 'HIAS and other agencies have more trust in CBOs than community leaders because [the agencies] worry about corruption and tribalism. CBOs have transparency – you can visit them, see what they are doing, it is out in the open.'

This is not to say that the only RCOs in Nairobi were those run by community leaders; but that RCOs depended on some form of networking to be able to operate effectively. For many organisations, these networks were not only those with implementing partners of UNHCR. Nairobi was the only site where formal community-based organisations run by Somalis were both numerous and reasonably well established. Many Somali RCOs had started during the heyday of the Kenya Transition Initiatives (KTI), which began in 2008 with the initial aim of countering interethnic and tribal conflict by promoting youth participation in politics. These organisations often had links to community leaders but did not depend on them for support; the networks they had grown during their time working with the international community, and flexibility in accommodating trends in funding priorities, were more significant in their trajectories.

Across both Congolese and Somali refugee communities, RCO trajectories reflect the 'inspiration/opportunity/network' cycle described elsewhere, in which ideas become harnessed to (sometimes 'chance') encounters through which some refugees are able to broaden their support bases. For the RCO and community leaders, these encounters tended to be with staff working in the formal refugee governance system with whom positive relationships could be built. Yet sometimes, important encounters happened with actors outside the UNHCR and implementing partner system. The example of the Somali RCOs that flourished under the KTI highlights this possibility, but it also shows that it has not always been the case that these relationships create more sustainable forms of support. Indeed, examples of long-term partnerships that have responded to refugees' own stated priorities are rare.

Congolese Community Leaders

Nairobi is a sprawling city, with Congolese refugees living on the outskirts in all directions. Since 2009, Banyamasisi refugees like Bahati had organised themselves through a leadership committee called the Union Refugees Banyamasisi in Kenya (URBK), which consisted of elected representatives from the areas of Kitengela, Kasarani, Kayole and Kayangali and an overall president, at that time a woman called Chantal. When Banyamasisi refugees arrived in Kenya, URBK was often their first point of call. 'In Kenya, the only way to survive is to be together' Chantal told us. 'Banyamasisi and Banyamulenge refugees here are fearful of the other tribes; we come together like a family because we have no family.'

Back in DRC, Chantal was a businesswoman, but her father had been a community leader and he passed on a lot of advice and knowledge to her. The organisation's activities included orientation of new refugees, identifying basic needs and helping out vulnerable people. Chantal met frequently with UNHCR and received training on leadership, which included conflict resolution and advocacy for refugees who were not getting adequate support. But often, Chantal found that the best place to refer refugees who needed immediate assistance was not to implementing partner organisations like HIAS, but to refugees who were well positioned within their communities to assist others.

Sometimes, these refugees were community leaders; other times, they ran their own community-based organisations. Sometimes they did all these things and more. But a key source of support came from churches. Part of the power of the church was in its centrality to refugees' lives. In Kasarani, we visited Antioch Church, which was actually three churches with over a thousand members, the majority of whom were refugees from the Great Lakes region and predominantly Congolese. Charles, one of its pastors, described the 'emotional, spiritual and material needs' that Antioch sought to meet. 'HIAS can do counselling, yes, but we are meeting the needs of the whole person.' This included social connectedness, which 'cannot be delivered by the Red Cross, but is vital. HIAS is not open on a Sunday, but the church is always there.' Simon, the bishop who heads Antioch, had been in Nairobi for seventeen years. A few years earlier he had started an alliance network called Shalom, which all Congolese churches in Nairobi were now part of. 'More refugees come all the time, which means the churches are growing.'

But, increasingly, Congolese churches were moving beyond redistributing charitable giving to church members in need. As with the growth of community initiatives for refugees outside 'traditional' systems of leadership and representation, we heard how churches were also seeking to capitalise on their connections to communities by marketing their activities through formal CBOs. RefugeeCare, for example, is a registered CBO based out of a branch of Harvest Church Ministries in Kitengela, where a makeshift mezzanine level above the pulpit housed two rooms. John was the bishop of Harvest Church. Before becoming a refugee eleven years previously, he had been an influential and wealthy bishop in Uvira. John quickly set up a new ministry in Nairobi under the umbrella name of Harvest, and in his role as a religious leader, attended training in counselling at HIAS.

HIAS was keen to draw on John's knowledge of the community and visited twice to see what they could do. They provided some mattresses and referred some of the congregation to entrepreneurship training at Danish Refugee Council. But John was frustrated; he could see there were other needs in the community that NGOs were either ignorant of or did not have the capacity to meet. Then in 2015, Frank joined Harvest, after 'the Bishop called on me to see how I could assist his congregation of God'. Frank had previously been a coordinator in Rwanda for the First Lady's Imbuto Foundation; he described development as 'his true calling'.

Together, John and Frank registered a community-based organisation called Refugee-Care. They hired a secretary, a field officer and a finance officer; Frank was RefugeeCare's coordinator, and Bishop John the director general. They initiated formalisation of the church's activities. When people came to ask for help, they were now asked to fill in forms and 'state their needs and vulnerabilities.' John and Frank reached out to a number of organisations to ask for help with RefugeeCare's programmes, which were at that time funded by contributions from the various Harvest churches, 'people motivated to provide by God'.

The large numbers of members of Harvest and the reputation of Bishop John had drawn in enough contributions for RefugeeCare to run a feeding programme and pay rent for twenty-one vulnerable families each month. But eventually, Frank explained, RefugeeCare would not depend on these contributions. 'Sixty percent will come from the church but the rest we are seeking from sponsors and partners' he told us. 'We are reaching out. There is an organisation called House of History which funds peace and reconciliation, we want to work with them to do that, and we are trying to work with Xavier Project too. We want to network so we are reaching out to Nairobi University. Even prayer is helpful to us. We are working hard on empowering RefugeeCare to get further resources.' Their eventual goal was expansion: 'We need to advocate and empower refugees worldwide, and our target is to one day work across Africa' Frank told us. Considering the reach of Bishop John's church, this did not seem ambitious; Harvest had fifty branches back in DRC, a further six in Nairobi in addition to the Kitengela branch that RefugeeCare worked out of, and even two in Kakuma camp.

Occupying multiple positions can expand the resources available to refugees who are working to assist their communities. One Congolese refugee who had learned this from experience was James, a well-known figure in advocacy among both refugees and refugee-serving organisations in the city. James had been in Nairobi since 2003. He was a top-level elected community leader for Congolese, and he also worked as a community worker for the National Council of Churches of Kenya, one of UNHCR's implementing partners. In addition to these two roles, James was also one of the founders of Zindua Afrika, 'one of the first refugee CBOs in Nairobi'. Zindua Afrika was run by, and served, both Kenyans and refugees.

James explained that whilst community-based organisations were important for refugees, 'CBO leaders must have connections and a network, links with implementing partner organisations who can provides services. They can do referrals.' The training James had received from UNHCR as a community leader had helped him to improve his community work, 'and through my community work I learn about issues which as a leader I can assist with on another level'. James had been able to access training from World Vision on business management and had worked with implementing agencies such as HIAS and DRC to map refugee needs. All these skills had been useful in setting up and building Zindua. 'I have written proposals to the USA, to Australia' James told us. Zindua had also been able set up an exchange programme with an Italian NGO called Karibu Africa through a connection based in Karen, a wealthy suburb of Nairobi.

James was optimistic that CBOs were the way forward when it came to advocating for changes in Kenyan law to increase the availability of work permits and business licenses. 'The Family Matters programme which the government is implementing was written by refugees,' he said. 'We are getting them on side to show that refugees are doing well. The government takes organisations seriously – they do not want to work with pastors or community leaders because they are only working in their own communities.' CBOs not only cross ethnic and tribal lines, but also the divisions between host and refugee communities.

On the other hand, what community leaders did – which CBOs could not always do – was 'cultural preservation and understanding', according to James. As community leaders represented their tribe, they were often seen as more trustworthy and reliable by their communities precisely because of their lack of neutrality; 'they protect individuals and are always looking out for their people'. James also thought that being unburdened by the processual obligations of working within the agency systems meant that community leaders could assist people much more urgently – a significant consideration for hungry and desperate refugees. However, community leadership and the favours that leaders were able to give out was organised on a more reciprocal basis. This was at odds with the norms of formal, non-partisan organisations, where James warned that 'you cannot expect anything in return from people who come to you as someone working for a CBO'.

Community Leaders in Eastleigh

Eastleigh, the main Somali area of Nairobi, had two designated refugee 'community leaders' in early 2018. Whilst neither of them had been officially elected, there were plans by UNHCR to formalise representation through a vote later that year. Said, the younger of the two, planned to stand as a candidate. He described the election as 'historic'. 'I was called by God. I started at home, helping my sisters to get an education, and then started helping others.' Bashir, an older man, described feeling equally strong in his motivations to help his fellow refugees. Shortly after his arrival in Kenya, he had started a CBO called Continental Africa Refugee Union, which aimed to root out corruption in the way protection and assistance was delivered by UNHCR and the government. 'Refugees are dehumanised here' he told us.

It is important to note that whilst churches were often the first point of call for Congolese refugees, the mosques in Eastleigh played less of a systematic role in delivering social protection and assistance. Somali refugees who arrived in the city were expected to seek out family and kin for support; the mosque might be able to help with this by directing Somalis to those who could provide material assistance, but it was unlikely to provide for them directly unless no other assistance could be found. Instead, Said and Bashir were recognised by Somalis in Eastleigh as being people who could represent and advocate for refugees with UNHCR and its partners.

Said had been a refugee in Kenya since 1994, and he had started advocating for his fellow Somalis from 2002 onwards. When he first became a refugee, he sold ready-made clothes. 'I am still a businessman, but not a very successful one, as one of my shops collapsed!' Said went to a good school in Somalia and knew English, Swahili and several Somali dialects, which was integral to his ability to intermediate between international organisations and refugees who were in need of assistance from them. Initially, helping people out was an informal activity done as a favour, as he was able to communicate on people's behalf with UNHCR. Said had worked with HIAS for several years as a community worker, received paralegal training from Kituo cha Sheria and believed in working within the current system; 'civil society and NGOs are important, because to effect change you have to work with the community'.

Whereas Said felt his status within the community came from his work with agencies, leading to his being recognised by UNHCR, Bashir was an elder who had been invited to consult with UNHCR directly on matters affecting Somalis in Eastleigh since 2007, and had a history of involvement in refugee CBO activities.

> I used to be the secretary of a CBO called Somali Elders Refugees and Kenyans Organisation (SERKO) and got support from the Kenyan government when I met with them to discuss our activities. Then UNHCR started consulting me when they heard from the government about my work. The previous Somali leadership were corrupt, so they were happy to work with me.

This was not always the case; his organisation CARU had identified that multiple Kenyan resettlement officers and UNHCR employees were accepting bribes in order to facilitate wealthy Somalis' resettlement. CARU was also meant to address the division of refugees based on nationality. However, CARU was stopped due to pressure by UNHCR. Bashir received warning after warning to stop his work, and he was jailed twice. Finally, one UNHCR Protection Officer told him that he should stop because his life was in danger. He finally closed CARU in 1996. Like Said, Bashir received training from Kituo cha Sheria on legal issues so he could help more effectively.

There had been a feud between Bashir and Said as long as anyone could remember; whether someone went to Bashir or Said for help depended on tribal identity – which, Bashir told us, divided everyone into two groups in Eastleigh. 'Said has spread rumours about me, saying that I take money from UNHCR and don't give it to the people I say I am helping' Bashir exclaimed. 'But the truth is there is no money!' The split between the two leaders was frustrating for refugees. Ayan, a social worker with RefugePoint, had had to navigate their politics in seeking assistance for vulnerable people in Eastleigh. 'If you go around saying 'you are my tribe so you have to help', it can ruin your name. If you have been in a bad situation yourself, you should not refuse to help another because of their tribe!' she told us disapprovingly.

Indeed, whilst community workers, community and religious leaders and refugee providers of social protection and assistance in the Congolese refugee community were intertwined and assisted each other, this was not the case for the Somalis. 'Community leaders and workers are actually very separate in Eastleigh' Kaltoun explained. 'There are people who UNHCR favour but who know little about what's happening in the communities they are supposed to represent. In reality, community workers are chosen for their competence, but community leaders are chosen for their connections.' In many conversations with Somalis in Eastleigh, we heard about distrust – particularly along tribal lines; one refugee told us that 'community leaders are the worst for tribalism and corruption'. Another said that she did not turn to community leaders at all, preferring to go to her neighbours. 'If you go to a community leader and ask for help, they will ask you what your clan is – if you're not one of them, they won't help you.' Some accused community leaders of taking advantage of their position as intermediaries with UNHCR and making money out of refugees who went to them for help.

Subcontracting in Nairobi

The relationships that some refugees were able to cultivate with implementing partners were key to the activities of their organisations. This 'subcontracting' model enabled a division of labour that could be mutually beneficial, if the RCOs who entered into such partnerships were content to remain implementers rather than set the agenda. Kintsugi was an RCO started by Bahati, a Congolese Banyamasisi refugee who had been an incentive worker for various implementing partner organisations since arriving in Nairobi. His most recent ongoing employment as a social worker for HIAS meant Bahati was also well-known to other Congolese refugees, as he spent much of his time out in the community meeting with people who had approached HIAS for help.

Because Kintsugi was able to respond fast to refugees in crisis, HIAS often referred refugees to Kintsugi for immediate shelter or food assistance. In return, Bahati was able to contact staff at HIAS and advocate for refugees who needed professional psychosocial support. Bahati explained that this was working well for Kintsugi; because organisations like HIAS had trained social workers and vetting systems in place to identify the needs of refugees before referring them on to refugee community actors like Kintsugi, this alleviated the pressure on Kintsugi to provide counselling and therapy, which many refugees were seeking but was, at that time, beyond the RCO's capacity. This division of labour meant that Kintsugi could focus on what they were good at; helping refugees to access resources, either through directly allocating what they could, or by referring them to agencies for services.

In 2016, Xavier Project heard about the activities of Kintsugi through refugees whom Kintsugi had helped and approached them to form a 'partnership'; Xavier Project would pay the rent on a building for Kintsugi if they could run their ICT and English language classes out of the shared space. The benefit to Xavier Project was a credible community base, key to their 'Community Enterprise Cycle'[2] model; for Kintsugi, having offices and a memorandum of understanding with an NGO increased their legitimacy and standing with other refugees.

Connections like these would not have been possible without Bahati's previous experience working with these agencies and his resulting knowledge of whom to call upon in different situations. The reputation that Kintsugi was able to build by working with implementing partners in this way generated social capital for Bahati and his RCO within the local community. Having a building where people could go to access a variety of services helped with legitimacy and was a big factor in Kintsugi's decision to work with Xavier Project. Those who have benefited from Kintsugi gave back; 'they are the first ones to come and support us and tell others what we do when it comes to fundraising' said Bahati.

Investment and Retreat

In Eastleigh, top-down modes of engagement had also characterised the funding of a number of Somali-led RCOs established during investment by USAID in 'community-based approaches' to countering violent extremism (CVE) under the Kenya Transitions Initiative (KTI). Started in 2008 and funded by the United States Agency for International Development (USAID), by 2011 the KTI had begun to focus its funding on countering violence extremism (CVE) in 'at-risk' populations, essentially piloting what would become its official CVE programme in Kenya (Khalil & Zeuthen 2014). Following the attack on Westgate Mall in downtown Nairobi in 2013, USAID directed significant amounts of money through the KTI towards youth initiatives in Eastleigh, which was home to large numbers of young Somalis who were not in formal employment. The grants available under the KTI were directed towards a range of activities aimed at livelihoods training, facilitating community debates on sensitive topics and treating post-traumatic stress disorder (PTSD) amongst refugees (Khalil & Zeuthen 2014).

This period saw a proliferation of refugee-led community organisations. One of these was YUSOM, which had been operating since 2011. 'Originally, YUSOM stood for Youth United for Somalia, but various people told us that this wasn't a good idea, so we became Youth United for Social Mobilisation' Farhan explained wryly. 'Our aim is helping voiceless and marginalised youth, especially refugees.'

When funding was withdrawn in 2013, there were consequences for the organisations whose work tied into its objectives. 'There were fifty-seven youth organisations by 2013, but many of them closed when USAID withdrew support. We think they got the information they wanted from us, and then left' Farhan told us. This was echoed by another youth initiative leader, Mahad, who ran an organisation called the East Africa Youth Community. Mahad estimated that in 2013 twenty-five organisations shut down overnight when USAID withdrew their funding. 'There are no jobs and no youth groups to help young people – they are just sitting around and talking. Everything that used to be there for them has shut down' he said. Those organisations which were still around were present in name only; 'they only have meetings if they know a visitor is coming'.

Some of the groups from this time survived through diversification of their activities; YUSOM began to operate as a social business as well as a youth mobilisation initiative.

---

[2] See: http://xavierproject.org/enterprise

Farhan told us that Somali refugees in Eastleigh were desperate for jobs, but they struggled in the face of the lack of employment opportunities and a saturated small-business market within Nairobi. YUSOM filled this gap by providing skills training in Nairobi, where young people were 'settled but had no jobs, and weren't being supported to get them' by the Kenyan government. Young men who had been trained by Farhan, who also had a shop selling imported items, worked for him in Nairobi and in other parts of Kenya.

Mahad and Farhan both told us that many young people were being driven to leave Nairobi by the high cost of living and police harassment. Whilst East Africa Youth Community now mainly worked in Mombasa, YUSOM worked in Somalia as well as Eastleigh to undertake peacebuilding activities and attempt to create links between youth in Kenya and businesses in their homeland so that young people could move back safely and find work there. 'Peace is not the main issue for us, it is jobs and skills. Our young people are not asleep. They only join bad groups and go to fight because they have no other option' Farhan explained. 'We are not ignorant, we just have to be optimistic that there will be peace in Somalia in the future, and we must prepare for it.'

These days, Farhan said, he saw his international relationships as much more important for YUSOM and its capacity to promote development for Somalis. 'Now as an organisation we are truly international: our finance manager is Congolese, our programme manager is Kenyan. YUSOM needs international experts, support from people in other countries and communities.' By travelling outside Kenya, Farhan could 'carry the message' of YUSOM and recruit support, which he had successfully done, partnering most recently with the Somalia Aid Foundation to work in Eastleigh. However, being able to travel was itself a privilege. Unlike Mahad, Farhan had been able to secure a Kenyan identity card, and this enabled him to leave and return to Kenya as freely as any citizen.

Refugees' Perceptions of Working with UNHCR

What had continued was the relationship Farhan had built with UNHCR during his time as a key figure in the Eastleigh youth empowerment scene. This continued to pay dividends; alongside his business activities, Farhan participated in international forums on refugee issues and continued to receive calls from international organisations working in Eastleigh when they needed help or advice. Yet Farhan remained critical of UNHCR's work with the Somali community. 'Somalis need strong voices, but UNHCR doesn't really want that; they want someone to agree with them.' Despite having been able to remain at the heart of the humanitarian sphere in Nairobi, Farhan felt that nothing would really get better for the Somali community as a result of the misuse and diversion of funds at much higher levels than he is involved at, describing corruption as 'inbuilt' in the institutions that worked with refugees. 'I did monitoring and evaluation work for UNHCR once and seventy per cent of the questions we asked the respondents weren't applicable, so people (UNHCR staff) just put in the answers they wanted.'

Frustrations with UNHCR were echoed elsewhere in Eastleigh. In 2009, a community organisation was started in Eastleigh 2009 by the father of its current director, a young Somali-Canadian called Afrah. Afrah's family had been resettled from Somalia to Ottawa, Canada in the early 1990s. In 2001, Afrah's father returned to Somalia and Kenya to work as a Child Protection Officer for UNICEF. However, he felt he could make a bigger impact with his own organisation, which would focus on youth empowerment; KOBCIYE means 'empowerment' in Somali. KOBCIYE actually began in Somalia but moved to Eastleigh in

2010. Through its community centre, KOBCIYE also gave members training in practical skills such as accounting and computer hardware, and a women's empowerment pro- gramme that offered training in makeup, henna design and speaking up in the community. They held various community events, including an annual sports tournament known as the Unity Cup, a youth conference on countering violent extremism, and a tech and entrepreneurship summit.

All of KOBCIYE's training and services were free to members, and the organisation sought to target the most vulnerable Somalis in Eastleigh, mainly those without formal education or a legal status in limbo, with Afrah estimating that between a quarter and half of beneficiaries were refugees. KOBCIYE was mainly funded by embassy grants, though Afrah, as the main fundraiser, regularly sought out additional resources. They had received grants or had had partnerships with a number of organisations, including the Turkish Development Agency, the African Development Youth Trust and UN-Habitat. However, Afrah expressed frustra- tion with the limited agency KOBCIYE had in the case of grants and joint endeavours with larger organisations, which often stipulated the activities and funding period. KOBCIYE's training required equipment and staff. This caused difficulties for KOBCIYE. 'We operate within their big bureaucratic reality,' Afrah told us, 'and often it seems like they create their policies without consulting organisations working with these communities every day.'

In 2013, two Congolese refugees called Majaliwa and Simbi started training other refugees in the skills they had learned back in DRC. Majaliwa was a master craftsman, and Simbi a tailor. Building up quite a reputation, they began to sell their products wholesale to the Salvation Army, who then sold them into high-end shops in Nairobi. In 2017 the organisation was joined by Gilbert and Munga, two Congolese artists with some experience in community-based organisations back in Bukavu. They decided to register 'L'Afrikana' as a community-based organisation, with the training they were offering on tailoring and crafts becoming a cornerstone activity. Both Kenyans and refugees were able to come and join L'Afrikana as members and receive training; then, with the profits they made, L'Afrikana funded various social protection and assistance programmes. These included a feeding programme and school sponsorship for orphans and vulnerable families, supporting forty children in 2017.

L'Afrikana had sought out relationships with formal organisations, but with varying degrees of success. They expanded into English training and computer access by working with Xavier Project, but this 'partnership' had not translated into financial assistance like salaries or building expenses, despite their dependence on the classrooms at L'Afrikana's workshop in Kawangware. There was not even money to pay the cook who catered for the teachers, and certainly no support to build the capacity of L'Afrikana to access further funding or opportunities. The agreement with Xavier Trust also caused tensions with UNHCR, who had wanted L'Afrikana to go through them to sign a partnership agreement. L'Afrikana were reluctant to do so, suspicious of what this might entail.

Christian, the paralegal whose work we mentioned earlier, had worked with L'Afrikana on navigating this situation. 'UNHCR steal data, proposals, information we have – they want to show those outside Kenya that they are the only ones helping refugees. There is so much co-optation, but refugees have no other choice' he said. Indeed, Gilbert and Munga were already suspicious of UNHCR, who had come to see L'Afrikana and promised to help them, but never delivered. 'We tried to apply to them for a HIV livelihoods project, but they gave the grant to a bigger organisation who they were already partnering with on health, so I don't know why they bothered to advertise it' said Munga.

James at Zindua Afrika was similarly frustrated by the experiences he had had with UNHCR and its various partner organisations. UNHCR staff had previously come to see what Zindua was doing, but in the past, James said they had taken Zindua's ideas to Kenyan organisations. Because of this, James felt that UNHCR 'are not ready to fund CBOs, they are not ready to register them or let them grow. They are not providing a platform. UNHCR see refugee-led organisations as temporary, because we are refugees, but they forget that CBOs can continue to work even if the head of the organisation leaves.'

Because of these issues, James felt that RCOs were deliberately being limited in what they were able to do. He added that the problems with refugee identity cards and mandates since RAS took over this service from UNHCR had made things even harder for people who wanted to help their communities, as they were afraid the police would find reasons to cause problems for them if they were seen to be stepping out of line. The efforts that James had been making in using the training he had received from UNHCR and its partner agencies in reaching beyond local institutions were driven by a reluctance to work within the current terms available to refugees.

Outliers

Within both the Congolese and Somali refugee communities in Nairobi, certain RCOs had managed to successfully 'bypass' UNHCR and its implementing partners. With a subcontracting model being the only way for RCOs to engage with these institutions, formalised and registered RCOs rejected the constraints and dependency that this relationship could potentially lead to. Obtaining support from outside of Kenya was an end goal for both Somali and Congolese RCOs. The 'inspiration/opportunity/network' cycle described earlier did not always guarantee positive outcomes due to the degree of uncertainty associated with personal connections. But being able to construct other types of partnerships was not accessible to all CBOs that were run by refugees.

Inspiration

Tawakal Clinic on Eastleigh's Fifth Street was started in 2006 as a private clinic by Dr Maimuna and her husband, both gynaecologists who fled Somalia in the 1990s. In 2010, four Somali boys were killed by the police just down the road from the clinic. 'I was devastated. I couldn't stop crying. I turned to my husband and said 'we have to do something' Dr Maimuna told us. The doctors went into the community and interviewed young people who were already involved in criminal activities. They found that the main problems were around identity and self-esteem, with young people wanting to belong to a group. 'They go to school with Kenyans, grow up feeling that they have a place here; but then they leave school and apply for jobs like their Kenyan peers, and are asked 'where are your documents? You are not Kenyan' Dr Maimuna explained. 'They get harassed by the police, they begin to feel that there is nothing here for them. They lose hope.'

But what troubled them even more was the lack of support and understanding that young people were getting from their parents and elders. 'They would praise the police when they kill someone, and it's because they don't know what to do about the crime levels either. We realised that we needed to support young people more.' Tawakal became more than just a clinic: Dr Maimuna and her husband set aside time to facilitate a youth discussion group, where young people could bring problems and come up with their own solutions. 'We trained them on peer counselling, and although we are always around, now we try not to be too visible, not let them feel our weight.'

Feeling that the unmet desire for a sense of belonging was a factor in poor self-esteem and led to young people's involvement in gangs, the doctors had the idea to teach the youth group Somali traditional dance. 'Many of the young people grew up here and don't even know about this beautiful tradition, and it builds their confidence to have something about being Somali that they can take pride in'. Dr Maimuna explained that for many young people who were born in Eastleigh, Somalia did not even feel like a real place. The popular discourse of Somalia in Kenya was about terrorism and violence. 'When Somalis hear nothing good about themselves, they lose hope and become angry' she said, 'but Somalis have a history that is longer than the war.' The dance that the young people performed was energetic and twisting, performed to traditional wedding music and strikingly different from the hip-hop that blasted from shops all over Eastleigh.

Opportunity

The main function of Tawakal was as a women's clinic. As time passed, and more refugees came to them for treatment, the doctors began to observe a pattern amongst the women who attended for consultations. 'They would come in, complaining of pain, headaches, fainting, inability to sleep. They were really suffering, and all in the same way. But the blood tests showed nothing was physically wrong with them that could explain these symptoms', Dr Maimuna explained. 'We contacted a professor at the University of Nairobi for a second opinion and he suggested that we were dealing with something psychosomatic – but it was very real for the sufferers.'

Dr Maimuna decided to go back to university and study trauma, enrolling at the University of Nairobi. She began to understand that what she was seeing amongst women in the Somali community was PTSD and depression, and that without medical assistance, people were turning to substance abuse to cope. 'We see a huge issue with *miraa* (a psychoactive stimulant drug cultivated in Somalia) – not just amongst youth and men, who are the usual users, but amongst middle-aged people, even women.' The doctors started a women's support group and free psychosocial counselling for refugees suffering from PTSD after fleeing Somalia.

Networks

Key to the success of Tawakal was the relationship between the doctors and Kenyans. Through the professor they had consulted about the symptoms they were seeing amongst their fellow Somalis, the clinic initiated a partnership with the University of Nairobi, which sent its students to get work experience by delivering free therapy to Somali refugees at Tawakal. This has been hugely beneficial to the community in Eastleigh, who can access quality counselling without the waiting times associated with official providers such as HIAS.

In addition to the student training programme they ran in partnership with the University of Nairobi, Kenyan NGOs had also worked with Tawakal; 'We cooperate with them and both benefit. They are able to get international assistance, and are looking for people to implement their ideas, and we have the capacity to do that.' For example, in 2016 Tawakal worked with an NGO that had funding from the US State Department to tackle violent extremism in Eastleigh by bringing the police and Somali community together to improve the relationship between law enforcement and community members.

Analysing 'Success'

Dr Maimuna and her husband cared deeply for their community. One weekend, Dr Maimuna had gone to a street gathering where a projector had been set up on the street to screen the swearing in of the new Somali president; a group of youths had attacked the party and started throwing bricks. Dr Maimuna was caught in the crossfire, and had a black eye to show for it. But she appeared most distressed on behalf of the youth cultural dance group, which had been performing at the gathering. They had been targeted too, and some of their instruments and traditional costume props had been stolen in the ensuing melee. 'They are the future' she said. 'They are the ones who will go back to Somalia and do good things. They have to carry with them the things they learn here and use them to promote a better way of life. We don't want them to lose hope.'

The longevity of Dr Maimuna and her husband's presence in Nairobi was part of the reason that it had been possible to build up the relationships that had enabled them to establish such a successful initiative. They both arrived in 1991 and had been working as doctors in Kenya for over twenty years. Tawakal had no interest in partnering with UNHCR or its partners, describing themselves firmly as part of Eastleigh – not just its refugee community, but all who lived there. The respectability of Tawakal was underscored by their founders being educated and well connected. Their skills were valued by Kenyan organisations as well as by the Somali community, garnering them respect across both refugee and host communities.

Having independence from UNHCR and remaining non-partisan conferred the advantage of a level of respectability and authority on the organisation. Dr Maimuna and her husband were distinctly non-political, so even though they existed independently from the mainstream refugee social protection systems in Nairobi, they did not present a challenge to them. 'Why would we want to be community leaders?' Dr Maimuna laughed when we discussed the elections in Eastleigh.

The financial detachment of Tawakal from UNHCR also meant that they were not subject to the funding priorities of refugee-serving institutions in the same way that other organisations in Eastleigh had found themselves over the years. Indeed, the successful continuation of YUSOM when many other Eastleigh ventures had collapsed was due to the ability of Farhan to redefine his work even when funding from the Kenya Transition Initiative ran dry. Interactions with international agencies and exposure to norms and expectations of working practices could help individual refugees in their pursuit of other opportunities – but only if they were able to transcend some of the legal and practical barriers that came with the 'refugee' label.

Conclusion

In contrast to Uganda, institutional support and even funding has been available over the years to RCOs in Kenya – in particular for activities targeting specific groups and issues, such as protecting LGBTI refugees. UNHCR and the government of Kenya have been keen to cut overheads and promote 'self-reliance' for refugees in line with the Comprehensive Refugee Response Framework; on the front line of refugee services, implementing partners have seen deploying refugees themselves as a way to meet these objectives, whilst also being effective in delivering services and accessing communities. This has created space for refugee-led organisations to position themselves as part of the humanitarian infrastructure of Nairobi.

In understanding the nature of institutional engagement with RCOs in Nairobi, personal connections are an important explanatory factor in understanding who was able to access opportunities and who was not. The trajectories of some RCOs were linked to the relationships of their leaders with UNHCR and its implementing partner organisations (IPs). Personal reputation became even more important as currency due to the lack of official criteria laid out by agencies regarding their conditions for working with refugee-led organisations. Those RCOs that had been successful in overcoming the 'chicken-and-egg' problem of needing to formalise in order to access institutional partnerships while lacking the capacity to do so were those whose leaders had been able to build such capacity through training, work and relationships in their roles as community leaders, incentive workers and elected representatives.

Whatever the narrative of 'community-based approaches', RCOs were largely treated instrumentally by implementing partner organisations. The partnerships that currently existed, like those offered by Xavier Trust, were sometimes more beneficial to the institutions than to the refugees who initiated them. They took pressure off the institutions; but organisations like L'Afrikana and Kintsugi struggled to keep up with demand from their communities for the free assistance that they offered. Regardless of these problematic dynamics, refugees in Nairobi remained keen for opportunities to work with institutions; this is evident in the way that RefugeeCare in Kasarani had sought to rebrand its tithe collection and redistribution and James, Christian and Bahati's development of various CBOs around their roles as intermediators between different stakeholders. Some organisations, like Kobciye and Tawakal Clinic, had opted out of the system by establishing partnerships with supporters outside the refugee governance structures – and even outside Kenya. But these were both outliers in that the education, histories and careful focus away from refugees specifically meant a different degree of networks and connections could be mobilised. Dependence on investment from outside was risky for refugees like Mahad, who did not have the social capital to access a broad range of funders – or to hold them to account.

Whilst formal institutions in Nairobi were much more engaged with RCOs than those working in Kampala, there are clearly problems with a system that is based on refugees' social capital and ability to appeal to individuals within implementing organisations. For one, it does not render 'legible' those refugees who may be important providers of social protection and assistance but remain outside this system for various reasons, such as language skills or level of education; Bahati of Kintsugi emphasised that learning to speak English had been one of the most important factors in being able to make inroads with UNHCR and start building relationships. Leaders were also reluctant to openly express distrust of the terms of engagement offered by UNHCR and its partners, for fear of being pushed out altogether; the climate of fear created by repressive government policies towards refugees in Kenya means that refugees who challenge the current system of RCO engagement might be accused of biting the hand that feeds.

6

Kakuma

Established in 1992 for Sudanese refugees, Kakuma camp in Kenya's remote Turkana County hosts 190,000 refugees; it is *de facto* Kenya's seventh largest city. But unlike most other cities, it is not connected to the electricity grid, its economic and social model is mainly based on international assistance and its inhabitants are required to reside within a designated area. Its residents are divided across four sub-camps, which get increasingly newer but poorer from Kakuma 1 to Kakuma 4, and Kalobeyei, a new 'integrated settlement' that opened in 2016. In Kalobeyei, refugees and hosts live alongside one another, and refugees themselves receive a greater proportion of their assistance through market-based models like cash-based assistance for food and shelter.

Kakuma has become a byword for innovation: the hashtag **#IamKakuma** alludes to a series of impressively unique features. It was the first refugee camp to host a TEDx event, the home of more than half of the Refugee Olympics team, and the venue for a pioneering study that revealed Kakuma to be a $56 million economy ripe for investment. Together, UNHCR and the Turkana County Government have been trying to reinvent Kakuma according to a market-based model, which could better serve both refugees and the host community; if development assistance and private investment could be secured, everyone would benefit. The Governor of Turkana, Josphat Nanok, became a champion for this new approach, most evident in the new Kalobeyei settlement.

But whilst this approach is improving lives for some refugees (Betts et al. 2019), Kakuma and Turkana County remain poor, and the majority of its residents are dependent upon international assistance or the aid economy. A vast array of non-governmental organisations serve as implementing partners to UNHCR and other UN agencies in Kakuma, delivering social protection and assistance. Refugee-led organisations were initially hard to find: early in our fieldwork, UNHCR staff struggled to name any, with one exception – Solidarity and Advocacy for Vulnerable Individuals and Crisis (SAVIC). SAVIC, which had won an innovation prize from UNHCR, had a large and well-equipped building and claimed to have an operating budget of US$200,000 a year. Yet, largely unknown to UNHCR, other RCOs were slowly growing in number in Kakuma. In 2017 there were more than twenty registered refugee CBOs, engaging in a range of social protection and assistance activities – in addition to countless 'self-help' groups and cooperatives. The work of RCOs across Kakuma's Somali, Congolese and South Sudanese communities included education and literacy programmes; organising within their communities to provide sanitation, building maintenance and environmental upkeep; and promoting peacebuilding and gender equality.

Figure 6.1 illustrates some of the refugee-led community-based organisations, or RCOs, we met and spent time with in Kakuma, and serves to underscore the varied nature of interactions between formal institutions and refugee-led social protection. A significant

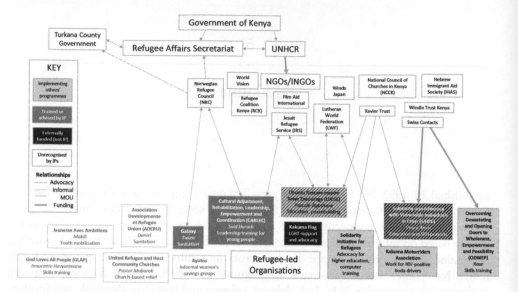

Figure 6.1 Refugee-led, national and international organisations in Kakuma

number of organisations were simply invisible to formal institutions. Those that were known to implementing partners (IPs) had tended to form relationships where they were positioned as 'subcontractors', implementing programmes on behalf of IPs within refugee communities. But this figure also reveals that a few organisations had managed to secure support from beyond Kakuma.

The Congolese population of Kakuma might be the smallest of the three nationality groups discussed, but they were the most prolific in setting up formal community-based organisations. The largest refugee organisation – in both size and reputation – was SAVIC, co-founded by two Congolese refugees who had moved to Kakuma from Tanzania. Their work had attracted funding from a number of US-based foundations. Their classrooms were impressively equipped with computers and projectors displaying instructions for learning basic Excel and PowerPoint. Their existence signalled to visitors that innovation did not just come from governments, international organisations or large corporations; it could also come from refugees themselves.

Yet SAVIC's co-founder, Vasco, explained that RCOs faced major barriers. Some are 'briefcase organisations' with 'personal interests' determining their work, he suggested. But many, he said, struggled for funding or recognition to get their activities off the ground. Unsurprisingly, few UNHCR staff could name any of the other RCOs indicated in grey on the chart shown in Figure 6.1. Whilst the Norwegian Refugee Council in particular had recently begun to reach out to refugees who were running their own initiatives in order to help them through the convoluted CBO registration process, a number of interventions by the Refugee Affairs Secretariat had made this challenging.

Consequently, while most of the large NGOs operating in Kakuma claimed to work with local organisations, few actually did so in a way that enabled refugees to take the lead on activities. The main way in which refugee-led initiatives were able to attract support was by implementing projects on behalf of the main agencies working in the camp. Organisations that did this included URISE (Ubuntu Restore Inspire Solve Encourage), which was started by Pascale, a graduate of the Arrupe Programme run by Jesuit Refugee Services. Drawing on his relationships with implementing partner organisations, he and his team delivered skills training on behalf of implementing organisations, including Xavier Trust. Other groups, including ODWEP and SAVIC, had partnered with another implementing partner, Swiss Contacts.

Fewer formal Somali or South Sudanese initiatives could be found in Kakuma. Refugees explained that this was due to several factors. The majority of South Sudanese in Kakuma were women, and whilst they did come together to discuss and resolve problems, the majority of their time was eaten up by subsistence farming and childcare. On top of this, many South Sudanese did not have the language abilities and the level of education required to work with implementing partner organisations, and therefore lacked the opportunity to build the connections that were necessary for building a formal RCO.

Whilst there is one Somali-led RCO in Figure 6.1, Cultural Adjustment, Rehabilitation, Leadership, Empowerment and Coordination (CARLEC), in general Somali social protection strategies were nebulous and informal. Yet they were significant for Somali survival: when asked to estimate what proportion of help they get from other Somalis rather than UNHCR and its institutions, Somalis put such assistance at a minimum of 75 per cent. Some of this happened through *ayutos*, traditional savings groups where money is collected from members and allocated each week to a different person. Like the South Sudanese, much assistance was determined and delivered through traditional structures and hierarchies, and thus not 'legible' to UNHCR and its partners in the same way that RCOs are.

Institutions

UNHCR and the 'Marketisation Agenda'

At the time of our fieldwork, UNHCR in Kakuma had engaged little with refugee-led organisations. Yet its operations staff were increasingly interested in the possibilities that refugee-led initiatives presented for partnership and delivery of services – an approach that could also feed into the UN Global Compact on Refugees and its emphasis on the economic self-reliance and socio-economic inclusion of refugees.

The centrality of self-reliance was particularly evident in the development of Kalobeyei settlement, located several miles to the north of Kakuma, where self-reliance was being promoted through initiatives that included encouragement of agriculture through 'kitchen gardens' and cash-based assistance programmes such as 'cash-for-shelter' and a form of digital currency called 'Bamba Chakula' (Betts et al. 2019). The International Finance Corporation – the private sector arm of the World Bank – highlighted the huge entrepreneurial potential of the camps, noting that over half of Turkana County's 4,000 retail shops were in Kakuma and Kalobeyei and that aggregate household expenditure in the camps was $56.2 million (World Bank 2018).

The policy vehicle for rolling out the Global Compact in Kakuma and creating opportunities for self-reliance was a fifteen-year strategy co-designed by UNHCR and the County Government known as the Kalobeyei Integrated Socio-Economic Development Plan (KISEDP). In its first iteration in 2016, KISEDP was simply a blueprint for the new Kalobeyei settlement, but by 2018, its focus had broadened to be a plan for the whole of the sub-county of Turkana West. Despite KISEDP's emphasis on self-reliance, its focus was mainly on *economic* self-reliance. The 106-page development plan includes only one brief reference to CBOs, and it is in the 'Private Sector and Entrepreneurship' section: 'Supporting value chain sub-sector initiatives that will strengthen firm-to-firm linkages and enterprise networking and strengthen mutual cooperation between business associations, including CBOs' (UNHCR 2018, p. 97).

Despite the conspicuous absence of CBOs from the main development strategy for the sub-county, UNHCR has had a vision for how it envisages the role of refugee-led organisations. UNHCR's chief of the Kakuma sub-office at the time of our fieldwork, Sukru, explained that he saw a role for such organisations as complementary to the broader vision for market-based development. Since 2017, he has been trying to get refugee-led, community-based organisations integrated into UNHCR's overall strategy. 'I want UNHCR to do less' he told us. 'Refugees are capable of doing lots of what (IPs) are currently doing.' He acknowledged that implementing partners could not be forced into also doing less – particularly if they were not entirely reliant on UNHCR for their funding. 'Agencies will be the barrier; we need to get them to understand this way of working' Sukru said. He described how, the previous year, many long-standing implementing partners applied to UNHCR to run programmes in Kalobeyei. 'We turned a lot of activities down because they were trying to do things the way they always had. But this is a new model of working with refugees.'

What Sukru envisaged was a system of social protection in which the market decides who provides what. RCOs could either subcontract from implementing partners, as some were already doing, or deliver services directly to the community for a fee. If the services provided by refugee CBOs were good enough, then refugees would vote with their feet and go to them for assistance. This was already happening with medical assistance; refugees were choosing to go to private providers rather than to the camp hospitals, associating a paid service with better quality. 'When people see the expense of a service, they value it more' Sukru said. 'Take the Cash for Shelter programme. Building shelters used to be done by Peace Wing Japan. When we gave refugees the money instead and got them to make decisions about their own housing, they saw how much things cost.'

Under this system, a refugee-led organisation could register as a partner with implementing agencies and UNHCR and provide services on their behalf. Sukru used Lokado, a local Turkana NGO, as an example of this already happening. Lokado worked with implementing partners, including the Danish and Norwegian Refugee Councils and Lutheran World Federation, as an intermediary with their communities; Lokado was able to draw on its comparative advantage in knowing each community's expectations and needs, and provided services, such as the buying, selling, and distribution of firewood, directly to them. One of the problems this could overcome was trust. As Sukru explained, 'refugees don't trust implementing partners. There are miscommunications all the time, and beliefs about bias at all levels. We constantly tackle it, but people find reasons not to trust us.' Enabling refugees to take services into their own hands and charge for them according to what people were willing to pay – and the transparency that this enabled – provided a solution to this dynamic.

A market-based approach made sense on one level: it promised quality and sustainability, with only 'quality' RCOs being able to succeed and grow. But on the other hand, it contributed to an environment in which refugee CBOs were generally unable to secure the recognition or funding needed to compete within the 'humanitarian marketplace' (Crisp 2009). Sukru acknowledged that for a market-based approach to work, the huge gap in the capacity of refugee-led organisations would need to be overcome. RCOs in Kakuma faced a chicken-and-egg problem: they needed sufficient capacity and competence to become viable partners to international NGOs, but they lacked the support that they would require to reach that stage. In the absence of recognition or funding, refugees struggled to build their capacity to assist each other in the ways that UNHCR envisaged being possible, with most initiatives remaining small in scope.

An IFC report described the main barrier to refugees' ability to participate and benefit in the 'marketplace' of Kakuma as being that they lacked the necessary education to be able to put their skills to use (World Bank 2018, p. 17). According to Sukru, a market-based approach necessitated an 'entrepreneurial mindset'. In order to foster potential future refugee service providers, a 'business incubator' would be built in Kalobeyei by its implementing partner, the Aurora Humanitarian Initiative (AHI). But just progressing through school in Kakuma was a highly competitive activity. There were only just over 1,000 Secondary School leavers each year in Kakuma, and fewer than 100 would progress to university.

Indeed, whilst a market-based approach was improving livelihoods for some refugees, it should also be noted that overall, Kakuma, and Turkana County in general, remained very poor places. Food assistance in Kakuma was limited to 1,200 calories per day and fluctuated with availability. Employment for refugees was limited mainly to 'incentive work' on behalf of NGOs, or small-scale, informal self-employment. Many homes struggled to afford electricity, and at night remote areas of the camp could be violent. And while education and health facilities in the camps were among the best in the county, they were still inadequate. Primary school class sizes averaged around 200 students per teacher, and secondary and tertiary education opportunities remained limited. Social protection was clearly necessary; despite the large numbers of implementing partners in the camps, however, formal sources of assistance were unable to meet demand.

Towards the end of our fieldwork, by late 2018, UNHCR began to recognise that it needed to do more to support community-based organisations. It created a one-off CBO fund of $25,000 and set-out a tender for applications for five one-off grants of $5,000 each. UNHCR chose five areas of eligible activity for the tender – all areas where they saw CBOs as helpful for UNHCR's work: voluntary repatriation awareness raising, hygiene awareness, social media training, distribution-related awareness and education awareness among the youth. All five areas related to 'awareness raising' and were driven by UNHCR priorities. However, UNHCR did not have time to disburse the allocated funds before the end of the financial year in 2018 and so it re-opened the call again in February 2019. Nevertheless, UNHCR Kakuma claims to have used the exercise to support CBO registration in Lodwar, the regional capital, and one senior staff member claimed that as many as 182 CBOs were registered. This figure, however, included two different legal categories for refugee organisations – CBOs and 'self-help groups', the former being non-profit and the latter often being for-profit – and our UNHCR informant suggested that the latter should be the preferred option.

However, a disconnect also existed between the ambitions of international agencies and local government on the one hand, and the remit of the government's Refugee Affairs Secretariat (RAS) on the other. RAS responded to refugee attempts to self-organise with suspicion. Whilst refugees were ostensibly being encouraged to formalise their activities, their ability to do so was undermined by the difficulties they faced in even obtaining movement passes to be able to travel to Lodwar and register with the local government. The security concerns of RAS, particularly over refugees' access to external sources of funding – which refugees and agencies alike saw as essential to enabling refugee-led organisations to grow – highlighted challenges for shifting paradigms of refugee governance during a time of heightened anxiety about terrorism in Kenya.

Refugee Governance in Turkana

Some of UNHCR's implementing partners were already encouraging refugees seeking to formalise their social protection activities through creating CBOs. Since 2015, the Arrupe diploma programme run by Jesuit World Learning (JWL) encouraged its graduates to build on the community service component of their degree to initiate their own social development projects in Kakuma. This had led to a burst of refugee community-based organisations, who, on the advice of the agencies in the camp, began registering in Lodwar. To register as a CBO or a self-help group – the two categories under which RCOs are able to formalise under Kenyan law – an RCO must have a constitution, a record of members, minutes of meetings and the relevant forms in triplicate. These are not demanding criteria, but it is a list that requires, at the very least, a basic knowledge of how to navigate bureaucracies and the use of printing facilities – something that refugees who were already involved with agencies like JWL in Kakuma were well-placed to access.

For other refugees, however, this process was more difficult. George, Grace and Niven, who coordinated NRC's Information, Counselling and Legal Advice (ICLA) programme at its Kakuma office, had worked on mapping refugee community-based organisations. They found that the majority of established and operational CBOs in Kakuma had registered before 2013; indeed, Niven was surprised that we had found any who had successfully registered as recently as 2017. This was because in 2016, when the Refugee Affairs Secretariat (RAS) took over responsibility for granting movement passes for refugees, it suddenly became more difficult to travel outside the camp. When refugees requested a movement pass, they had to have a reason to leave and provide evidence for it. To register a CBO, it was necessary to travel to the office of the Turkana County government's Social Development department in Lodwar, three hours from Kakuma. From 2016 onwards, this became more complicated. Refugees seeking to travel to Lodwar were told by RAS to get a letter from UNHCR, confirming that their organisation had legitimacy and that its members were indeed refugees. However, UNHCR's response was to tell refugees that they needed to be registered before they could obtain this letter.

Stuck in the middle like this, a group of refugees seeking to register their CBO came to NRC asking for assistance and intermediation. NRC was already assisting both refugee and host community groups with registration because the documentation could be challenging to put together, and the process for approval of CBOs in Lodwar did not differentiate between refugee and host community groups. NRC raised this with RAS, which immediately objected on the grounds that the Westgate attack in Nairobi in 2013 had been linked to international remittances that had come through groups registered in Dadaab refugee camp, and so giving refugees the opportunity to access international funding channels without proper vetting was a huge security risk.

RAS came back to NRC with a list of criteria for permitting refugees to register. These included not only a ban on all international financial transfers, but further restrictive measures as well, including a stipulation that refugee CBOs must obtain written permission from the police, the camp commandant and the UNHCR head of sub-office if they held a meeting. Niven told me that they had thirty-two refugee groups on hold for registration, waiting for clarifications; meanwhile, every one of the Turkana host community groups that had come to NRC for assistance was now up and running.

Indeed, by late 2018, the central government actually suspended refugees being able to register CBOs in Lodwar, arguing that it should be a right that should only be available to citizens. The suspension was part of the roll-out of a new initiative called the Huduma-Biashara Centres, designed to provide a simplified 'one-stop shop' regulatory space for all citizens and residents' civic registration and business advisory needs. At the time of writing, it was unclear when, or whether, the suspension would be lifted.

Subcontracting and Implementation

Whilst NRC had been an important mediator for refugee organisations, two other implementing partners in Kakuma had been trialling working through refugee CBOs to deliver their programming. Swiss Contacts was a relatively new UNHCR implementing partner in the livelihoods sector. Since 2014 they had been providing support to businesses in the refugee and host communities to develop various livelihoods projects, and since 2016 they had been piloting an initiative to do the same with refugee-led organisations in Kakuma. Faith, their programme officer, told us that after working in Kakuma for four years and training local host organisations and businesses in the Skills for Life methodology, they decided to put out a tender for refugee community-based organisations. It was the first time they had worked with refugee CBOs, and Faith told us that the project was seen as a learning platform for the Swiss Development Agency for future work in humanitarian contexts 'as part of a paradigm shift towards more sustainable interventions'.

Swiss Contacts paid skilled tradespeople to deliver training on various potential income-generating activities such as baking, tailoring and shoe repair. After the training was completed, the trainees got to keep the equipment used during teaching and were helped to start a savings group amongst themselves for future expansion. For the CBOs themselves, Swiss Contacts undertook an assessment to determine where organisations needed capacity development, such as monitoring, compliance and reporting. However, this was specifically so that the CBOs could deliver on the Skills for Life programme outputs: Faith shook her head firmly when we asked whether Swiss Contacts was interested in supporting refugee CBOs to deliver their own programming. 'We know our methodology works, and this is what we specialise in, so this is what we are supporting them in doing.'

IsraAid, an Israeli-based humanitarian organisation, had been delivering psychosocial programmes in the camp since 2014. Recently, it had begun trying to take a community development approach to its work in order to increase community ownership and investment in the counselling and rehabilitation services it offered to refugees. It had been undertaking mapping of refugee CBOs, but the eventual aim was for IsraAid to set up its own 'refugee community-based organisation' as an arm to deliver IsraAid training in counselling and support. When asked if this would really constitute a 'community-based' initiative, however, it was clear that IsraAid saw encouraging total independence as risky; the primary aim was to more effectively deliver their project.

These examples reflected Sukru's idea of 'subcontracting'. By delegating work like counselling and business training to refugees, organisations like IsraAid and Swiss Contacts would be free up to do more 'high-value' activities like management, reporting and monitoring and evaluation. This would also mean that implementing partners would still be able to meet the high demand for on-the-ground services, or even increase the numbers they could claim to service, which they simply did not have the capacity to meet through core staff alone.

However, a big challenge is external funding to support a subcontracting model. According to UN agency staff, Danish Church Aid (DCA) is one of the 'better' IPs in terms of its willingness to work with CBOs, and it has a reputation for working with local NGO partners. However, even DCA is actually working formally only with host community CBOs. For example, they have worked for seven years with Lokado and more recently with another host-community CBO called Sapcone. Both partnership agreements exist because they bring additional funding to DCA. For example, the work with Lokado is based on a Memorandum of Understanding that outlines potential areas of shared interest. Practical collaboration is dependent upon joint funding, which they currently have as part of a DANIDA-funded project. Similarly, the collaboration with Sapcone is based on a grant from UNICEF. This example highlights how some international NGOs are willing to work with local partners but that doing do depends upon external funding sources, which currently do not prioritise collaboration with refugee-led organisations to the same extent they do with host-community organisations.

Refugee Agency

In Kakuma, the narrative of refugee self-reliance and empowerment coming from UNHCR and its partners was largely at odds with refugees' own experiences of being prevented from actually leading on or expanding their own social protection initiatives. However, one outcome of the narrative that refugees can overcome barriers to establish competitive organisations, was the light it shone on individual leaders. In Kakuma, as in other sites, the heads of established RCOs were invariably young men, many of whom were frustrated by the limited opportunities available in the isolated and economically challenging environment of Kakuma.

As in our other research sites, it was Congolese refugees who had the most long-standing RCOs in Kakuma; however, refugees of other nationalities had also begun to create and register organisations. From 2015 onwards, the Arrupe diploma programme run by Jesuit World Learning had encouraged its graduates to build on the community service component of their degree to initiate their own social development projects in Kakuma. This had contributed to a proliferation of refugee community-based organisations, who, on the advice of the agencies in the camp, began registering in Lodwar until the stalemate with RAS from 2017 onwards. These organisations, started by young men of all nationalities, attempted to balance the gender ratio of their committees and include members from all different ethnic communities, in line with the requirements of UNHCR and its implementing partners.

Given the limited options available to refugees in this climate, if UNHCR saw a place for refugee-led groups to deliver services, then setting up a community-based organisation was as good a survival strategy as any. This is not to say that RCO leaders were not invested in the outcomes for their communities, but that within a discourse of market-based approaches, being seen as competitive and cost-effective was more important than altruism for those seeking to work within the 'subcontracting' model that was on offer. Yet to position oneself in this way also required refugees to be non-threatening to IPs, which may like the idea of 'community-based approaches' yet be reluctant to hand over the reins completely and risk losing their foothold as UNHCR partners.

For some Congolese organisations, circumventing the partnership model on offer from UNHCR and its associated agencies was made more possible by links to diasporas in Europe and the United States. With many Congolese having been resettled from Kakuma over the years, some refugee-led organisations have been able to receive and network with international visitors to Kakuma through their international networks. The two most long-running CBOs in Kakuma – ODWEP and SAVIC – were initiated by Congolese who had since been resettled yet continued to act as CEOs from a distance, representing and marketing their organisations beyond Kenya. The feasibility of this option, however, should not be overstated: many more refugees sought international support than were successful in establishing sustainable partnerships with external donors.

The largest group of refugees in Kakuma and Kalobeyei were also the most recent arrivals: South Sudanese refugees who had fled the country during ongoing surges of interethnic conflict since 2013. The 80,000 South Sudanese made up nearly half of Kakuma's total population; yet during the time of this research, South Sudanese CBOs could not be identified in Kakuma. Both Dinka and Nuer communities also expressed a preference for resolving problems within their communities through customary law, rather than in ways that would engage with formal institutions. Ongoing conflict between Dinka and Nuer communities was a major worry for South Sudanese refugees, but traditional structures of authority were seen by both groups as the most acceptable means of resolving differences. This was a sentiment echoed by Somalis in Kakuma; both South Sudanese and Somali refugees felt that Kenya was hostile to their cultural norms, and both groups preferred to maintain their distance from the Kenyan staff of implementing partner organisations.

To successfully engage with institutions, RCOs were expected to embody particular markers of legitimacy. This included having educated leadership capable of understanding and translating the norms of social protection and assistance in the way they framed their own activities. RCOs, ideally, can present an alternative space for action that does not depend on support 'from above' – those who are unwilling or unable to play the political games required of a 'refugee leader' can recruit support from other places. But as discussed here, this was much more difficult in Kakuma, where geographic and economic marginalisation, combined with the reluctance of the Refugee Affairs Secretariat, made retaining independence as an RCO much less likely. Under these conditions, opting out of forming community-based organisations that were legible to the international community – as Somalis and South Sudanese in Kakuma were doing – might be understood as resistance to the limited notions of 'refugee empowerment' on offer from UNHCR.

Transforming Access to Education

With refugee 'capacity' being a key condition for strong RCOs capable of partnership and delivery, it is worth considering the limited numbers of refugees able to access further education. One RCO had been attempting to find solutions. Solidarity Initiative for Refugees, based in Kakuma 2, was started by a group of young Congolese refugees in 2014. Honore, its director, had been working for the Norwegian and Danish Refugee Councils as a translator and social worker since his arrival in 2013, but felt unfulfilled by the opportunities available in the camp and was worried about stagnating in Kakuma.

I got my diploma in International Relations back in 2011 in DRC, and wanted to complete my bachelor's [degree], but the war stopped me. I came here, hoping I might find opportunities. But I found that UNHCR thinks that completing secondary school is enough for a refugee, because it's enough to get you work here (with implementing partners). But people here are thinking of their futures. We have time, and we can use it to prepare for going home or being resettled.

Solidarity Initiative's aim was to increase the numbers of refugees accessing higher education. Before the organisation started, Honore's friend Fabrice had told him about a free distance learning initiative by the University of Geneva (Switzerland) called Chiron, which he himself had enrolled on. 'When I heard about Chiron, I thought "this should be available to everyone! We should tell people about it!"' Fabrice and Honore began to tell people about Chiron and compiled a long list of people interested. The only challenge that Fabrice and Honore had to overcome was that it would be difficult for refugees to complete the online modules, given that there was such limited computer access in the camp and what little there was usually came at a price.

Yet in the camp was an education centre called Arrupe Learning Centre, which was run by Jesuit World Learning (JWL). It had computers, and JWL's remit as an implementing partner of UNHCR was to expand education for refugees. Fabrice and Honore met with JWL and requested that they open their centre up for additional hours so that people could enrol in the Geneva University courses and use the Chiron platform to study. But to their dismay, the Arrupe staff were not impressed. 'They did not agree with what we were trying to promote; they called it disruptive. They themselves didn't offer bachelor's degrees at the time and said it would distract their students studying on their diploma programme.'

Fabrice and Honore were back to square one, but the idea had set in, and they were determined to find a way to help those they had told about the programme. It was a chance encounter with some volunteers that gave them the idea to start Solidarity Initiative. 'These students from Outreach Australia came and we talked to them about Chiron. They were so excited about it and went home and fundraised for thirteen laptops so we wouldn't need to rely on Arrupe. They helped us come up with the name of "Solidarity Initiative for Refugees".'

Solidarity Initiative operated in small brick building in the middle of a field, surrounded by several trees and encircled by a barbed wire fence, with a gate and a security guard. At the back of the building, in a lean-to with a tin roof, around twelve students sat and worked on laptops as a class on computer programming was being delivered by a young Sudanese teacher. They signed an agreement with the INGO Xavier Trust to fund their internet connection in exchange for also delivering Xavier Trust's Good Start programme, which taught financial literacy, psychosocial wellbeing and Scratch, a basic IT course. 'This is our organisation's classroom' Honore explained.

> The building you see next to it is a library. Some researchers came to visit us from Harvard and put pressure on UNHCR to help us get a building, but it is used by Windle Trust Kenya as a library. UNHCR told Windle Trust that they should share the plot with us, and that they should build something next to it which would be a mirror image, but they refused and created this structure for us instead. We just share the fence – but our organisation pays for the security guard.

Barriers to Progress

With Solidarity Initiative up and running, Honore contacted the University of Geneva to tell them about the now 250 refugees who had signed up wanting to study via the Chiron platform. Solidarity Initiative proposed to set itself up as an 'implementing centre' for the university. But now things stalled again – and this time it was not a barrier that could be overcome through sheer determination. With Chiron, students study as distance learners for two years only. At that point, students who have fulfilled the online portion of the course requirements are expected to complete their degree in person in Geneva. The university's response to the sudden huge number of applications from Kakuma was to state firmly that they would not support any students to travel overseas from the camp. Refugees from Kakuma were welcome to study the online portion of the course – but would not receive transcripts or certificates, even for the section that they had completed.

This was a huge blow to Solidarity Initiative. Many of the students who had enrolled in the Geneva University programme dropped out, though some continued to study using the laptops provided by the 'friend' from Outreach Australia, perhaps hopeful that there might be a change of heart. Solidarity Initiative's classroom was still being used to implement the Xavier Project programmes, and they delivered more advanced classes in IT themselves. 'We had visitors from Harvard who agreed this was unjust. They said they wanted to see refugees succeed. They invited us to write a blog post for them about our work and said they would try to find out more from the administrators of the Chiron platform, but we have still not heard any feedback' Honore said. 'Our students are becoming disaffected.'

Henri and Honore saw formalising Solidarity Initiative as a key means of obtaining the legitimacy they would need to find another partner who could support refugee education, or advocate for them with the University of Geneva. They had, however, been struggling with the registration process for CBOs, and still did not have a certificate.

> We started the process in 2014, but the government in Lodwar told us repeatedly that they could not grant us a certificate because they had a limited number available and had to share them between refugees and host organisations. We went to the Norwegian Refugee Council to get them to advocate for us, but even then, our application was rejected. The government in Lodwar told us that we should get a Kenyan CEO and Finance Officer and then we could pay taxes through them but UNHCR rejected this idea because they want to link refugee CBOs to their implementing partners. We were going around in circles. We are still waiting now: since April [2018] the Norwegian Refugee Council have had all of our information.

One driver for Honore and his friends to set up their own organisation was the treatment of refugees by agencies, which was described by many as disrespectful and exploitative. Solidarity Initiative's growth was due to being able to capture the imaginations of refugees who were also seeking a way to move beyond the positions and status available to them within the camp. Indeed, Honore himself was not interested in going back to work for the implementing partners as an incentive worker. 'With education you gain status. Here there is respect for those with higher education because they are so few. They become leaders and role models in the community' he explained. 'At the agencies, I earned ten times less than a Kenyan who only went to primary school' (Jansen 2018).[1]

Rose, a Rwandan refugee who had been employed by World Vision Rwanda before coming to Kakuma, was the finance officer for a CBO called Orphans, Disabled, Widows

---

[1] Such status in Kakuma is described by Jansen (2018) as 'campital' – the combined social, human and financial capital that determined how refugees could manoeuvre through the camp environment and expand their agency.

and Educational Programmes. Generally known as ODWEP, it had been implementing a programme on behalf of Swiss Contacts, which, as discussed earlier, is an implementing partner of UNHCR. Rose told us that initially Swiss Contacts only wanted to pay the trainers who were delivering their content, and not ODWEP staff who would be providing the administrative support. 'We complained about that because it was not fair, and now ODWEP staff are paid too, but the Kenyan trainers get higher salaries than the refugees.'

When Rose first arrived in Kakuma she worked as an incentive worker for World Vision in the camp. As she explained,

> In Rwanda, I got a good salary. This is why I applied to work for them again. But I saw that the refugees working for World Vision in Kakuma were poor and were treated terribly. Their Kenyan staff had a bus to take them to the field offices, but we weren't allowed to get on it. They brought drinking water to sites and we weren't permitted to take a bottle. This is why we have the motivation to make CBOs – to show the world and Kenyans that we can run things too.

A disrespectful dynamic, in which refugees were treated instrumentally rather than as genuine stakeholders, was not only ethically problematic but also affected the capacity of refugees to work effectively with their communities. Rose told us, 'a few years ago UNHCR commissioned ODWEP to collect some information – to go and hear complaints from the community, mainly about water issues. We wrote a report for them but got no feedback. We lost credibility in the community. People told us everything and never got anything from UNHCR. ODWEP lost the community's trust because of this.'

Strategies for Overcoming Barriers

What are some of the options for transcending these dynamics? For many refugees, the answer was to try and find support from outside Kenya. Refugees who were both knowledgeable about the way the international aid system works, and well positioned to use this information, were most able to play an effective leadership role in establishing RCOs. Rose, ODWEP's finance officer, explained that the organisation was started by Shogonya, a Congolese refugee who was now in Canada. When Shogonya had still been in Kakuma, ODWEP had been much more active on the ground; but since his departure their activities had dwindled. Rose told us that as Shogonya was a student now, his capacity to support ODWEP was limited. In contrast, the online presence of ODWEP, had grown hugely since Shogonya's resettlement. The organisation had a very professional website that detailed ODWEP's work on women's empowerment, sexual and reproductive health and alternatives to violence, as well as a number of other activities, despite, according to Rose, there being only one current active programme – the Skills for Life project ODWEP was implementing on behalf of Swiss Contacts.

Indeed, with external 'legibility' being key to generating external support, the Internet offered refugees an important medium for engaging with potential supporters, advocates and donors. Refugee Flag Kakuma (RFK) was an LGBTI group run by Namala, one of around 200 Ugandan refugees in Kakuma. Namala was very active on social media; the majority of support that RFK received had been through a JustGiving page linked to their Facebook account, to which he posted regular, harrowing accounts of the challenges of life in the camp for LGBTI people. Through social media, Namala encouraged supporters of LGBTI rights to advocate for refugees' security and access to the services that they needed.

LGBTI refugees in Kakuma were confined for their own safety to a protection space in Kakuma 3 run by Lutheran World Federation, a small tented area with heavy security. 'As soon as people here know you are Ugandan and a refugee, they know you are gay' he told us. Yet there were services that LGBTI refugees were not receiving, such as HIV testing and treatment, hormones for transgender members and psychosocial support. 'IRC gives us medication but no STI screening. It's difficult to explain why we need this to their health workers because of homophobia' Namala explained. 'UNHCR are trying its best, put we need to put pressure on them and remind them of their mandate to protect.'

Personal relationships were often crucial to organisational development. International interest in the plight of LGBTI refugees and the blurring of boundaries through the Internet had enabled RFK to lobby more sympathetic audiences than those available within the camp, where Namala recounted refugees being subject to discrimination from implementing organisations staffed by Kenyans, and violence and aggression from other camp residents. 'Our allies are others like us. Most of our support base is LGBTI. They are not well off financially, but they are good at writing letters, and advocate for us in Geneva, Sweden, Japan, other places' Namala explained. Whilst such money was not a reliable stream of funding, refugees had more flexibility on how to deploy money from outsiders, especially when it was generated informally, than they did with money obtained through 'partnerships', which might come with conditions attached.

Pascale, the Congolese graduate of the Arrupe programme who started an organisation called Ubuntu, Restore, Inspire, Solve, Encourage (URISE) told us about getting funding from an organisation in the UK called Sky School. The only verification they required was by one of the staff checking with UNHCR's Education Officer that Pascale was who he said he was. Other 'friends' of URISE included a yoga teacher who visited and then raised US$1,000 for them through her studio. Pascale explained that connections with visitors who knew what was possible had been essential for creating 'partnerships' in other countries, which then gave URISE credibility, which then attracted more visitors. 'We used the thousand dollars to do community outreach. Another friend is trying to fundraise for us now in Canada.'

URISE had been able to establish itself because of Pascale's effective use of his own connections within Kakuma as well as outside. Pascale explained that 'the best thing we were taught by Regis University (the Arrupe programme's certifying institution) was to value human beings'. Their message was palatable and accessible. 'Youth here are involved in drugs, they are unemployed, they fight – they want to regain their dignity. But because of culture and different beliefs, there is conflict. If people understand each other, we can create peace. That is our goal' Pascale explained. 'We welcome all people in the community. Our members are from all nationalities, it is an initiative for Africa.' Pascale had been able to mobilise support from individual staff at LWF, JRS and UNHCR, who had assisted him in securing a building and an internet connection so that URISE could run the Sky School programme. The programme provided high school education online to refugee youth who had dropped out of school, extending what was already provided by the schools in the camp, although the programme was yet to be certified.

Somali Adaptation

For Somalis in particular, cultural practices offered an important means to provide social protection beyond formal organisations. Somalis in Kakuma had been refugees in Kenya for a long time, and over the years they had developed both commerce and social protection strategies which made them less reliant on external services. In Kakuma 1, Habibo and her neighbour Kafi elaborated on how social protection was organised among Somalis in Kakuma. 'There are several different kinds of charitable giving amongst Somalis in Kenya' Kafi explained. 'Here in Kakuma there are small collections, like for burials and things for women immediately after they give birth. These are organised mainly by women.' Somali refugees in Kakuma had a great number of households headed by women, and the everyday burden of care for the proportionately high numbers of children and older people in the camp tended to fall on women. Somali women looked after the domestic sphere, but they also had to find opportunities to make money. Many of them owned small businesses and were part of *ayutos* (informal savings schemes in which all members put in a set amount of money each month; every month, members take turns to receive the money collected to invest or spend as they like) in the camp. Hodan and Hali were part of an *ayuto*, which replicated the savings groups they were both part of at home. 'The *ayutos* here are only small, you get a few hundred shillings. Back home the *ayutos* were enough to buy plots of land to truly expand one's home and business.'

The big challenge in Kenya, Kafi said, was that whereas back in Somalia there was always a host of relatives around the corner to help out, here people depended on the kindness and generosity of their neighbours. Habibo also remarked upon the significance of being near to other Somalis for overall wellbeing. She came to Kakuma in 2009 from Dadaab, and she said that it was a better place to live as a Somali. 'Dadaab was much better because there were more of our people there. It was also closer to Somalia, so we could visit and come back easily. We could even buy camel milk there.'

But Hodan and Hali thought that Somali interconnectedness felt different in Kakuma to how things were back home. 'Back in Somalia, we never really knew exactly what was happening in our neighbours' lives. Everyone was working and too busy for each other', Hali explained, 'but coming to the camp has created unity. Here, if there is an incident, all Somalis are your relatives.' Becoming refugees had changed the ways in which Somalis helped each other by bringing them closer together and creating a sense of a united Somali identity. 'Regardless of conflict', Hali said, 'we have learned something new about ourselves, and if we can ever return home, these lessons will come with us.'

For many Somalis, connections with Nairobi were an important source of social protection. Kakuma is two days from Nairobi by road, but many families sent their children to Eastleigh for school, or moved there themselves for work, keeping Kakuma as their base. Kafi had two young people living with her whose parents were working in Nairobi; they went to school in Kakuma, but once they finished they had to also contribute to her household financially or move on. Indeed, the lack of opportunities in Kakuma had resulted in extensive movement of Somali adults of working age between the camp and cities like Nairobi. Once they had finished school, young people went to Nairobi to find work; if they did not have family there, they would be taken in by other Somalis and contribute both to that household and send money back to Kakuma to bolster the finances of their families who remained in the camp.

Strategies for livelihoods in Kakuma were impossible to disentangle from their relationship to places like Eastleigh in Nairobi. The networks that were generated and solidified through Somali mobilities were hugely important to Somali social protection strategies. As well as movements of people, once a year in Eastleigh there was a big collection of *sadaqah* (a type of non-obligatory *zakat* – a type of charitable tax under Islamic law). During this time, Kafi explained that 'delegations of Somalis travel from Kakuma to Nairobi to advocate for the money to come to the camp to help vulnerable people here'. This advocacy was usually done by men. The money was used for building houses and paying travel and medical expenses for sick people; but it also reinforced the connection between Somalis in Nairobi and those living in the camp.

The increasing restrictions on movement since RAS had taken over management of the camp was also creating challenges for the continuity of the strategy of sending young people to work in Nairobi. The worries over what this meant for young people's futures in Kenya that Habibo and Hodan expressed to us formed a driver for youth-led CBOs like CARLEC, the only Somali-led initiative we met with in Kakuma. Led by a young Somali man called Said, CARLEC stands for Cultural Adjustment, Rehabilitation, Leadership, Empowerment and Coordination. Like Pascale of URISE, Said was a graduate of the Jesuit World Learning Arrupe Programme, where he learned about 'community development' and had been encouraged to think about what activities he could do to benefit the camp. CARLEC sought to address issues like radicalisation, gender inequality and interfaith conflict, which were all major concerns for the Somalis we met, and Said and his team had established a peer mentoring programme. At the end of 2018, CARLEC were still awaiting their certification from Lodwar, but they were hopeful that the intervention of the Norwegian Refugee Council would help them to obtain CBO status too.

Whilst many Somalis sent their children to Nairobi for work, others feared what would happen to them in the city. Stories of a 'killer cop' in Eastleigh had reached the camp, and the police were nightmarish spectres. 'I fear to send my children to Nairobi because of the risk of harassment and detention and violence by the police' Habibo explained. Hodan expressed her fears about the alternative: 'our children feel stuck and suffocated here in Kakuma and I worry about trafficking. A friend's son was trafficked. He went to Egypt but then died in the Mediterranean on his way to Europe.' Adults felt ill-equipped as individuals to deal with the structural issue of the lack of opportunities available to their children, which saw them spending time online, communicating with Somalis in other parts of the world. 'The problem is the few that make it to Europe – they post photos on Facebook showing their new life and asking their friends "why do you stay in Kakuma, look what you could have!"' exclaimed Hodan.

Cultural Continuity and the South Sudanese

Many South Sudanese felt that their cultural modes of social protection were difficult to reconcile with formal institutional mechanisms. Rather than creating RCOs, traditional ways of ensuring community cohesion and justice that focussed on the role of elders were the main means of ensuring protection and assistance in the camps. A key component of this was the use of customary law[2]. Nuer and Dinka South Sudanese elders explained that their own traditional system of courts, established by tribal elders to hear grievances and provide mediation, was generally preferred to involving the Kenyan police. 'Police involvement takes control away from the communities. We're usually able to resolve issues like conflict between our youths and unmarried pregnancies ourselves, so we prefer to do so

---

[2] This system existed alongside the formal, UNHCR-approved systems of Block Leaders and community peacekeepers, which were promoted by the Lutheran World Federation (LWF).

using traditional systems' Jonju, a Nuer elder from Kakuma 4, explained. Often, the police were not informed at all; according to Jonju, this was because many people did not like the constitution of Kenya, which takes precedence over tribal customs. By keeping problems out of the host country's legal system, South Sudanese were able to implement justice that was respected as legitimate within their own communities.

Disruption to South Sudanese society had, however, created significant challenges for peaceful coexistence with other tribes and nationality groups in Kakuma. At a community centre in Kakuma 1, Dinka elders, many of whom have been here since the early 1990s, met to play card games every day. Abraham, one of these elders, told us that his community particularly struggled as refugees because wealth and status for the Dinka is tied up in cattle and farmland – physically impossible to bring to Kakuma. Dinka living in Kakuma were therefore dislocated from markers that a) were intrinsic to their individual identities, and b) structured community dynamics.

Abraham explained that, in the camp, concerns about mitigating the effects of this disruption boiled over into regular conflicts over the key issue of dowries.

> At home, a baby girl is a source of income for her family, but here, someone can just take her and pay nothing. There are no cows, so they just do not pay. So families try to take their daughter back, but what if she is pregnant? Then if a Dinka girl marries a Congolese, we don't even have the right to claim a dowry from them – but we cannot take her back because they will go to the police. The police will be on their side and say "it is her right to marry who she wants" and send us away.

Daif, another Dinka elder, spoke up to corroborate these concerns: 'Back home I had so much, but here I just have daughters. It is wealth that people can just take away.'

A system of community oversight that recognises elders as authorities, and operates separately from the formal legal system, is the norm in South Sudan, with disputes regulated and resolved within families and communities through customary law (Milos 2011). Such norms do not disappear when people move en masse. But whereas supporting community-based mechanisms like the block leader system in Kakuma had been an important part of organisations like LWF's work to promote peace in the camp, truly community-initiated mechanisms like customary law found themselves at odds with national law – even if they had other features, such as quick emergency assistance and conflict resolution, that UNHCR and its partners valued.

Rather than adapt to Kenyan legal norms, the Dinka men said their communities should instead find ways to ensure that customary law could be sustained. 'Men and women can still marry in the camp, but instead of paying the dowry up front, their families put the payments on hold until we all return to South Sudan. If they get resettled, then they can send back money, rather than pay the dowry in cows' Abraham elaborated. It was notable that both the presumption of an eventual return to a peaceful South Sudan and ensuring recognition of customary law by international actors working in South Sudan were also key goals of South Sudanese human rights defenders like Simon in Kampala. But the South Sudanese elders' distress showed that these were not just desirable objectives; they were framed as necessary conditions for the continuity of the South Sudanese way of life. 'We just came here for protection', Abraham stated, 'but now our culture is being changed.' Under these terms, retaining as much control as possible over social assistance and protection becomes an act of cultural survival. Forming RCOs would not serve this purpose.

Self-Reliance at the Margins

The discussion so far has centred on refugee-led social protection and assistance in Kakuma. But just 3.5 kilometers from the Kakuma camps is the new Kalobeyei settlement, where a 'self-reliance' model was being implemented. Over 70 per cent of refugees in Kalobeyei were from South Sudan, three-quarters of whom were women (Betts et al. 2018). Macklena was an elected neighbourhood leader for the block where she lived alongside several other families – most of which, like hers, were headed by women. She was thirty-six years old, had ten children and she and her sister had been living in Kalobeyei since arriving in Kakuma in 2016. Macklena had positive things to say about Kalobeyei, especially in comparison to what she had heard about Kakuma. 'Here we have a better system. There is a lot of conflict in Kakuma between refugees and the host community, especially over matters like rape, but here they are living alongside us and we can solve problems together.'

Macklena echoed other South Sudanese in Kakuma on where people go for assistance when issues like the distribution and theft of firewood and water, which were in limited supply, occurred. 'Before anyone, we tell community leaders.' However, when refugees needed help with something that required more assistance than their leaders could arrange, there was nowhere to turn. Macklena said that a frequent problem in Kalobeyei was delay in payments from Bamba Chakula, the electronic payment system through which refugees in Kalobeyei received money to buy their food at selected shops, instead of receiving food aid from a distribution centre. Community leaders like Macklena were limited in their capacity to act on such delays because there was no central authority in Kalobeyei to whom they could appeal. For refugees to be able to negotiate with agencies over rights and protection, it was first necessary for those agencies to recognise their claims in the first place, but 'we feel we are not allowed to complain' Macklena told us. 'If people run out [of money], they just have to wait for the next payment. Sometimes you can get credit by leaving the Bamba Chakula card at the shop, and sometimes neighbours will donate small things. But people have very little here to share.'

As well as lacking resources, new arrivals like the South Sudanese in Kalobeyei also felt detached from the social connections that enabled people who had been displaced for longer periods of time to survive. This feeling of detachment, when added to the minimal intervention from UNHCR and its partners, made refugees like Macklena feel that they were on their own. There had been some support from agencies like the Danish Refugee Council for groups to start businesses – but those that had received assistance from the IP had then just helped their own relatives. 'If you're here with no family and friends, then you get nothing' she added. 'We are also all spread out, and it's so hot and difficult to move around, so it's difficult to even get people together.' But regardless of these socioeconomic difficulties, Macklena thought Kalobeyei was a better place for South Sudanese to live than Kakuma because they could at least live in a community where they comprised the majority of the population. 'Cultural diversity is difficult for us. It brings many challenges' she explained.

Outliers

As seen throughout this and other chapters, many refugee-led organisations perceived external support as key to building their capacity, and few organisations had been successful in accessing the gold standard of funding – formal international supporters for one's own programmes. The feasibility of this option, however, should not be overstated; only SAVIC and indeed URISE have successfully obtained international support, and only SAVIC has found sources of funding that did not simply position them as 'subcontractors' but allowed them to run projects of their own design.

Inspiration

SAVIC's head of programmes in Kakuma, Vasco, was friendly and welcoming, with excellent English. SAVIC was currently registered not as a CBO but as an NGO, which required a significant turnover and impressive staff capacity just to meet the reporting expectations of the government. 'Our next aim is to be an INGO – we want to open a branch of SAVIC in Tanzania, Congo, other parts of Africa.' Vasco told us. Their backstory was impressive. Vasco had only arrived in Kakuma in 2010. He and his friend Muzabel, who had been resettled to the United States in 2014, had started SAVIC as a self-help group to tackle the challenges facing youth in the camp. 'There was a lot of early marriage and pregnancy, and girls were dropping out of school, so we wanted to do something' he explained.

Opportunity

Vasco and Muzabel knocked on the doors of various NGOs to ask for help with registration, and they were eventually given a recommendation letter by UNHCR and directed to Lodwar. At first 'it was just us volunteering, no profits, doing training in schools. We started sexual and reproductive health (SRH) clubs to educate students, and then realised we needed to integrate those who had dropped out already as well, so we started community clubs too.' The success of the clubs, Vasco explained, gave them the idea to expand their activities into English and Swahili language training. Both he and Muzabel spoke English, and they noticed that the lack of ability to communicate amongst the many nationalities was a key driver of conflict in the camp.

However, these classes required resources. 'We asked a little money from those who attended, but it wasn't enough to cover the cost of running them. So we started to write proposals to try and get grants to fund our work' Vasco explained. In 2013, SAVIC got lucky and signed a memorandum of understanding with the National Coalition of Churches in Kenya, an implementing partner of UNHCR in the camp. As Vasco told us proudly,

> We partnered with them on their sexual and reproductive health work. The money they gave was only for resources and not salaries, but we started having a huge impact. An NGO did a survey and found that people living in Kakuma 2, 3 and 4 (where SAVIC worked) had more SRH knowledge than those in Kakuma 1. And people were saying that this knowledge came from SAVIC!

Networks

This validation was significant for SAVIC's credibility. Over the next three years they were given grants by the Segal Family Foundation, the Franklin Foundation, the Anderson Arojas Foundation, and Free the Mind Foundation. Their activities grew and they expanded into vocational training and entrepreneurship, with the help of Swiss Contacts, who partnered with SAVIC to deliver training on dressmaking, tailoring and baking. Whilst their partnership with Swiss Contacts was as a subcontractor, SAVIC did not rely on this relationship to provide them with funds or equipment. What Swiss Contacts could provide SAVIC with was an expanded beneficiary base to add to its figures of over 6,000 refugees trained since 2010, bolstering its legitimacy. In 2016, SAVIC registered in Nairobi as an NGO. 'We aren't waiting for UNHCR to give us money. We don't want to have to close our doors if our partnerships in the camp end' Vasco said.

Like HOCW in Kampala, SAVIC recognised the importance of capitalising on relationships with people from overseas. In 2017, a young woman from China visited Kakuma and met with SAVIC. This was a turning point; when she returned to China, she and her wealthy family helped to connect SAVIC to charities they knew back home. Vasco told us that SAVIC received over $200,000 that year from China, which funded their impressive building. Having a physical base was deemed by refugees seeking to carve out a significant role in social protection provision to be essential for legitimacy, visibility and getting further support – both from refugees and the international community. Their focus now was on continuing fundraising so that they could complete the building.

In future, SAVIC planned to expand beyond Kakuma and into Kalobeyei. 'We are meeting with UNHCR to discuss this. They want us to expand our programmes, but right now we don't have the money for that' Vasco explained. UNHCR's Head of Sub-Office, Sukru, was dismissive of SAVIC – 'Muzabel is the creator of SAVIC, not Vasco' he told us – but to us, Vasco was doing an excellent job of promoting and representing SAVIC in Muzabel's absence.

Analysing 'Success'

The success of SAVIC was not simply due to chance encounters. Like many of the leaders of successful organisations discussed throughout this book, both Muzabel and Vasco had experience working for and with international humanitarian and development organisations, both in Kakuma and beforehand. Vasco and Muzabel met in 1996, when they were youth chairmen in Kigoma camp in Tanzania. Vasco received training from World Vision on leadership, which included proposal writing. He went on to work for UMATI, a sexual and reproductive health organisation, which partnered with International Planned Parenthood Federation in Tanzania.

When the refugee camps in Tanzania were closed, Muzabel and Vasco were sent to Kenya, where Vasco got a job at Lutheran World Federation as a gender equality and human rights officer. He then worked for the World Food Programme. The good relationships that the staff of SAVIC had personally maintained, and the formal knowledge that they had of the expectations of other organisations, helped to explain the success of SAVIC. 'Even without UNHCR funding, we need to report to them,' said Tom, SAVIC's programmes officer, 'so it's important that we keep them involved.' 'Successful CBOs are those which can access funds from outside Kakuma', Vasco explained, 'but it's hard to get funds as refugees. You need links and people to recommend you. Success is a matter of collecting those links.'

The introduction of the Comprehensive Refugee Response Framework and its requirement for initiatives to benefit both refugees and the host community posed new challenges for SAVIC as a self-described 'refugee NGO'. Vasco found himself under pressure to ensure that he cultivated good relationships with Kenyans, and in particular local Turkana people. 'Now, if you want support from agencies, Kenyans need to be either heads of the CBOs or working with them. Kenyans want to see their colleagues involved before they will help.'

When Vasco last saw Joseph Nanok, the governor of Turkana, he was asked how many Kenyans were involved.

> He told me that it would be impossible for them to help us get support unless we hire Kenyan staff. He told me "you're in Kenya! You must hire Kenyans." So now we're thinking of hiring two Kenyans. Even Swiss Contacts asked us about our impact for the host community. Everyone is under pressure. Even UNHCR are under pressure to hire more Turkanas because the host community says they just have Kikuyus working there.

Conclusion

The last few years have seen refugee CBOs in Kakuma gradually proliferate. Yet international agencies continue to position RCOs as potential contractors of services rather than setting agendas based on what they see is needed within their communities. Implementing partners appear reluctant to take risks by supporting refugees to design their own programming and choose their own direction. The most successful RCOs are those that can effectively mimic humanitarian narratives on what refugees need and show themselves as well-placed to deliver these pre-determined objectives. Examples of this include UNHCR's vision of 'managers', refugees to whom work can be outsourced within a competitive marketplace, and Israid's idea of setting up their own 'RCO' to deliver Israid-designed psychosocial programming. This instrumental approach prevents refugee-led social protection and assistance from challenging existing paradigms of the humanitarian system too much; RCO engagement is treated as an innovation from above.

With the proper support and recognition, refugee-led social protection and assistance can not only meet gaps in services, but also give purpose and hope to ambitious and intelligent people and keep them from becoming dulled by camp life. Yet dismissive treatment, whether real or perceived, has had powerful effects on refugees' perception of partnership opportunities. Refugees have sought to reach beyond UNHCR and its partners in seeking support for their work not simply because they do not trust them, but because the available modes of partnership are of limited appeal and cannot be negotiated. This also appears to be a driver for refugees to seek assistance from outside Kakuma. And whilst inequalities of power did not disappear when funders were beyond the camp boundaries, they were perhaps less visible at a distance and did not contribute to the everyday experience of marginalisation.

As in Nairobi, interactions between refugee-led initiatives and implementing partners in Kakuma also unfolded within a politicised context under the new Refugee Affairs Secretariat (RAS). At the same time as refugee groups were seeking recognition through registering as community-based organisations, RAS was taking an increasingly restrictive stance on refugee initiatives. In seeking to render refugee-led organisations visible, agencies such as the Norwegian Refugee Council in Kakuma unfortunately also exposed them to the demands of RAS and a particular operational agenda. This saw refugee initiatives not in terms of positive community action but in terms of financial flows potentially being diverted to groups of non-citizens, which might in turn present a security concern to Kenya's national interest. This deterred meaningful capacity-building, and created tensions between UNHCR, implementing partners and different arms of government. Outliers like SAVIC established themselves before these changed conditions came about, serving to highlight further that the narrative of promoting 'self-reliance' – which had been used as justification for the reduction of institutional services in the camp – had little meaning in the face of other structural dynamics that constrained the agency of refugees.

Occasionally, external attempts to promote 'community-based approaches' have contributed to the proliferation of organisations that appear meaningful but, in practice, engage in few concrete activities. Only refugees who were able to formalise their activities into recognisable structures that conformed to the norms of international agencies were rendered 'legible'. Whilst this led to a proliferation in registered groups in Kakuma, often encouraged by UNHCR implementing and operational partner agencies, much of what refugees were doing to assist each other was actually happening outside this system and remained 'illegible'. Indeed, the camp's market-base narrative emphasised opportunities for individuals who could 'speak the language' of humanitarian assistance, rather than supporting the forms of protection and mutual help that refugees themselves valued and prioritised[3].

---

[3] The dependence of small organisations on larger ones has been seen elsewhere in humanitarian assistance to produce increasingly uniform behaviours – and therefore decreased capacity to respond flexibly and innovatively to social problems (Wallace, Bornstein & Chapman 2006).

Conclusion

Our basic claim is simple: refugee-led organisations exist, and they deserve recognition for the important roles they play. Many of them offer social protection to other refugees, within or beyond the communities of their leadership. They fill gaps left by national or international providers in areas as diverse as education, vocational training, psychosocial support, health, microfinance, sport, youth engagement and legal representation. They vary in scale, focus and capacity, demonstrating the many ways in which refugees mobilise to support vulnerable members of the community. They are providing protection and assistance – the very services normally associated exclusively with international aid agencies and NGOs. And for many refugees, especially those in cities, such sources of community support are perceived as more relevant to their lives than those provided by large-scale aid organisations.

In spite of this, however, refugee-led organisations rarely receive recognition or funding from the international humanitarian system. The rhetoric at the global level sometimes suggests differently: localisation has become a major theme in elite policy circles, and refugee leaders are occasionally invited to discussions in Geneva and New York. In addition, policy documents like UNHCR's Community-Based Protection Policy ostensibly promote collaboration with refugee-led initiatives. At the local level, however, the reality is different. Practice varies from country to country, reflecting the absence of a clear policy framework at the global level. For example, in Nairobi a number of RCOs are at least invited to collaborate with some of the United Nations' implementing and operational partners. In Kampala, by contrast, ties between UNHCR and refugee-led organisations are virtually non-existent. In Kakuma, RCOs are encouraged to register with the government but are told to compete with more established providers, and there is also a prevailing sense that organisations from host communities are privileged over refugee organisations. In Nakivale, the relationship between UNHCR and RCOs is characterised by mutual distrust.

RCOs face a chicken-and-egg dilemma. In order to receive recognition and funding, they need to have capacity. But in order to have capacity, they need recognition and funding. UNHCR delegates service delivery to 'implementing partners' and collaborates with 'operational partners'. In practice, RCOs are simply unable to meet the standards required to be conferred with such a status. Instead, UNHCR encourages them to partner with international and national NGO implementing partners. However, few implementing partners actually engage RCOs, and on the rare occasions they do it is usually as an interface with communities to facilitate access and extend their own services, as seen in Nairobi. Without the capacity to meet accounting and audit standards, most RCOs find it a challenge to independently raise funding from traditional donors. For the most part, they are locked out of the international humanitarian system.

Against the odds, though, some outliers emerge and thrive. Organisations like Bondeko, YARID, HOCW, SAVIC, Kinsugi, URISE, Wakati, Sesi and Kobciye have emerged from humble beginnings to serve literally thousands of refugees each. They are registered organisations, have constitutions, staff and premises, and have found some sources of funding from outside the humanitarian system. They have grown mostly in spite of, rather than because of, the United Nations system. Why have they succeeded? Usually because of charismatic individual leaders who, through previous experiences and chance meetings, have built networks enabling them to transcend traditional national and international funding sources.

Comparative Analysis

We began with a question: what explains variation in the scale and scope of refugee-led social protection? Our empirical focus on East Africa does not enable us to draw globally representative conclusions. It does, however, give us a basis on which to derive a context-specific answer and to begin to build theory that may have wider applicability. A common and fairly parsimonious story emerges from across all four of the sites in which we worked. Like most answers in the social sciences, ours is built around the interaction of structure and agency.

International institutions play a key role in constraining and enabling refugee-led social protection. Without a clear global policy framework on how to engage refugee-led organisations, within UNHCR or elsewhere, national UN representations have discretion in how they engage refugee-led social protection. Across our research sites, working with RCOs is not an organisational priority for them, and so variation is largely an outcome of the general culture of the national offices. In Kampala, InterAid is the only implementing partner. This reflects UNHCR's dominant concern – to retain a good relationship with a national government that favours InterAid and bans refugees' political mobilisation. In Kakuma, a market-based logic has been adopted, not just for RCOs but more broadly: they are, in theory, encouraged – but only if they can compete.

Despite the variation, RCOs are largely sidelined in all four contexts; there is simply no definitive way for them to acquire funding or status within the humanitarian system. The Finnish Refugee Council is the only major international NGO operating in the two countries that has a structured programme to build the capacity of RCOs. Urban Refugees has a similar programme but does not operate in these countries; UNHCR does in theory have a Social Protection Fund, but this mainly supports economic self-reliance and does not operate in Kenya or Uganda. The RCOs that do emerge vary significantly in scale, capacity and perceived effectiveness. What makes the difference about the types of organisations that emerge is a series of factors relating to the agency of refugees themselves. In particular, identity, interests and individuals represent key sources of variation.

Nationality and Culture

Without wishing to essentialise national or ethnic groups, an important source of variation in the character and focus of RCOs has been the cultural and political provenance of the organisation or network. This is partly because many post-crisis protection practices are adaptations of norms that existed prior to refugees' flight from their countries of origin

(Staniland 2014). Congolese refugees appear the most likely to register and build organisations, as distinct from networks. Comfortable with market-based competition, but with strong Christian norms of charity and solidarity, Congolese organisations frequently support activities relating to self-reliance, reflecting both market-based and Christian ideals. In contrast to other groups, many Congolese embrace their refugee identity, being more willing to advocate on behalf of all refugees irrespective of nationality. This is reflected in the relative inclusivity of some of the Congolese CBOs, including their greater likelihood to lead and promote networks like RELON that work across national and ethnic groups.

In contrast, the Somali community is more likely to rely on networks and traditional social norms than RCOs for social protection. We find comparatively few registered Somali CBOs. Clan and kinship shape social protection obligations alongside Islamic practices of social support. Norms, rather than organisations, support the direct provision of charitable assistance through *zakat* or based on notions of *sadaqah* (friendship). Meanwhile, rotating savings and credit schemes called *ayutos*, often with a social insurance scheme, frequently operate. Many of these *ayutos* focus on particular groups such as single female heads of household. And remittances are a central dimension of social protection across the community. Where organisations such as Kobciye – meaning 'empowerment' in Somali – do emerge, the focus is often on training young people in entrepreneurship and business skills. This reflects a cultural emphasis on commerce as a viable livelihood opportunity. Across each site, the umbrella Somali Community Association serves a role overseeing conformity with many of the norms that govern reciprocal obligations to community-based social protection.

The South Sudanese community is based on cooperative structures: institutionalised cooperatives are the dominant mode of meeting social protection needs and ensuring effective risk management relating to loss of crops or cattle. Among South Sudanese, cattle ownership is traditionally a primary source of authority and status, and it is used to mediate other social norms – for instance, those relating to marriage. A significant proportion of social protection creates reciprocal obligations to sustain insurance mechanisms in the event of loss, or to sustain intergenerational obligations that support the young and elderly when they are unable to sustain a pastoral holding. In exile, one of the striking changes is the loss of cattle, which has led to normative adaptation across a range of areas, with implications for social protection. In exile, leaders and elders remain the primary sources of protection. These norm-based structures regulate mutual obligations. Meanwhile, there is a parallel set of RCOs that mainly focus on peacebuilding activities rather than offering direct assistance to refugees.

Another important aspect of identity that shapes refugee-led social protection is gender. The public face of RCOs is more likely to be male, even though women actively participate behind the scenes in leading some of the most successful organisations, like HOCW, Bondeko and YARID. Men are more likely to be involved in advocacy and women in small-scale assistance programmes. It is common among the activities of RCOs to have projects on themes such as 'women's empowerment' that speak to gender issues but frame them in ways that hint at underlying gendered conceptions. The intersection between nationality and gender also shapes variation in the focus of activities. Among the Somali community, women are often involved in support groups run by women, for women. However, these tend to be separate from men's social protection activities. Among the South Sudanese, women are involved in refugee CBOs alongside men, albeit mainly in support roles. Among the Congolese, women play the most active role in CBOs, although they are not usually in leadership positions.

Political Economy

The RCO landscape, however, should not be viewed in culturally deterministic terms. Crucially, there is a political economy relating to refugee-led social protection. At the outset, we highlighted our desire to avoid romanticising refugee-led social protection. Motives and interests are complex, and power, hierarchy and status are as much a part of local-level institutional politics as they are of global-level institutional politics.

Although relatively few resources are available to support refugee-led social protection, such activities exist within a political economy in which flows of money shape incentives and behaviours. Purporting to 'protect' creates opportunities to seek money and authority. As Vasco, the co-founder of SAVIC, pointed out, many refugee organisations are doing great work – but some are 'briefcase organisations' with 'personal interests'. While we do not wish to assert whether this is true, there are clearly multiple and competing narratives about which refugee leaders are working primarily on behalf of their communities, and which ones are more focused on improving their own status and their organisation's funding.

Choices of specialisation are often shaped by the availability of earmarked funding. Many of the funded South Sudanese RCOs in Kampala focus on peacebuilding activities, tapping into sources of donor funding intended to finance transformation within South Sudanese politics. By positing a diasporic connection with Juba, several are able to access grants earmarked for peacebuilding. Similarly, in a context of scarce resources, small amounts of donor funding can have a disproportionate influence on the focus of RCOs' work. For instance, Youth United for Somali Mobilisation (USOM) in Nairobi received its only significant grant from USAID at a time when the US government prioritised community-based approaches to counterterrorism. Even after USAID ended the funding, USOM's leadership continued to focus on a narrative connecting social protection to risks of terrorism and insecurity. Meanwhile, some organisations have been able to access funding simply because they have a niche focus that leads to limited competition: CESSI, for example, received funding from gay rights activists in Europe because it specialised in an area in which there was a need, a gap and available funding.

Furthermore, a cast of potentially 'unhelpful helpers' often gets involved within the landscape of refugee-led social protection. Foundations, philanthropists, advocacy organisations and academics all appear in the story, eager to assist organisations and individuals who have potential. It is not that they mean badly; many are crucial to RCO progression. But they often expand opportunities for the visible outliers while ignoring the wider landscape. By helping the few that are already succeeding, little is done to push for systemic transformation based on more equitable access to opportunity.

Charismatic Leadership

Individuals matter. There is a common story behind most of the more successful outliers. Usually, it involves an individual refugee arriving in the host country, experiencing personal challenges, and then, following interaction with another NGO, deciding to create a CBO. The key event that leads to takeoff is often a chance meeting with an actor from outside the community who connects the refugee leader to a wider transnational network of supporters and funders. This story of inspiration-opportunity-networks lies behind the narrative of nearly every successful refugee social entrepreneur we met in Uganda and Kenya.

For example, Felicity Suzan came alone as a teenage girl from the DRC to Kampala. Fostered by a pastor, who paid for her schooling but insisted she find a part-time job to pay for her own transport to school, she created URISE after chance encounters with the Dutch Butterfly Foundation and Kamperwitz, which enabled her to fund the organisation's initial activities around music, design and youth participation. Bolingo Ntahira came to Kampala and initially lived on a bus with dozens of other refugees. He met a priest, whom he brought to the bus to see the conditions. The priest established a foundation called AGAPE and gave Bolingo land on which to create HOCW. AGAPE helped HOCW identify initial volunteers for its work. One such volunteer went on to get a job at the Slovenian Foreign Ministry, opening up the opportunity for the Slovenian Embassy to give HOCW its first large grant. Robert Hakiza has been able to scale the work of YARID through a combination of his own leadership skills and a series of meetings that have in turn led to new opportunities. The Xavier Project provided computers, leading to an expansion of support for youth education. This in turn facilitated access to wider transnational networks, culminating in YARID receiving the Joyce Pearce Foundation's Ockenden Prize and Robert Hakiza receiving invitations to become an Aspen Fellow and to speak at TED Global.

Bahati Ghislain arrived in Nairobi in 2013, unable to speak either English or Swahili. After living on the streets, he taught himself both languages and went to HIAS to seek help to find work. He began translating for the Congolese community and working as a social worker for HIAS. He also became involved with Congolese community organisations like the Family of Banyamulenge in Kenya (FBK) and the Union Banyamasisi in Kenya (UBK). These opportunities enabled Bahati to create Kinsugi, providing a reception centre for newly arrived refugees, offering psychosocial support, and serving as a gateway to other services. Also in Nairobi, Charles Kyazze attended a UNHCR self-help group on LGBTI rights, and, inspired by the consultant, was able to set up CESSI, which provides support to LGBTI refugees. Through guidance from a UNHCR consultant, he was able to access a unique pot of funding through a German gay rights organisation, enabling him to establish his CBO. Musabel Welongo was able to found SAVIC, the largest RCO in Kakuma, both because of both his own ability and opportunities unavailable to other refugees in Kakuma. He had been a refugee in Tanzania, where he worked as a community organiser, and then lived in Nairobi before choosing to come to Kakuma to open SAVIC. There he was able to collaborate on a Xavier Project funding application to UNHCR Innovation, which subsequently opened up wider network opportunities.

These examples highlight that it takes exceptionally driven individuals, usually inspired by personal experience, to transcend institutional constraints. However, a key additional ingredient has been access to transnational networks. The connections have often emerged through chance encounters with other sympathetic individuals with access to networks. These have allowed refugee leaders to bypass the formal humanitarian system and create viable CBOs. However, the success of these individuals further highlights the failure of the system: refugees should not have to have particular traits, or rely on chance opportunities for transnational networking, in order to establish sustainable activities on behalf of the refugee community.

So what does leadership mean in relation to these success stories? While many leadership theories focus on personal traits and characteristics as the basis for leadership – and the sources of authority that underlie them – leadership can also be theorised as inherently social (Grint 1997). Effective leadership is context and audience specific. One of the paradoxes of refugee CBO leadership is that different characteristics seem to be valued differently by *external* (i.e. international) actors and *internal* (i.e. refugee) actors.[1] The great challenge faced by refugee leaders has been how to simultaneously demonstrate traits that are valued by both audiences. The ways in which *competence* and *likeability*[2] are judged by external and internal audiences are likely to be quite different.

For an external audience, what appears to mark out competence is a willingness to serve a 'translation' role, serving as an effective intermediary between international priorities and local implementation. For example, in Kakuma the Turkana NGO Locado is valued precisely for playing this role. What determines likeability seems to be 'humility', a willingness to deferentially observe and respect international hierarchies and standards. For example, refugee leaders – such as Pecos Kulihoshi Musikami in Kampala – who are overtly critical of international actors find themselves excluded from global networks.

For an internal audience, competence is defined largely by the ability to bring 'resources' to the community. Creating networks that lead to funding is the basis for organisational longevity and hence community support. As Bolingo Ntahira put it, 'If you invite someone for dinner, the food also has to be good'. Without funding, many organisations have fallen by the wayside, unable to engage the community. Likeability appears to be related to 'authenticity' – the ability to build legitimacy through honest relationships and values-based actions (Gardner et al. 2011). Nearly all the successful refugee leaders we met are respected within their communities for their ethical and values-based conduct.

The refugee leader's dilemma is how to be perceived as legitimate by both external and internal audiences simultaneously. External legitimacy comes from complementing the priorities of international actors; internal legitimacy comes from effectively addressing community needs. While these goals are not necessarily in tension, it currently takes exceptional individuals to mediate between these priorities and thereby retain authority.

Implications for Theory

Our biggest theoretical contribution is the concept of the 'global governed'. It represents an ontological commitment to examine global governance from the perspective of the putative beneficiaries. It is an attempt to turn global governance on its head: starting from the bottom rather than reifying the centrality of the powerful. It offers, we have argued, an especially useful means to critically re-examine the provider–beneficiary relationship that characterises a range of policy fields, including development, humanitarianism, health and peacekeeping.

We have boldly posited that the term serves as an umbrella concept for a cluster of existing literatures on post-development, post-humanitarianism, and post-protection. These literatures, we have argued, are germane for our purpose because they are fundamentally about the role of power in global governance. They have in common that they offer frameworks for critiquing the 'global' while rendering visible the 'local'. They render

---

[1] 'Internal' and 'external' environmental factors are commonly distinguished within the organisational leadership literature.

[2] 'Competence' and 'likeability' are traits identified as important for social network formation within the leadership literature but which are often in tension with one another (Casciaro & Lobo 2005).

visible hidden power relations and unquestioned institutional assumptions while reasserting the subjectivity and agency of the marginalised.

We have suggested, though, that while the post-development literature and its embryonic analogues are derived from post-structuralist and predominantly Foucauldian roots, there is no necessity that their underlying agenda be advanced from any particular epistemological perspective. An insistence on a Foucauldian approach, we have argued, risks romanticising the local, neglecting material interests and sidelining agency.

Certainly, the work of James Ferguson, for instance, offers a crucial starting point for our exploration of the 'global governed'. However, while Ferguson's ethnographic account of the World Bank's encounter with the rural population of Lesotho mirrors our goal of problematising the relationship between international institutions and the populations they supposedly serve, it is too structurally weighted for our purposes. The key themes within our analysis – identity, interests and individuals – are all largely invisible from the perspective of the post-development literature. And yet, for us, they are crucial to understanding both the position of the global governed and the potential to transcend hierarchy and subjugation.

For us, global governance does not represent a single, totalising discourse, with singularly inevitable outcomes for a 'local' population. It is complex, varied, and political at all levels – even among the subject populations. Beyond dichotomies of global and local or top-down and bottom-up, reinforced more so by Escobar than Ferguson, there is diversity and contradiction within international institutions, just as there is at the community level. To avoid simply demonising the global and romanticising the local, a research agenda for the 'global governed' must include an account of variation, contingency and agency. It must ultimately be a story about individuals with identities and interests that are constrained and enabled by their institutional context. Therein, after all, lies the potential for transformative alternatives.

Post-Protection

The area of governance on which we focus in this book is 'protection'. It is an area that has many features in common with 'development'. It appears inherently benevolent, it legitimates intervention, and yet it is poorly defined and almost infinitely malleable. To protect is to govern: it is to assert a relationship of power between the 'protector' and the 'protected'. This is not to suggest that some activities occurring under the umbrella of 'protection' are ethically indefensible or even unnecessary: saving lives, improving welfare and enabling individuals and communities to have greater entitlements and capabilities – all are important activities that often take place within this framework. Protection, though, has a more complex dimension, and is inextricable from power.

In the case of the refugee system, protection is the underlying organising principle that legitimates hierarchy. States have responsibility for their own citizens; when they fail, that responsibility transfers to the international community; it is then delegated downwards to host states or United Nations agencies like UNHCR. These actors then have discretion on how they choose to delegate that authority and resources to their implementing partners and operational partners, and they are able to select and exclude. The justification throughout is a protection mandate. Even though a cursory genealogy of the concept of protection reveals its historical and cultural contingency, its universality is asserted by dominant protection organisations, and it takes on quasi-religious status.

One of the problems is that, following Ferguson (1990), protection has an anti-political quality. It depoliticises, or rather, renders invisible, the power, interest and ideas that shape and naturalise particular norms, behaviours and outcomes. And yet protection is an inherently political act. It legitimates the concentration of resources, decision-making authority, and the right to govern within the hands of the designated protector. It is no wonder that, historically, the language of protection has justified a range of actions that have led to contradictory and clearly harmful outcomes: from safe havens in Srebrenica to refugee camps in Dadaab to the use of depleted uranium shells in Kosovo.

Our argument, again, is not that 'activities seeking to ensure access to rights under refugee law, human rights law and humanitarian law' (as protection is sometimes defined) is a bad thing. It is that 'protection' as a discourse can have deeply perverse consequences when putative humanitarians ignore its inherent relationship to power. Our focus on refugee-led social protection offers insights into this process. It shows how, because the authority to protect resides primarily with the powerful, alternative providers of social protection face structural barriers created by international protection actors. It is ironic that 'protection' becomes a justification to prevent communities from mobilising to provide social protection.

From a research perspective, ours is a call to Refugee Studies and Humanitarian Studies to engage in a project of post-protection research that applies and adapts many of the valuable insights of the post-development literature. It is a project that requires historical, anthropological and political research in order to render visible how power and contingency shape when and how protection is deployed to entrench arbitrary, and sometimes unnecessary, sources of authority. From a practical perspective, the implication is that we should seek to restore autonomy to 'protected' populations, ensure that consent and participation are present within protection and, wherever possible, seek to encourage the localisation of protection responses.

Localisation and Delegation

The politics of protection is most evident in the interface between localisation and delegation: the way in which the legitimacy to protect is passed down through levels of governance. Within the International Relations literature on global governance, localisation and delegation are major themes. But neither literature extends the analysis downwards as far as the 'beneficiary' populations. Localisation focuses mainly on how international norms adapt in their encounters with regional and national norms (Acharya 2004). Meanwhile, the delegation literature is mainly about how states devolve power to international organisations or how international organisations delegate it to international NGOs (Abbott et al. 2015). Our focus on refugee-led organisations connects the themes of localisation and delegation, and it invites an extension of the focus to include the 'global governed' as actors within those processes.

The process by which localised delegation takes place represents an intriguing area for empirical research. For example, how does politics shape the status of 'implementing partners' and 'operational partners', not only within humanitarian fields but more broadly across global governance? It emerges as a distinctly original context for research precisely because our research shows how, far from being merely technocratic, it is a highly political process in which no actor – international, national or local – is outside the politics. Power and interests are at stake at every level of delegation.

Take, for example, the puzzle of how InterAid – despite being viewed by many refugees as ineffective – has retained its status as UNHCR's sole implementing partner in Kampala for two decades. It is an intriguing question, and the causes and consequences of this privileged relationship of delegation are highly political. The relationship between UNHCR and the government partly underlies the designation of a monopoly status, but the consequences for refugee-led organisations are, invariably, ongoing marginalisation and alienation.

Participatory Governance

Beyond our primary interest in a subset of international regimes involving provider–beneficiary relationships, the work has wider implications for global governance as a whole. In particular, it opens up a series of broader normative issues relating to the meaning and content of participatory governance. What relationship should exist between the 'governors' and 'the governed' within international regimes? What normative principles should define the interaction? Under what conditions are consultation, consent, co-design – or even the delegation of decision-making authority – requirements for participatory governance? How do they vary in different types of governance arrangement?

The literature on participatory development has been a central part of Development Studies (Chambers 1981). It argues that benevolent external helpers should reflect critically on the motivations and assumptions they bring to development interventions and find ways to address power relations through collaborative work with those they are trying to assist. At a minimum, this should involve consultation and a commitment in good faith to listen to and consider their concerns. However, this literature has often been critiqued for assuming that participation can be meaningful when the terms of the discussion are themselves weighted towards the agendas of powerful, external actors (Cooke & Kothari 2001). Furthermore, the challenge has always been: whose voice matters? Given power dynamics within a given community, including those relating to gender and status, how can participatory approaches be designed to assure a genuinely representative voice from that community?

In the humanitarian context, participation is further complicated by the apparent urgency of intervention, as well as its occasionally technical nature. This is especially the case in conflict and crisis settings, in which the priority is to save lives. Analogous to life-saving treatment in health, the degree of participation that is possible may be limited by urgency and the threshold of expertise required for meaningful engagement. Nevertheless, many aspects of contemporary humanitarianism, including daily life in refugee situations, have neither the constraints of urgency nor significant technical barriers to entry. Consultation and informed consent, at least, are usually possible and generally practised.

But once an emergency phase has passed, participation surely involves more than consultation and consent. It should presumably entail the possibility to participate in agenda-setting, negotiation and implementation relating to programming. It may even include elements of self-governance. If a community can self-govern and wishes to do so, then it should presumably be able to progressively acquire such rights. Of course, for refugees this is somewhat complicated. They are on the territory of another state, under the legal and political authority of that state, and some of the tasks relating to governance may have been delegated to the international community. But insofar as the international community has the authority to include approaches to participatory governance, there seems little basis on which to discourage it.

Specifying the degree of participation required across particular domains represents a normative challenge, as does institutional design to accommodate participation. But one way to resolve such dilemmas should perhaps be to begin from a radically different starting point – a presumption of self-governance – and then arrogate authority upwards only on an ethically justifiable case-by-case basis. In other words, apply a principle of subsidiarity to participatory governance, letting provision take place at the smallest level of governance except where clashes of interest cannot be reconciled, or unless levels of efficiency and competence in delivery strongly justify a greater external role. The approach, then, is to normatively mirror the book's wider analytical move: to ontologically situate the 'global governed' at the centre of the analysis. These are just preliminary propositions, and this book has not been based on a substantive normative analysis, but it is clear that more reflection, both academic and practical, is needed on how to localise and democratise protection.

Implications for Practice

Organisations like UNHCR should adopt a global policy framework relating to refugee-led community-based organisations. These are important actors, and yet they are almost entirely neglected in the organisation's main strategic documents, as well as in the Global Compact on Refugees. In the absence of a clear policy framework at the global level, there is enormous variation in the practice of how international organisations work with refugee-led organisations at the field level. However, the general picture is that refugee-led initiatives find themselves locked out of the formal humanitarian system, and those that succeed do so largely by bypassing formal delegation structures. Four specific recommendations stand out, which should form the basis of a global policy framework.

First, *mapping and recognition*. One of our contributions in this book has been to literally develop maps of the RCO landscape for each of our four sites. These make visible and legible the range and diversity of refugee-led social protection initiatives and the ways in which they currently relate to the formal humanitarian system. And yet this kind of mapping is not used by international organisations. In that sense, one of the practical innovations of this book is our method for RCO mapping. Given the large number of UNHCR staff we spoke to who struggled to even name refugee-led CBOs in the camps, settlements or cities in which we were working, we think our book's approach to visually mapping this landscape could be adopted, adapted and improved. Understanding what exists is the first step towards being able to make sensible policy decisions about whether, and how, to partner with such organisations.

Second, *capacity-building*. Refugees perceive the current humanitarian system as being set up in a way that reproduces inequalities between international organisations and refugees, excluding their voice and participation. At the same time, many of the international organisations are concerned that RCOs may be inefficient or lack the capacity to be given responsibility for key protection tasks. This leaves refugee leaders facing a chicken-and-egg dilemma: many refugee organisations do not have the capacity to obtain funding and recognition, but they cannot build capacity without funding and recognition. There is a logical way out of this dilemma: develop ways to systematically build capacity for community leadership. Just as entrepreneurship and business leadership are increasingly encouraged in refugee camps, so too should community leadership capacity be supported.

Basic skills like management, accounting, auditing, strategy and coaching could improve community leaders' ability to lead and manage viable partner organisations. Meanwhile, to make this feasible, training, mentorship and seed funding should be made available on a more consistent basis.

Third, *direct funding and bypassing*. At the moment, only very small amounts of funding are available to refugee-led organisations through UNHCR and other actors working within the UN humanitarian system. As our analysis shows, the main sources of grants are eclectic and based on personal networks. One problem that most refugee leaders have is that they cannot meet the onerous accounting and auditing standards required by most traditional donors. However, donors have much to gain from piloting direct funding for refugee-led organisations: with appropriate support, they may represent much more cost-effective ways to allocate resources than working through multilayered processes of delegation. While risk levels may well be higher with supporting small-scale refugee-led organisations, piloting, learning and innovating about direct financing schemes would be worthwhile. At the moment, some NGOs such as the Finnish Refugee Council do offer grants to RCOs, but these opportunities are few and far between.

Fourth, *partnership and process*. At the moment, it is generally unrealistic for refugee-led organisations to become implementing partners, or even operational partners, of UNHCR. Indeed, most could not take on large-scale delivery tasks within the humanitarian system as it is currently designed – at least not without significant capacity-building over time. Nevertheless, it is clear from the successful outliers observed in this book that many RCOs have the potential to fill important niches in key areas and to be important intermediaries between international organisations and the community. Rather than having to consistently work outside the humanitarian system, a range of institutional opportunities for RCOs to engage UNHCR and its implementing partners in direct and regular dialogue needs to be created. The processes for localisation and delegation need to be made much more inclusive and transparent. At the very least, partnership must involve inclusion of refugees' own priorities in the shaping of responses, rather than simply the inclusion of refugee capacity within responses designed by others.

Final Thoughts

Many areas of global governance are shaped by hierarchy. Powerful governments design international institutions, international institutions select their NGO partners, and NGO partners choose how to engage with community-based organisations. Such hierarchies are especially pronounced in policy fields with so-called beneficiary populations, including development, humanitarianism, health, peacekeeping and child protection. The underlying justification for the appropriation of governance authority is often 'protection'. An immediate threat to a subject population is used to legitimate external intervention in order to mitigate that threat and restore a particular vision of normality. Protection can play an important role in safeguarding life and ensuring human welfare, but to protect is also to govern. Protection is mediated by power and, if prolonged, can lead to subjugation and the erosion of autonomy.

In this book, we have explored the ways in which so-called beneficiaries can be important and neglected actors within global governance. We have done so by looking in depth at one particular policy field: the international refugee system. For refugee governance, as with humanitarian governance and even child protection, for instance, there has been a recent trend towards using the language of localisation, participation and agency. And yet, what we have found in our work is a mismatch between the global rhetoric and the local reality. The practice varies significantly across national and local contexts. In general, refugee-led organisations face significant structural barriers to receiving recognition or funding, even when they are providing widely valued sources of protection and assistance. Despite this, some refugee-led organisations are thriving against the odds, and doing so largely by going through their own transnational networks to bypass the formal system. We hope that our work will inspire further empirical and theoretical research on the interaction between international institutions and their beneficiary populations. More importantly, we also hope that it will lead to more consistent and principled ways to promote participatory forms of global governance.

Our research for this book is mainly qualitative. However, we also ran a small, complementary survey with refugees and host community members across our four contexts of interest. In order to do this, five questions were put to a representative, randomly selected sample of Congolese refugees, Somali refugees and members of the local host community in Kakuma, Nairobi, Nakivale and Kampala. They survey questions were included as part of the wider 'Refugee Economies' survey implemented by the Refugee Studies Centre. The total sample size for the questions was n=8159:

The following questions provide an illustration of the descriptive statistics that emerge from the findings relating to social protection. They highlight that refugees, like the surrounding host community, are generally far more likely to rely on their own families, networks and communities for a range of sources of social protection. Of course, it should be noted that UNHCR nevertheless provides the underlying social protection base in camps and the national government provides much of the social protection base in cities. But the results highlight refugees' perceptions of the sources of social protection that they understand to be most relevant to them under particular circumstances.[1]

Table A.1 Breakdown of survey respondents by nationality and location

	Congolese	Somalis	Hosts	Total
Kakuma	445	459	605	1509
Nairobi	712	556	1191	2469
Nakivale	804	823	667	2294
Kampala	473	459	955	1887
Total	2434	2307	3418	8159

[1] For each of the figures, DRC = Congolese refugees; SOM = Somali refugees; TUR = Turkana; KENinSOM = Kenyans in Somali areas; KENinDRC = Kenyans in Congolese areas; UGAinDRC = Ugandans in Congolese areas; UGAinSOM = Ugandans in Somali areas.

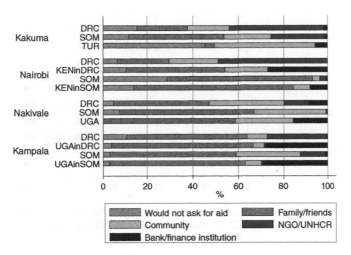

Figure A.1 Answers to Survey Question 1: 'Who would you ask for help to finance the creation of a business?'

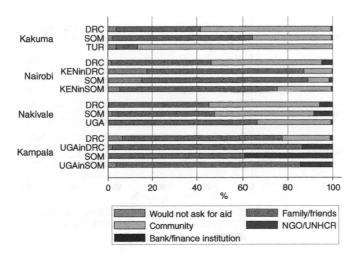

Figure A.2 Answers to Survey Question 2: 'Who would you ask for help if you did not have enough food to eat?'

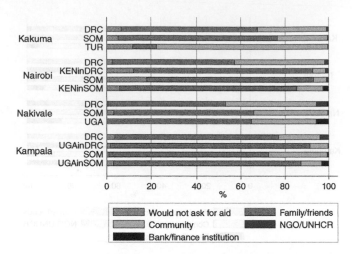

Figure A.3 Answers to Survey Question 3: 'Who would you ask for help if you faced an emergency?'

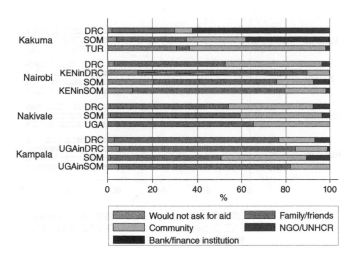

Figure A.4 Answers to Survey Question 4: 'Who would you ask for help if you needed to find a job?'

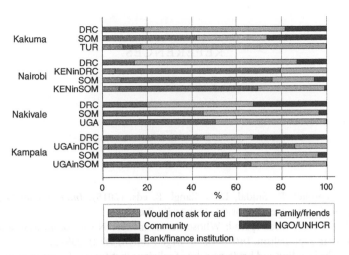

Figure A.5 Answers to Survey Question 5: 'Who would you ask for help if you were in trouble with the police?'

REFERENCES

Abbott, K. W., Genschel, P., Snidal, D. & Zangl, B. eds. (2015). *International Organizations as Orchestrators*. Cambridge: Cambridge University Press.

Acharya, A. (2004). How ideas spread: Whose norms matter? Norm localization and institutional change in Asian regionalism. *International Organization*, **58**(2), 239–275.

Allen, R. (2010). The bonding and bridging roles of religious institutions for refugees in a non-gateway context. *Ethical and Racial Studies*, **33**(6), 1049–1068.

Asian Development Bank. (2001). *Social Protection Strategy*. Mandaluyong: Asian Development Bank.

Autesserre, S. (2010). *The Trouble with the Congo: Local Violence and the Failure of International Peacebuilding* (Cambridge Studies in International Relations). Cambridge: Cambridge University Press.

Autesserre, S. (2016). The responsibility to protect in Congo: The failure of grassroots prevention. *International Peacekeeping*, **23**(1), 29–51.

Baines, E. & Paddon, E. (2012). This is how we survived': Civilian agency and humanitarian protection. *Security Dialogue*, **43**(3), 231–257.

Barkawi, T. & Laffey, M. (2002). Retrieving the imperial: Empire and international relations. *Millennium: Journal of International Studies*, **31**(1), 109–127.

Barnett, M. (2011). *Empire of Humanity: A History of Humanitarianism*. Ithaca, NY: Cornell University Press.

Barnett, M. & Finnemore, M. (2004). *Rules for the World: International Organizations in Global Politics*. Ithaca, NY: Cornell University Press.

Barrientos, A. (2011). Social protection and poverty. *International Journal of Social Welfare*, **20**(3), 240–249.

Barrientos, A. & Hulme, D. (2009). Social protection for the poor and poorest in developing countries: Reflections on a quiet revolution. *Oxford Development Studies*, **37**(4), 439–456.

Bekai, A., Antara, L., Adan, T., Arrighi de Casanova, J.-T., El-Helou, Z., Mannix, E. . . . Zakarvan, T. (2018). *Political Participation of Refugees: Bridging the Gaps*. Stockholm: IDEA.

Bellis, A., Fraser, L., Houghton, A. M. & Ward, J. (2005). Connecting Policy and Practice in the Refugee Integration Agenda. Paper presented at 35th Annual SCUTREA Conference. Brighton, UK: University of Sussex.

Betts, A. (2013). *Survival Migration: Failed Governance and the Crisis of Displacement*. Ithaca, NY: Cornell University Press.

Betts, A. (2018, November 22). Refuge, reformed. Online article. https://foreignpolicy.com/2018/11/22/refuge-reformed-kenya-refugees/

Betts, A., Bloom, L., Kaplan, J. & Omata, N. (2016). *Refugee Economies: Forced Displacement and Development*. Oxford: Oxford University Press.

Betts, A. & Jones, W. (2017). *Mobilising the Diaspora: How Refugees Challenge Authoritarianism*. Cambridge: Cambridge University Press.

Betts, A., Chaara, I., Omata, N. & Sterck, O. (2019). *Refugee Economies in Uganda: What Difference Does the Self-Reliance Model Make?* Report. Oxford: Refugee Studies Centre.

Betts, A., Omata, N., Rodgers, C., Sterck, O. & Stierna, M. (2019). *The Kalobeyei Model: Towards Self-Reliance for Refugees?* Oxford: Refugee Studies Centre.

Betts, A., Omata, N. & Sterck, O. (2018). *Refugee Economies in Kenya.* Oxford: Refugee Studies Centre.

Betts, A. & Orchard, P., eds. (2014). *Implementation and World Politics: How International Norms Change Practice.* Oxford: Oxford University Press.

Bloch, A. (2008). Refugees in the UK labour market: The conflict between economic integration and policy-led labour market restriction. *Journal of Social Policy,* **37**(1), 21–36.

Boer, R. D. (2015). Liminal space in protracted exile: The meaning of place in Congolese refugees' narratives of home and belonging in Kampala. *Journal of Refugee Studies,* **28**(4), 486–504.

Bond, B. H. (1986). *Imposing Aid: Emergency Assistance to Refugees.* Oxford: Oxford University Press.

Booth, K. (1991). Security and emancipation. *Review of International Studies,* **17**(4), 313–326.

Bornstein, E. (2012). *Disquieting Gifts: Humanitarianism in New Delhi.* Stanford, CA: Stanford University Press.

Bradley, M., Milner, J. & Peruniak, B., eds. (2019). *Refugees' Roles in Resolving Displacement and Building Peace: Beyond Beneficiaries.* Washington, DC: Georgetown University Press.

Burns, K., Male, S. & Pierotti, D. (2000). Why refugees need reproductive health services. *International Family Planning Perspectives,* **26**(4), 161, 192.

Campbell, D. (1998). Why fight: Humanitarianism, principles, and post-structuralism. *Millennium: Journal of International Studies,* **27**(3), 497.

Campbell, S. (2018). *Global Governance and Local Practice: Accountability and Performance in International Peacekeeping.* Cambridge: Cambridge University Press.

Carrier, N. C. (2016). *Little Mogadishu: Eastleigh, Nairobi's Global Somali Hub.* Oxford: Oxford University Press.

Casciaro, T. & Sousa Lobo, M. (2005). Competent jerks, lovable fools, and the formation of social networks. *Harvard Business Review,* 83, 92–99, 149.

Chambers, R. (1981). Rapid rural appraisal: Rationale and repertoire. *Public Administration and Development,* **1**(2), 95–106.

Chambers, R. (1986). Hidden losers? The impact of rural refugees and refugee programs on poorer hosts. *The International Migration Review,* **20**(2), 245–263.

Cholewinski, R., Perruchoud, R. & MacDonald, E., eds. (2007). *International Migration Law: Developing Paradigms and Key Challenges.* The Hague: T. M. C. Asser.

Chouliaraki, L. (2005). *The Soft Power of War.* Amsterdam: John Benjamins Publishing Company.

Chouliaraki, L. (2006). *The Spectatorship of Suffering.* London: SAGE Publishing.

Chouliaraki, L. (2008). The mediation of suffering and the vision of a cosmopolitan public. *Television & New Media,* **9**(4), 1–34.

Chouliaraki, L. (2012). *The Ironic Spectator: Solidarity in the Age of Post-Humanitarianism.* Cambridge: Polity Press.

Chouliaraki, L. (2013). Mediating vulnerability: Cosmopolitanism and the public sphere. *Media, Culture & Society,* **35**(1), 105–112.

Cloward, K. (2014). False commitments: Local misrepresentation and the international norms against female genital mutilation and early marriage. *International Organization,* **68**(3), 495–526.

Cooke, B. & Kothari, U. (2001). *Participation: The New Tyranny?*, 1st ed. New York: Zed Books Ltd.

Cordero-Guzmán, H. R. (2007). Community-based organisations and migration in New York City. *Journal of Ethnic and Migration Studies,* **31**(5), 889–909.

Crisp, J. (2009). Refugees, persons of concern, and people on the move: The broadening boundaries of UNHCR. *Refuge,* **25**(1), 1–4.

Davis, P. & Baulch, B. (2009). Parallel realities: Exploring poverty dynamics using mixed methods in rural Bangladesh. *Journal of Development Studies,* **47**(1), 118–142.

Der Derian, J. (1989). The boundaries of knowledge and power in international relations. In Der Derian, J., & Shapiro, M. J., eds., *International/Intertextual Relations: Postmodern Readings of World Politics.* Lexington, MA: Lexington Books, pp. 3–10.

Devereux, S. (2002). *Food Security in Sub-Saharan Africa*. London: ITDG Press.

Devereux, S. & Sabates-Wheeler, R. (2004). Transformative Social Protection. IDS Working Paper 232, pp. 1–36.

Dicklitch, S. (2001). NGOs and democratization in transitional societies: Lessons from Uganda. *International Politics*, 38(1), 27–46.

Dicklitch, S. & Lwanga, D. (2003). The politics of being non-political: Human rights organizations and the creation of a positive human rights culture in Uganda. *Human Rights Quarterly*, 25(2), 482–509.

Dryden-Peterson, S., & Hovil, L. (2004). A remaining hope for durable solutions: Local integration of refugees and their hosts in the case of Uganda. *Refuge: Canada's Journal on Refugees*, 22(1), 26–38.

du Toit, A. & Neves, D. (2009). Trading on a Grant: Integrating Formal and Informal Social Protection in Post-Apartheid Migrant Networks. BWPI Working Paper 75, University of Manchester.

Duffield, M. R. (2001). *Global Governance and the New Wars: The Merging of Development and Security*. London; New York: Zed Books; Palgrave USA.

Duffield, M. R. (2018). *Post-Humanitarianism: Governing Precarity in the Digital World*. Cambridge, UK: Polity.

Edkins, J. (1999). *Poststructuralism and International Relations: Bringing the Political Back In*. London: Lynne Rienner.

Enloe, C. (2014). *Bananas, Beaches and Bases: Making Feminist Sense of International Politics*, 2nd ed. Berkeley: University of California Press.

Eribon, D. (1991). *Michel Foucalt*. Cambridge, MA: Harvard University Press.

Escobar, A. (2011). *Encountering Development, The Making and Unmaking of the Third World* (revised edition). Princeton, NJ: Princeton University Press.

Ferguson, J. (1990). *The Anti-politics Machine: 'Development', Depoliticization and Bureaucratic Power in Lesotho*. Cambridge: Cambridge University Press.

Fiddian-Qasmiyeh, E. (2015). *South-South Educational Migration, Humanitarianism and Development: Views from Cuba, North Africa and the Middle East*. Oxford: Routledge.

Foucault, M. (1965). *Madness and Civilization: A History of Insanity in the Age of Reason* (trans. Richard Howard). New York: Vintage Books.

Foucault, M. (1979). *The History of Sexuality*. London: Allen Lane.

Gallie, W. B. (1955). Essentially contested concepts. *Proceedings of the Aristotelian Society*, 56, 167–198.

Gardner, W. L., Cogliser, C. C., Davis, K. M. & Dickens, M. P. (2011). Authentic leadership: A review of the literature and research agenda. *The Leadership Quarterly*, 22(6), 1120–1145.

Gill, S. (1993). *Gramsci, Historical Materialism and International Relations*. Cambridge: Cambridge University Press.

Gold, S. J., (1992). *Refugee Communities: A Comparative Field Study*. Newbury Park, CA, and London: Sage Publications.

Grabska, K., (2006). Marginalization in urban spaces of the Global South: Urban refugees in Cairo. *Journal of Refugee Studies*, 19(3), 287–307.

Grant, B. & Dollery, B. E. (2010). Place-shaping by local government in developing countries: Lessons for the developed world. *International Journal of Public Administration*, 33(5), 251–261.

Griffiths, D., Sigona, N. & Zetter, R. (2006). Integrative paradigms, marginal reality: Refugee community organisations and dispersal in Britain. *Journal of Ethnic and Migration Studies*, 32(5), 881–898.

Grint, K. (1997). *Leadership: Classical, Contemporary, and Critical Approaches*. Oxford: Oxford University Press.

Hall, R. B. & Biersteker, T. J. (2002). *The Emergence of Private Authority in Global Governance*. Cambridge: Cambridge University Press.

Hallward, M., Masullo, J. & Mouly, C. (2017). Civil resistance in armed conflict: Leveraging non-violent action to navigate war, oppose violence and confront oppression. *Journal of Peacebuilding & Development*, 12(3), 1–9.

Halperin, D. M. (1995). *Saint Foucault: Towards a Gay Hagiography*. New York: Oxford University Press.

Hammond, L. (2004). *This Place Will Become Home: Refugee Repatriation to Ethiopia*. Ithaca, NY: Cornell University Press.

Hawkins, D., Lake, D., Nielson, D. & Tierney, M. (2006). *Delegation and Agency in International Organization*. Cambridge: Cambridge University Press.

Hear, N. V., Molteno, S. & Bakewell, O. (2016). *From New Helots to New Diasporas: A Retrospective for Robin Cohen*. Oxford: Oxford Publishing Services.

Held, D. (1995). *Democracy and the Global Order: From the Modern State to Cosmopolitan Governance*. Stanford: Stanford University Press.

Herzfeld, M. (2005). Political optics and the occlusion of intimate knowledge. *American Anthropologist*, **107**(3), 369–376.

Hilhorst, D. (2017). Gender, sexuality, and violence in humanitarian crises. *Disasters*, **42**(S1), S3–S16.

Hilhorst, T. (2016, 20 May) The other half of gender: Are humanitarians blind to the vulnerabilities of male refugees? ALNAP Blog. www.alnap.org/blog/147.

Holzmann, R. & Jorgensen, S. (1999). Social protection as social risk management: Conceptual underpinnings for the social protection sector strategy paper. *Journal of International Development*, **11**(7), 1005–1027.

Hopkins, G. (2006). *Somali Community Organisations in London and Toronto: Collaboration and Effectiveness*. Oxford: Oxford University Press.

Horst, C. (2006). Buufis amongst Somalis in Dadaab: The transnational and historical logics behind resettlement dreams. *Journal of Refugee Studies*, **19**(2), 143–157.

Horst, C. (2008). The transnational political engagements of refugees: Remittance sending practices of Somali refugees in Norway: Analysis. *Conflict, Security and Development*, **8**(3), 317–339.

Horst, C. (2019). Refugees, peacebuilding, and the anthropology of the good. In Bradley, M., Milner, J. & Peruniak, B., eds., *Refugees' Roles in Resolving Displacement and Building Peace: Beyond Beneficiaries*. Washington, DC: Georgetown University Press, pp. 39–54.

Ilcan, S., Oliver, M. & Connoy, L. (2015). Humanitarian assistance and the politics of self-reliance: Uganda's Nakivale refugee settlement. *CIGI Working Papers*, 86, 3–10.

Inter-Agency Standing Committee (IASC). (2006). The international legal framework for protection. In Inter-Agency Standing Committee (IASC), *IASC Gender Handbook*. Geneva, CH: IASC.

International Finance Corporation, World Bank Group. (2018). Kakuma as a Marketplace: A Consumer and Market Study of a Refugee Camp and Town in Northwest Kenya. Report. Washington DC: International Finance Corporation, World Bank Group.

Jacobsen, K. (2005). *The Economic Life of Refugees*. Bloomfield, CT: Kumerian Press, Inc.

Jacobsen, K. (2019). Durable solutions and the political action of refugees. In Bradley, M., Milner, J. & Peruniak, B., eds., *Refugees' Roles in Resolving Displacement and Building Peace: Beyond Beneficiaries*. Washington, DC: Georgetown University Press, pp. 23–38.

Jansen, B. J. (2018). *Kakuma Refugee Camp: Humanitarian Urbanism in Kenya's Accidental City*. London: Zed Books.

Jentzsch, C., Kalyvas, S. N. & Schubiger, L. I. (2015). Militias in civil wars. *Journal of Conflict Resolution*, **59**(5), 755–769.

Johansson, P. (2019). Displaced persons as symbols of grievance: Collective identity, individual rights and durable solutions. In Bradley, M., Milner, J. & Peruniak, B., eds., *Refugees' Roles in Resolving Displacement and Building Peace*. Washington, DC: Georgetown University Press, pp. 132–150.

Johnson, T. (2014). *Organizational Progeny: Why Governments are Losing Control over the Proliferating Structures of Global Governance*. Oxford: Oxford University Press.

Johnson, T. (2016). Cooperation, co-optation, competition, conflict: International bureaucracies and non-governmental organizations in an interdependent world. *Review of International Political Economy*, **23**(5), 737–767.

Jones, W. (2013, 30 June). The UNHCR is much better than its reputation in Uganda suggests (and needs to say so). Web log comment. Democracy in Africa.

Jose, B. (2018). *Norm Contestation: Insights into Non-conformity with Armed Conflict Norms.* Cham, CH: Palgrave Macmillan.

Jose, B. & Medie, P. A. (2015). Understanding how and why civilians resort to self-protection in armed conflict. *International Studies Review*, 17(4), 515–535.

Kaplan, O. (2013). Nudging armed groups: How civilians transmit norms of protection. *STABILITY: International Journal of Security and Development*, 2(3), 1–18.

Khalil, J. & Zeuthen, M. (2014). A case study of counter violent extremism (CVE) programming: Lessons from OTI's Kenya transition initiative. *STABILITY: International Journal of Security & Development*, 3(1), 1–12.

Kibreab, G. (1987). *Refugees and Development in Africa: The Case of Eritrea.* Trenton, NJ: The Red Sea Press.

Kibreab, G. (2002). When refugees come home: The relationship between stayees and returnees in post-conflict Eritrea. *Journal of Contemporary African Studies*, 20(1), 53–80.

Krause, U. (2013). *Linking Refugee Protection with Development Assistance: analyses with a case study in Uganda.* Berlin: Nomos.

Lindley, A. (2010). Leaving Mogadishu: Towards a sociology of conflict-related mobility. *Oxford Academic Journal of Refugee Studies*, 23(1), 2–22.

Lindley, D. A. (2009). The early-morning phone call: Remittances from a refugee diaspora perspective. *Journal of Ethnic and Migration Studies*, 35(8), 1315–1334.

Lischer, R. (2005). *The End of Words: The Language of Reconciliation in a Culture of Violence.* Grand Rapids, MI; Cambridge, UK: Eerdmans.

Luft, G. (2002). *The Cultural Dimension of Multinational Military Cooperation.* Baltimore, MD: Johns Hopkins University Press.

Lyon, F. & Porter, G. (2009). Market institutions, trust and norms: Exploring moral economies in Nigerian food systems. *Cambridge Journal of Economics*, 33, 903–920.

Lyons, T. (2007). Conflict-generated diasporas and transnational politics in Ethiopia: Analysis. *Conflict, Security & Development*, 7(4), 529–549.

Macey, D. (1993). *The Lives of Michel Foucault.* London: Vintage.

Masullo, J. (2017). A Theory of Civilian Noncooperation with Armed Groups: Civilian Agency and Self-Protection in the Colombian Civil War. PhD Thesis, European University Institute, Florence.

Masullo, J. & O'Connor, F. (2017). PKK violence against civilians beyond the individual: Understanding collective targeting. *Terrorism and Political Violence*. Online article. DOI: 10.1080/09546553.2017.1347874.

Maystadt, J.-F. & Duranton, G. (2019). The development push of refugees: evidence from Tanzania. *Journal of Economic Geography*, 19(2), 299–334.

Maystadt, J.-F. & Werwimp, P. (2009). Winners and losers amongst a refugee hosting population. CORE Discussion Papers 2009034. Ottignies-Louvain-la-Neuve, Belgium: Universite catholique de Louvain, Center for Operations Research and Econometrics (CORE).

McConnachie, K. (2012). *Burma's Refugees: Self-Governance in Comparative Perspective.* Oxford: Oxford University Press.

McDowell, L. (2018). Moving stories: Precarious work and multiple migrations. *A Journal of Feminist Geography*, 25(4), 471–488.

Miller, S. D. (2016). *Political and Humanitarian Responses to Syrian Displacement.* New York: Routledge Focus.

Milos, D. (2011). South Sudanese communities and Australian family law: A clash of systems. *ARAS*, 32(2), 143–159.

Morris, J. (2019). From Phosphate to Refugees: The Offshore Refugee Boom in the Republic of Nauru. Unpublished PhD thesis, Oxford University.

Mylonas, H. & Shelef, N. (2017). Methodological challenges in the study of stateless nationalist territorial claims. *Territory, Politics, Governance.*, 5(2), 145–157.

Norwegian Refugee Council/International Human Rights Committee, (2017). Recognising Nairobi's refugees: The challenges and significance of documentation proving identity and status. Report. Nairobi: NRC/IHRC.

Paddon Rhoads, E. (2016). *Taking Sides in Peacekeeping: Impartiality and the Future of the United Nations.* Oxford: Oxford University Press.

Paris, R. (2001). Human security: Paradigm shift or hot air? *International Security*, 26(2), 87–102.

Percy, S. (2007). *Mercenaries: This History of a Norm in International Relations.* Oxford: Oxford University Press.

Phillimore, J. (2012). Implementing integration in the UK: Lessons for integration theory, policy and practice. *Journal of Public Finance and Public Choice*, 40(4), 525–545.

Phillimore, J. & Goodson, L. (2008). Making a place in the global city: The relevance of indicators of integration. *Journal of Refugee Studies*, 21(3), 305–325.

Purkey, A. (2019). Transformative justice and legal conscientization: Refugee participation in peace processes, repatriation, and reconciliation. In Bradley, M., Milner, J. & Peruniak, B., eds., *Refugees' Roles in Resolving Displacement and Building Peace.* Washington, DC: Georgetown University Press, pp. 75–94.

Rahnema, M. & Bawtree, V., eds. (1997). *The Post Development Reader.* London: Zed Books.

Ramadan, A. (2010). In the ruins of Nahr al-Barid: Understanding the meaning of the camp. *Journal of Palestine Studies*, 40(1), 49–62.

Rao, A. & Kelleher, D. (2010). Is there life after gender mainstreaming? *Gender & Development*, 13(2), 57–69.

Resch, R. P. (1992). *Althusser and the Renewal of Marxist Social Theory.* Berkeley: University of California Press.

Richmond, A. H. (1988). *Immigration and Ethnic Conflict.* Basingstoke: Palgrave Macmillan.

Richmond, A. H. (1993). Reactive migration: Sociological perspectives on refugee movements. *Journal of Refugee Studies*, 6(1), 7–24.

Ritchie, H. A. (2017). Gender and enterprise in fragile refugee settings: Female empowerment amidst male emasculation – A challenge to local integration? *Disasters*, 42(S1), S40–S60.

Ruiz, I. & Vargas-Silva, C. (2015). The labor market impacts of forced migration. *American Economic Review*, 105(5), 581–586.

Ruiz, I., & Vargas-Silva, C. (2018). Differences in labour market outcomes between natives, refugees and other migrants in the UK. *Journal of Economic Geography*, 18(4), 855–885.

Russell, A. (2011). Home, music and memory for the Congolese in Kampala. *Journal of Eastern African Studies*, 5(2), 294–312.

Sabates-Wheeler, R., & Feldman, R. (2011). *Migration and Social Protection: Claiming Social Rights beyond Borders.* London: Palgrave Macmillan UK.

Sachs, W. (1997). Introduction. In Sachs, W., ed., *The Development Dictionary: A Guide to Knowledge as Power.* London: Zed Books, pp. xv–xx.

Sachs, J. (2015). *The Age of Sustainable Development.* New York: Columbia University Press.

Salehyan, I. (2009). *Rebels Without Borders: Transnational Insurgencies in World Politics.* Cornell: Cornell University Press.

Schmidt, A (2013). Status determination and recognition. In Betts, A. and Orchard, P. eds., *Implementation in World Politics: how norms change practice.* Oxford: Oxford University Press.

Scholte, J. A. (2002). What Is Globalization? The Definitional Issue – Again. CSGR Working Paper 109/2. Warwick: Centre for the Study of Globalisation and Regionalisation.

Scott, J. C. (1977). *The Moral Economy of the Peasant: Rebellion and Subsistence in Southeast Asia.* New Haven: Yale University Press.

Scott, J. C. (1998). *Seeing Like a State: How Certain Schemes to Improve the Human Condition Have Failed*. New Haven: Yale University Press.

Scott, J. C. (2009). *The Art of Not Being Governed: An Anarchist History of Upland Southeast Asia*. New Haven: Yale University Press.

Scott-Smith, T. (2016). Humanitarian dilemmas in a mobile world. *Refugee Survey Quarterly*, 35(2), 1–21.

Seth, S. (2011). Postcolonial theory and the critique of international relations. *Millenium: Journal of International Studies*, 40(1), 167–183.

Smirl, L. (2015). *Spaces of Aid. How Cars, Compounds, and Hotels Shape Humanitarianism*. London: Zed Books.

Staniland, P. (2014). *Networks of Rebellion: Explaining Insurgent Cohesion and Collapse*. Ithaca, NY: Cornell University Press.

Suarez, C. (2017). 'Living between Two Lions': Civilian protection strategies during armed violence in the eastern Democratic Republic of the Congo. *Journal of Peacebuilding & Development*, 12(3), 54–67.

Sutton, R. (2018, 28 June). Safeguarding 'distinction' inside the wire: Humanitarian-peacekeeper interactions in South Sudan's Protection of Civilians sites. Online article. https://ilg2.org/2018/06/28/safeguarding-distinction-inside-the-wire-humanitarian-peacekeeper-interactions-in-south-sudans-protection-of-civilians-sites/

Tickner, J. A. (1992). *Gender in International Relations: Feminist Perspectives on Achieving Global Security*. New York: Columbia University Press.

Ticktin, M. I. (2011a). *Casualties of Care: Immigration and the Politics of Humanitarianism in France*. Berkeley: University of California Press.

Ticktin, M. (2011b). The gendered human of humanitarianism: Medicalising and politicising sexual violence. *Gender & History*, 23(2), 250–265.

UNHCR. (1994). UNHCR Statute Para 8. In United Nations General Assembly Note on International Protection. Geneva, CH: United Nations General Assembly.

UNHCR. (2014) Encouraging Self-reliance. UNHCR Global Report 2014. Geneva, CH: United Nations High Commissioner for Refugees.

UNHCR. (2018). The Kalobeyei Integrated Socio-Economic Development Plan for Turkana West. Geneva, CH: United Nations High Commissioner for Refugees.

Van Hear, N. (1998). *New Diasporas: The Mass Exodus, Dispersal and Regrouping of Migrant Communities*. London: UCL Press.

Von Billerbeck, S. B. (2017). *Whose Peace? Local Ownership and United Nations Peacekeeping*. Oxford: Oxford University Press.

Vrasti, W. (2008). The strange case of ethnography and international relations. *Millennium – Journal of International Studies*, 37(2), 279–301.

Waever, O., Buzan, B., Kelstrup, M. & Lemaitre, P. (1993). *Identity, Migration and the New Security Agenda in Europe*. London: Pinter Centre for Peace and Conflict Research, Copenhagen.

Wallace, T., Bornstein, L. & Chapman, J. (2006). *The Aid Chain: Coercion and Commitment in Development NGOs*. Rugby, UK: ITDG.

Weiss, T. & Wilkinson, R. 2018. The Globally Governed: Everyday Global Governance. *Global Governance*, 24(2), 193–210.

Werker, E., 2007. Refugee camp economies. *Journal of Refugee Studies*, 20(3), 461–480.

White, S. (1996). Depoliticising development: The uses and abuses of participation. *Development in Practice*, 6(1), 6–15. DOI: 10.1080/0961452961000157564.

Wilde, R. (2010). *International Territorial Administration: How Trusteeship and the Civilizing Mission Never Went Away*. Oxford: Oxford University Press.

Williams, L. (2006). Social networks of refugees in the United Kingdom: Tradition, tactics and new community spaces. *Journal of Ethnic and Migration Studies*, 32(5), 865–879.

Windle Trust Uganda. (2013). Towards Holistic Education for Children and Youth Affected by Conflict. Kampala: Windle Trust Uganda. Annual report. https://windleuganda.org/wp-content/uploads/2018/03/WTUAnnualReport2013_Final.pdf

World Bank. (2018). Kakuma as a Marketplace: A Consumer and Market Study of a Refugee Camp and Town in Northwest Kenya (English). Working Paper. Washington, DC: World Bank Group. http://documents.worldbank.org/curated/en/482761525339883916/Kakuma-as-a-marketplace-a-consumer-and-market-study-of-a-refugee-camp-and-town-in-northwest-Kenya

Zetter, R. & Pearl, M. (2000). The minority within the minority: Refugee community-based organisations in the UK and the impact of restrictionism on asylum-seekers. *Journal of Ethnic & Migration Studies*, **26**(4), 675–697.

Zetter, R., Sigona, N. & Hauser, M. (2002). Survey on Policy and Practice Related to Refugee Integration. Report. Oxford: Department of Planning, Oxford Brookes University.

Zetter, R., Griffiths, D. & Sigona, N. (2005). Social capital or social exclusion? The impact of asylum-seeker dispersal on UK refugee community organizations. *Community Development Journal*, **40**, 169–181.

INDEX

Introductory Note

References such as '178–179' indicate (not necessarily continuous) discussion of a topic across a range of pages. Wherever possible in the case of topics with many references, these have either been divided into sub-topics or only the most significant discussions of the topic are listed. Because the entire work is about 'refugees', the use of this term (and certain others which occur constantly throughout the book) as an entry point has been minimised. Information will be found under the corresponding detailed topics.